RoM

Get **more** out of libraries

Please return or renew this item by the last date shown.

You can renew online at www.hants.gov.uk/library

Or by phoning 0300 555 1387

Hampshire
County Council

D1332012

C016069673

Sage 50 Accounts

FOR DUMMIES®
A Wiley Brand

3rd Edition

by Jane Kelly

FOR DUMMIES®
A Wiley Brand

Sage 50 Accounts For Dummies® 3rd Edition

Published by: **John Wiley & Sons, Ltd.,** The Atrium, Southern Gate, Chichester, www.wiley.com

This edition first published 2015

© 2015 John Wiley & Sons, Ltd, Chichester, West Sussex.

Registered office

John Wiley & Sons Ltd, The Atrium, Southern Gate, Chichester, West Sussex, PO19 8SQ, United Kingdom

For details of our global editorial offices, for customer services and for information about how to apply for permission to reuse the copyright material in this book please see our website at www.wiley.com.

For general information on our other products and services, please contact our Customer Care Department within the U.S. at 877-762-2974, outside the U.S. at (001) 317-572-3993, or fax 317-572-4002. For technical support, please visit www.wiley.com/techsupport.

For technical support, please visit www.wiley.com/techsupport.

A catalogue record for this book is available from the British Library.

ISBN 978-1-119-05230-2 (paperback); ISBN 978-1-119-05231-9 (ebk);

ISBN 978-1-119-05233-3 (ebk)

Printed in Great Britain by TJ International, Padstow, Cornwall

10 9 8 7 6 5 4 3 2 1

Contents at a Glance

Table of Contents

Introduction

Sage is a well-known accounting system used in more than three-quarters of a million small- and medium-sized businesses in the UK. The range of business software continually evolves, and Sage's developers pride themselves on listening to their customers for feedback on how to improve the software. This results in regular revisions and updates that add new features to Sage each time.

This book offers you a chance to understand how Sage 50 Accounts can help you run your business effectively. Thoroughly revised to cover all the latest Sage updates, I hope you get a lot out of this third edition, which covers the 2015 edition of Sage 50 Accounts.

About This Book

The aim of this book is for you to get the most from Sage. I use lots of screenshots to help you navigate your way around the system and offer tips to help you customise the programs and reports contained in Sage in language you can understand, even if you're not an accountant.

Wherever possible, I show you the quickest way to do something, because you can often do the same thing in more than one way. I understand that you want a quick start, so I show you the easiest methods of doing things. You can always add details later, when time permits.

This book presents information in a modular fashion so that you get all the information to accomplish a task in one place. I don't ask you to remember things from different parts of the book; if another chapter has information relevant to the discussion at hand, I tell you where to find it, so you don't have to read the chapters in order. You can read the chapters or sections that interest you when it suits you.

This book includes a lot of instructions on how to proceed with various tasks in Sage. Wherever possible, I use numbered lists to indicate the order in which to do things.

✔ *Italics* are used to highlight new terms and for emphasis.

✔ **Boldfaced** text indicates the action step in a numbered list or text that you type into Sage.

✔ Monofont is used for web addresses and on-screen messages.

✔ Names of windows, screens and menu choices are capitalised.

✔ This little arrow ⇨ indicates the path you click through in a series of menu options.

Because examples can help you see how a concept works in real life, I created Jingles, a fictitious party-planning company, and I use its owner Jeanette to demonstrate some of Sage's reports and functions.

Foolish Assumptions

While writing *Sage 50 Accounts For Dummies*, 3rd Edition, for the 2015 version of Sage, I made some key assumptions about who you are and why you picked up this book. I assume that you fall into one of the following categories:

✔ You're a member of staff in a small business who's been asked to take over the bookkeeping function and will be using Sage.

✔ You're an existing bookkeeper who has never used Sage before or who needs to refresh your knowledge.

✔ You're a small-business owner who wants to understand how Sage can help in your business.

Icons Used in This Book

Every *For Dummies* book uses icons to highlight especially important, interesting or useful information. The icons used in this book are:

Look at this icon for practical information that you can use straightaway to help you use Sage in the most effective way.

This icon indicates any items you need to remember after reading the book – and sometimes throughout it.

The paragraphs next to this icon contain information that is, er, slightly technical in nature. You don't *need* to know the information here to get by, but it helps.

 This bombshell alerts you to potential problems you may create for yourself without realising it. Don't ignore this icon!

 This icon indicates that a function is available only to users of Sage 50 Accounts Plus and Sage 50 Accounts Professional.

 Some functions are included only if you run the Professional version of Sage, and – guess what? – this icon indicates those functions.

Beyond the Book

In addition to the material in the print or ebook you're reading right now, this product also comes with some access-anywhere extras on the web.

Head to `www.dummies.com/cheatsheet/sage50accountsuk` for a useful cheat sheet which includes a handy keyboard shortcut checklist, a list of at-a-glance UK tax codes and information on how to contact Sage. You can also find a table comparing the features in the Sage 50 Accounts product range to ensure you're using the best version for you.

Check out `www.dummies.com/extras/sage50accountsuk` for some great free bonus Sage-related articles.

Where to Go from Here

You're now ready to enter the world of Sage. If you're a complete beginner, starting at the beginning and gradually working through is probably best. The appendix provides a handy glossary of important terms used in this book that you may not be familiar with. If you're an existing user, but a little rusty in certain areas, you can pick the chapters that are most relevant to you, probably in Parts IV and V. This book is designed for you to dip in and out of. I hope that you find it a useful tool for developing and managing your business.

Part I

Getting Started with Sage 50 Accounts

In this part . . .

✔ Meet the Sage product range and decide which product is going to be the most useful to you.

✔ Install the Sage software and go step by step setting up your records and Chart of Accounts.

✔ Discover the tricks and tips for navigating around the system.

✔ Find out how to enter and check your opening balances.

Chapter 1

Introducing Sage 50 Accounts

*I*n this chapter, I introduce you to the Sage 50 Accounts software range. I show you how easily you can install the software and give you a guided tour, so that you can get up and running quickly – essential for busy people.

Sage works on the principle that the less time you spend doing your accounts, the more time you spend on your business, so it makes each process as simple as possible.

I also discuss SageCover, an optional technical support package, which is an addition worth considering. If you experience software problems, SageCover can help. For small businesses, this support is like having an IT department at the end of the phone.

Looking at the Varieties of Sage

Sage's developers understand that every business is different and each business has different needs. As a result, they've developed a range of accounting software designed to grow with your business, whatever it is. The three levels of Sage 50 Accounts software start with basic features and finish with a product that contains all the bells and whistles you can possibly want. These versions of Sage are:

- ✔ **Sage 50 Accounts:** This is the entry-level program. Sage 50 Accounts provides all the features you need to successfully manage your accounts. You can professionally handle your customers and suppliers, manage your bank reconciliations and VAT returns, and provide simple reports, including monthly and year-end requirements. This basic version is suitable for small businesses with a simple structure, and businesses that need basic stock systems but don't need systems for project costing, foreign currency, or sales/purchase order processing.

- ✔ **Sage 50 Accounts Plus:** This contains all the features of the entry model but also lets you manage project costs versus budgets and control costs of manufactured and assembled products, and has an improved stock control system to produce bills of materials and allocate stock.

- ✔ **Sage 50 Accounts Professional:** This includes all the features of Accounts Plus but adds sales and purchase order processing, foreign trading, bank account revaluation, and Intrastat support. Accounts Professional can handle up to ten users and manage multiple companies. This product is suited to both small- and medium-sized businesses and offers customers a product flexible enough to suit a multitude of different businesses, including those that trade in both the UK and abroad.

By the way, from Sage 50 Accounts 2014 onwards, you can buy a separate foreign currency module for all variants of Sage 50.

Deciding on SageCover

You can purchase SageCover at the same time as you buy Sage. SageCover gives you technical support in case you have any problems using Sage. It may seem an additional cost burden to begin with, but I think SageCover is well worth the money in case you a software problems.

Most people who use accounting packages know something about accounting but don't necessarily know much about computer software. When your screen pops up with an error message that you simply don't understand,

a quick phone call to your SageCover support line can soon solve the problem.

For Sage 50 Accounts, you can choose between three different types of cover:

- ✔ **SageCover Online:** The key features are the opportunity to use the web chat facility, where you can communicate with Sage advisors in real time by sending instant messages online. Email support is available for more detailed questions. You also get Ask Sage, which gives you online access to thousands of frequently asked questions. Finally, you receive a monthly e-newsletter containing the latest technical tips for your software.

✔ **SageCover:** This provides telephone support during normal office hours, as well as email and online question and answer support. You also get a monthly e-newsletter. If you have Sage 50 Payroll, you also get human resources advice as standard and software updates to your software is always up to date with the latest legislation. Sage also offers a data repair service should your Sage data become lost or corrupted.

✔ **SageCover Extra:** This includes all the benefits of SageCover, plus software upgrades, so you always have access to the latest

version. You can request three customised reports for Sage 50 Accounts users. You also gain the benefit of an express data repair service rather than just the standard service. You're given priority telephone support with SageCover Extra, including a call-back option, and also have additional remote support, which means that, with your permission, Sage technicians can remotely access your PC to help solve your queries.

Sometimes the Help button just doesn't answer your question. Having someone on the end of the phone to talk you through a problem is a real bonus. The technical support team can help you solve the most awkward problems that would otherwise have you throwing your laptop out of the window in pure frustration.

Installing the Software

There is more than one way to install your Sage 50 software. You may prefer the traditional method of buying the product off the shelf and loading the CD, or you may prefer the digital download method. Whichever you choose, Sage guides you seamlessly through the process to ensure you load the software as efficiently as possible.

Check the technical specifications required to run your software: Ensure your laptop or PC is sufficiently powerful to run the software. Sage is quite a big program and needs a relatively powerful computer to run it.

Getting what you need before you get started

Whichever method of purchase you use, you should receive a serial number and activation key. Without these two pieces of information, you can't successfully load the software. But don't worry: If you purchase a genuine copy of Sage software, you have the necessary activation information.

You also need some details about your company:

- ✔ **When your company's financial year begins:** If you're not sure of this date, ask your accountant.

- ✔ **Whether you use a VAT scheme:** Your accountant can tell you whether you operate the VAT cash accounting scheme or the standard VAT scheme. If you have a VAT registration number, keep it handy.

Moving to the installation

Follow the download instructions or insert your CD into the disk drive and follow the instructions on screen. The Installshield wizard runs and proceeds to install Sage on your computer.

Sage lets you know when the program has installed successfully. Then you can really get cracking.

Setting Up with the Active Set-Up Wizard

Of course, you're champing at the bit and want to get going with Sage, so double-click the new Sage icon on your desktop to get started. The Activate Sage Software window opens, as in Figure 1-1. Sage asks you to enter your activation key and serial number. If you don't have this information, click the My Sage button and follow the online instructions.

After you enter your activation key and serial number, click Continue and the Active Set-up wizard opens. The wizard guides you through seven different screens where you enter information as requested.

The first screen, shown in Figure 1-2, gives you three options:

- ✔ **Set up a new company:** If you're new to Sage, choose this first option. Sage guides you through the automatic steps of the Active Set-up wizard.

- ✔ **Use an existing company stored on your network:** If you already use Sage and are upgrading, choose this option, which lets you copy accounts data from your previous Sage installation.

- ✔ **Restore data from a backup file:** Choose this option if you're restoring data from an earlier version. If your backup was taken from an earlier version than V14 (2008), contact Sage for further support.

Figure 1-1:
Activating
your Sage
Software.

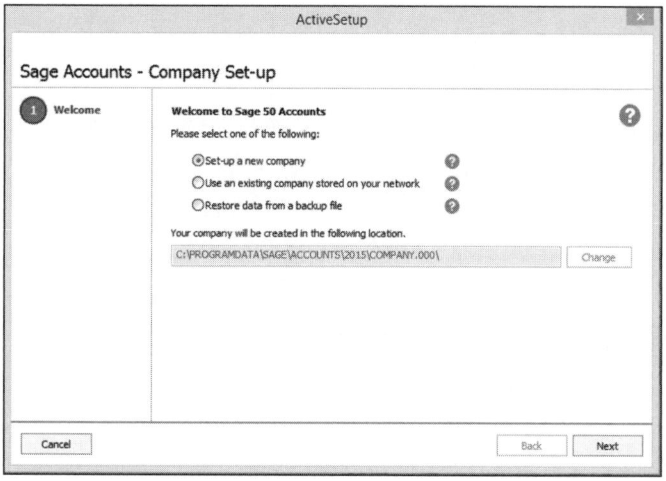

Figure 1-2:
Putting the
Set-up wiz-
ard to work.

Choose whichever option is best for you and click Next.

The following steps take you through the process of setting up Sage for the
first time.

1. Click Set Up a New Company and then click Next.

The Network Sharing screen opens, as in Figure 1-3.

2. Click Next and then enter your company's details.

Sage prompts you to enter your company's information, such as name,
address, and contact details, as in Figure 1-4. Make the set-up speedier

by putting in just the company name. You can complete the other information later by clicking Settings on the main toolbar and then selecting Company Preferences.

3. Click Next.

A screen appears that prompts you to Select Business Type, as shown in Figure 1-5.

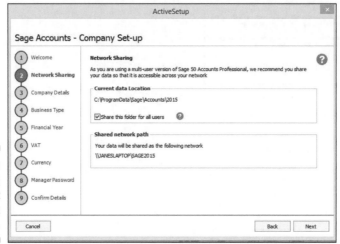

Figure 1-3: Asking about network sharing.

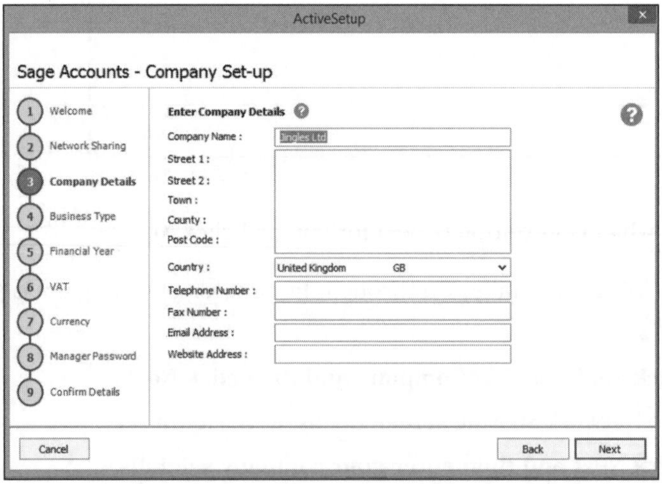

Figure 1-4: Asking for your company's info.

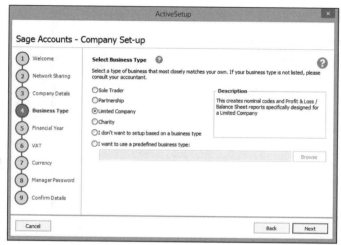

Figure 1-5:
What type
of business
are you?

4. Click the appropriate business type.

For example, I chose Limited Company for my fictional greetings card company Jingles. If you don't know your business type, ask your accountant. Whichever business structure you choose, Sage applies the appropriate nominal codes and profit and loss and balance sheet reports for your accounts.

If you don't want to select any of the categories shown, you can click Customised and create your own business type. You can then use your existing nominal codes if you transfer accounts from a different system.

5. Click Next and select your financial year.

Jingles ends its financial year on 31 March 2015, so the financial start date is April 2014, as in Figure 1-6.

6. Click Next and fill in your VAT details.

If you're not VAT registered, click No and go to Step 6.

If you're VAT registered, enter your registration number and use the dropdown arrow to select the appropriate VAT rate, as in Figure 1-7. You must enter the current standard VAT rate if that's the rate you've selected. Our example Jingles Ltd is VAT registered.

Don't enter any transactions until you're certain of which VAT scheme you operate. Failure to use the correct scheme means Sage calculates your VAT incorrectly. Applying the wrong VAT scheme can be extremely messy.

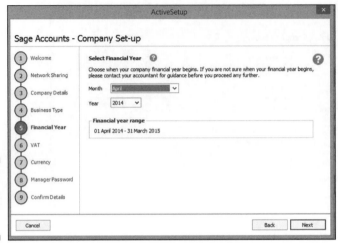

Figure 1-6:
Beginning
the financial
year.

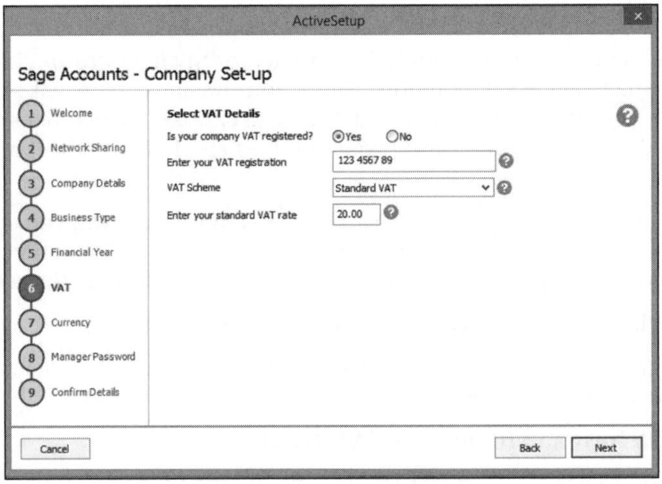

Figure 1-7:
Registering
your VAT
status.

7. Click Next and choose the type of currency you use, as in Figure 1-8.

Click Next again. Note the currency option is available only if you use Sage 50 Accounts Professional.

8. Click Next to open the Manager password screen.

Create a password, which you can then use every time you login to Sage, as in Figure 1-9.

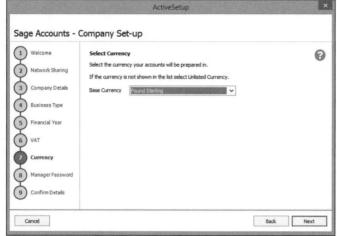

Figure 1-8:
Telling Sage
what cur-
rency to
use to pre-
pare your
accounts.

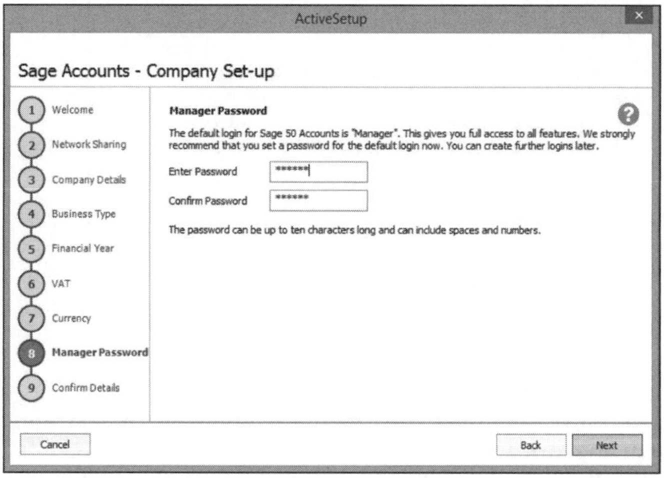

Figure 1-9:
Entering a
manager
password.

9. **The final screen summarises the data you entered on your Active Set-up wizard, as in Figure 1-10.**

   If you need to make any changes to your data, can click Back and revise the information.

10. **Select Create when you're satisfied the information is correct.**

    You've finished!

    The system now configures and asks you for your login details, as in Figure 1-11.

Figure 1-10:
Confirming
your details.

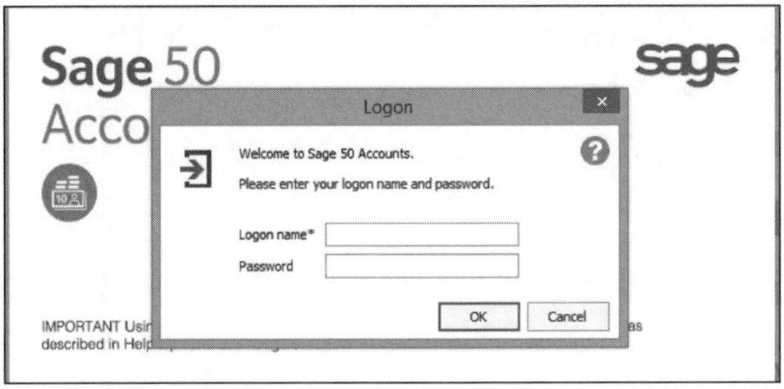

Figure 1-11:
Requesting
your login
details

After you successfully log in, Sage asks if you want to customise your company, as in Figure 1-12. Click the Customise company button, and a wizard style menu appears, where you can choose to set up the defaults for your customers, suppliers, bank, products, financials, and administration. Sage offers some helpful videos to assist you in setting up the individual modules. Fill the tickboxes as you completed each section.

If you click Setup Now, Sage automatically takes you to the default screen for whichever module you want to set up. Figure 1-13 shows an example of the Customer Default window.

If you prefer to use a step-by-step process, Setup Now is probably the way for you. However, in this chapter I work through setting up the modules manually so you can see where all the options are within Sage. To set up manually, click No on the Customisation screen and return to the Getting Started page.

Figure 1-12:
Customising
your
company.

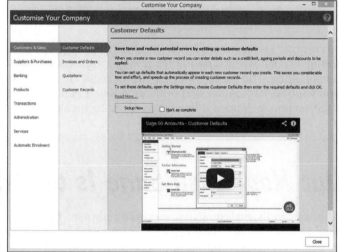

Figure 1-13:
Customer
customi-
sation!

If you need a break, close the Customisation screen, which takes you to the Getting Started page. To return to the customisation screen, click Help on the Menu bar and then Customise Your Company.

Registering Your Software

After you install Sage, when you next open Sage it may prompt you to register it. You have the option to register now or later, as in Figure 1-14.

Registering straight away is quick and easy. Click Register Now and the next screen prompts you to complete your personal details.

Figure 1-14:
Registering
your
software.

After you complete your details, click Register Now. Sage checks your details. If registration is successful, a new activation key appears on the screen and in your email inbox. The email confirms you've registered your product and shows you your Serial Number and Activation Key. Keep this information in a safe place, as you may need it if you ever need to speak to Sage customer services.

Finding Out How Easy Sage Is to Use

Sage is a user-friendly system, using words and phrases that people easily understand rather than accounting jargon. Sage also has a lot of graphics to make the pages look more appealing and easy to navigate. For example, an icon appears next to the Bank module that looks like the entrance to a grand building – like the Bank of England, perhaps.

Burying the accounting jargon

Sage uses terms that users understand and combines a mix of accounting terms with words such as *customers* and *suppliers*, instead of *debtors* and *creditors*. Accounting terminology isn't done away with altogether, however – for example, Sage refers to *nominal codes* and you still have to print aged debtors and creditors reports.

Navigating Around Sage

When you open Sage, the first screen you come across is the Getting Started screen, as in Figure 1-15. This screen provides useful links and various Help pages, including a page that shows you what's new in Sage 50 Accounts.

At the top of the Getting Started screen is the name of your version of Sage – Sage 50 Accounts Professional 2015, for example – followed by the company name you entered when you set up Sage. (Refer to the 'Setting Up with the Active Set-Up Wizard' section, which walks you through getting Sage up and running.)

Figure 1-15: Getting started with Sage.

The Sage 50 desktop is divided into three key areas:

- ✔ **Menu bar:** This bar runs horizontally across the top of the screen and is one method of navigating around Sage 50. (I give more info on this area in the section 'Exploring the Menu bar'.)

- ✔ **Navigation bar:** This bar runs vertically down the left side of the screen. It lists key topics and areas that you may use regularly within Sage. For example, you can access your customers and suppliers, create sales orders, check your stock in the products section, and carry out many other tasks that I cover in this book.

✔ **Work area:** This is the main central space of your screen. You can configure your viewing preferences by choosing Tools and then Options from the Menu bar. You can change your screen view to List format, Process Maps (similar to a flowchart), or Dashboard (a graphical display). The screen automatically defaults to the List format, which is the screen that I use throughout this book.

Exploring the Menu bar

The Menu bar runs horizontally across the top of your screen and provides many navigational tools to help you find your way around Sage.

By clicking the different Menu bar options, you gain access to submenus and different parts of the system. I talk about each option on the Menu bar in the following sections.

File

Clicking File gives you options to create, access, save, and share data. The submenu options are:

✔ **New Report:** This takes you into Sage Report Designer, where you can use the Report wizard to design new reports.

✔ **New Batch Report:** This lets you bundle a set of individual reports together and view, export, print, or email them at the same time. Click F1 for Sage Help and type `batch reporting` for more details.

✔ **Open:** This lets you access the demonstration data and practice data from here, open a report, and open previously archived data, including the VAT archive.

✔ **Close:** This closes the dropdown menu.

✔ **Backup:** This lets you back up your data. You can also back up your data when you exit the program. I recommend you back up your data each time you use Sage, or at least at the end of each day. Backing up more often during the day is a good idea if you process significant amounts of data. For the low-down on backing up your data, check out Chapter 9.

✔ **Schedule Backup:** This new feature in Sage 2015 includes the option to schedule your backups for a specific time each day. Use the Settings tab to determine the details of the backup that you require. I cover this in more detail in Chapter 9.

✔ **Maintenance:** This lets you correct data, delete records, check data, and even rebuild data. I talk about maintenance in more detail in Chapter 9.

✔ **Restore:** This helps you retrieve data from a previous backup. You may need this function if your data has been corrupted and you want to return to a known point in time when the data was free of problems.

✔ **Import:** This lets you import records, such as customer, supplier, stock, assets, nominal accounts, and project records, from other sources, such as Microsoft Excel, as long as they're in a predetermined CSV (comma-separated values) format. This option is very useful when you set up Sage and want to import information. You can speed up the data-entry process if you import information instead of keying in each individual record. I cover importing and CSV formatting in more detail in Chapter 19.

✔ **Microsoft Integration:** Using this option, you can export data to Microsoft Excel, Word, or Outlook.

✔ **Send:** This lets you send a message by using your default email program.

✔ **Log off:** Clicking this option logs you out of Sage.

✔ **Exit:** Clicking this exits you from Sage. You can also exit Sage by clicking the black cross in the top right corner of the screen.

Edit

You can use Edit to cut, copy, paste, insert or delete rows, duplicate cells, or memorise or recall data.

View

The *status bar* is the narrow strip across the bottom of your screen, showing the name of your Sage product, today's date, the start of the financial year, and the current transaction number. You can switch this bar on and off. You can also view the user list, which shows who is currently logged in to Sage.

Modules

The *modules* are essentially the different components that form the whole of the Sage accounting system. The modules include the usual accounting ledgers, such as customers, suppliers, bank, nominal ledger, and reporting functions, but they also include (depending on which version of Sage you purchased) additional components, such as projects, sales order processing, and purchase order processing. You can also access invoicing, quotations, fixed assets, departments, VAT, and transactions functions, wizards, and a diary.

Settings

The settings include the Configuration Editor and Company Preferences, which hold some of the basic information about your company and the way you installed Sage. Settings also include many of the default screens for the ledgers, which save you time when setting up records at a later date. If you use the Customisation Wizard when you install Sage, you may have already seen these default screens. If you need to change the system date or check the financial year, you can do it within settings. Settings also give you access to your Sage security settings and passwords to protect your accounts data. The settings include the following:

- ✓ **Configuration Editor:** This holds the basic information you enter when you complete the Active Set-up wizard. Some of the things you can do here include editing your customer and supplier trading terms, amending your VAT codes, and managing your project cost types and cost codes.

- ✓ **Company Preferences:** This lets you enter extra information if you didn't add everything when you used the Active Set-up wizard. You may want to update your address information or check your VAT details, for example.

- ✓ **Customer/Supplier/Bank/Product/Invoice and Order/Email Defaults:** These settings let you amend parts of the default data you set up on installation.

- ✓ **Financial Year:** This identifies the start of the company's financial year. This date is fixed when you start to enter data.

- ✓ **Change Program Date:** This lets you change dates when you run a month-end or year-end report. The date is normally set to the current day's date, but there may be times, such as period ends, when you wish to change the date temporarily.

- ✓ **Lock date:** Here you can enter a *lock date* into the system, which means you can prevent postings before a specific date. This is useful when you process year ends. Only users with access rights to lock dates can post.

- ✓ **Currencies:** This lets you edit your currency requirements if you use multiple currencies.

- ✓ **Countries:** This lists all the countries in the world and their country codes, and identifies countries that are currently members of the EU. The Sage 50 Accounts Professional package uses this information to comply with Intrastat reporting requirements. (I talk more about Intrastat in Chapter 17.) You can amend the Countries table as and when countries enter or leave the EU.

- ✓ **Control Accounts:** This gives you an at-a-glance list of all the control accounts within Sage. A *control account* is a summary of all entries within a specific ledger. For example, the sales ledger control account includes all transactions for all sales ledger accounts – the balance on the control account tallies with the sum of the sales ledger accounts. Control accounts are used as a check on the numerical accuracy of the ledger accounts and form part of the double-entry system that Sage performs when you enter transactions.

If you want to change the control accounts, do so before you enter any transactions – otherwise leave them alone!

You can reconcile a control account. Just click Help and follow the instructions for reconciling debtors or creditors.

✔ **Change password:** This lets you change your password periodically as part of your data protection and security routine.

✔ **Internet Resources:** This gives you an Internet Resources list that you can use to set your courier and credit bureau information. You can launch your website browser from within Sage and go to your credit bureau to check the status of a customer or go to a courier's website to track the progress of a parcel.

Tools

The Tools option is a hotchpotch of items. You can run the Global Changes wizard, carry out contra entries, run period ends, open up Report Designer, and convert reports, to name but a few. I outline the options below:

✔ **Global Changes:** Here you can globally change customer or supplier credit limits, turnover values, nominal budgets, product sales or purchase prices, reorder details, and discount table values.

✔ **Activation:** This lets you upgrade your program and enable third-party integration with the Construction Industry Scheme (CIS) and foreign traders (if you have Sage 50 Accounts Professional). Third-party integration lets you use add-on software tailored to your specific industry. Sage has a separate module for CIS and the recording of payments to subcontractors. You can activate this scheme by clicking Tools and then Activation for businesses that fall under the scheme.

You can use the Upgrade Program option to register after your initial 30-day Sage trial period runs out.

✔ **Opening Balances:** This gives you a series of actions that you need to complete to enter your opening balances. In Chapter 4 I guide you through the Opening Balances wizard.

✔ **Period End:** This lets you run the month end, allowing you to post accruals, prepayments, and depreciation. This option also clears the current-month turnover figures. You can run your year end, which sets your profit and loss nominal accounts to zero for the new financial year.

✔ **Consolidation:** You can use this to create multi-company accounts. You also have the opportunity to clear stock, delete stock, and clear your audit trail. (In Chapter 16 I talk more about clearing stock and audit trails.) You can also archive company data so at a later point you can compare current year values against archived data.

✔ **Transaction Email:** This lets you exchange invoices and orders with your customers and suppliers via Microsoft Outlook. You can import any orders or invoices that you receive via email directly into your Sage accounts.

✔ **Report Designer:** Here you can edit and create new reports customised for your business.

✔ **Event Log:** This shows a history of system events. If you contact the Sage helpline with a system problem, your event log may come in handy.

✔ **Options:** This gives you options to change the settings and appearance of Sage. For example, you can change the default view of the Customers and Suppliers screens from the process map to customer or supplier lists, using the View tab.

✔ **Batch reporting:** You can generate several reports from any area of the Sage software at the same time. Type `batch reports` into the Search field in Sage to find more information.

✔ **Data Service Manager:** The Sage Accounts Data Service runs on the computer or server where your Sage Accounts data is held. The service acts as a gateway and controls the reading and writing of data. Using this service increases the robustness of the system, improves data security, and helps optimise performance. You shouldn't need to change or amend this in any way.

✔ **Internet Options:** Here you can vary the Sage update criteria, enter Sage Cover login details, and enable Sage Mobile by clicking the Mobile tab.

Favourites

You can store your favourite reports here. To find out how to set up favourite reports, use the Help menu supplied with Report Designer, which you access via Tools on the Browser toolbar. In Chapter 18 I go into more detail about the Report Designer.

Weblinks

Weblinks gives you a number of links to useful websites, such as Sage shop and HM Revenue & Customs.

Help

Help is the last entry on the Menu bar but probably one of the most useful. If you want to understand more about the system and want to know how to do something, click the Help option. You have several help options to choose from, all of which take you to a Webhelp page where you can enter your keyword and click Search to find answers to your problems. In addition you can find the Customise Your Company wizard here, which you may have discovered when you first installed Sage. You can access these screens and amend your module defaults and other administrative functions at any time.

The About page now contains a raft of information about your computer, including system details, licence information, and contact details for Sage. Sage support staff often find this page very useful if you ask them for help with software problems.

Using Wizards

A number of wizards wield their technological magic through Sage. Their job is to help you through a wide variety of set-ups and tasks. You can access these helpful creatures from the Browser toolbar by clicking Modules and then Wizards.

A wizard's job is to make your work easy. All you have to do is follow the prompts and enter the information the wizard requests. Magic!

Wizards can help you in setting up Sage and day-to-day processing. They can help you set up new records for customers, suppliers, nominal accounts, bank accounts, products, and projects. You can also use wizards to do the tricky double-entry bookkeeping for items such as opening and closing stock, fuel-scale charges, and VAT transfers. Sage even provides a wizard to help you set up the foreign trader features. In Chapter 22 I offer lots more info about Sage's wizards.

Chapter 2

Creating Your Chart of Accounts and Assigning Nominal Codes

In This Chapter

▶ Getting familiar with some accounting concepts

▶ Charting your accounts

▶ Adding nominal codes in your chart of accounts

▶ Changing your chart of accounts

*I*n this chapter, I get down to the nitty-gritty of the accounting system – the chart of accounts (COA), which is made up of nominal codes. Think of the COA as the engine of the accounting system. From the information in your COA, you produce your profit and loss report, your balance sheet, your budget report, and prior-year reports. Set up your COA properly and the chart grows with your business – but set it up wrongly and you'll have problems for ever more.

Luckily, Sage gives you a lot of help and does the hard work for you, but you still need to understand why Sage is structured in the way that it is and how you can customise it to suit your business.

Understanding as Much as You Need to about Accounting

To use Sage, it helps if you have an appreciation of accounts and understand what you want to achieve. But you certainly don't need to understand all the rules of double-entry bookkeeping. In this section I give you the basics of accounting principles so you can use Sage more comfortably.

Dabbling in double-entry bookkeeping

Accounting systems and accounting programs such as Sage use the principle of *double-entry bookkeeping,* so called because each transaction is recorded twice. For every debit entry, you record a corresponding credit entry. Doing the two entries helps balance the books.

For example, if you make a cash sale for £100, your sales account receives a £100 credit and your cash account gets a £100 debit.

Some knowledge of double-entry rules helps when you use Sage. That way, you can interpret information a little more easily. The following is a short summary of the rules of double-entry bookkeeping:

- ✔ **Asset and expense accounts:** Debit the account for an increase and credit the account for a decrease in value.
- ✔ **Liability and income and sales accounts:** Debit the account for a decrease and credit the account for an increase in value.

Fortunately, you don't need to book yourself into a bookkeeping evening class, as Sage does the double-entry for you . . . phew! (If you're intrigued by the double-entry system, though, pick up a copy of *Bookkeeping For Dummies* by Jane Kelly, Paul Barrow, and Lita Epstein (Wiley), which explains double-entry and more.)

Having said that, understanding the double-entry method does help with Sage, particularly if you intend to do your own nominal journals. This knowledge also comes in handy if you intend to produce monthly management accounts. Sometimes, you need to post nominal journals to correct mistakes, and understanding the principles of double-entry bookkeeping lets you confidently process journals. Don't panic, though – Sage has many wizards that can post things like depreciation, accruals, and prepayments for you – so if you struggle with journals, leave them to your accountant or at least seek advice if you aren't sure.

Naming your nominals

In accounting and in Sage, you bump into the term *nominal* quite a bit. And for good reason, as several key concepts use the word:

- ✔ **Nominal account:** Every item of income, expense, asset, and liability is posted to a nominal ledger account. The nominal ledger accounts categorise all your transactions. The individual nominal accounts are grouped into ranges and can be viewed in your COA.

✔ **Nominal code:** A four-digit number is given to each account that appears in the nominal ledger. For example, 7502 is the nominal code for office stationery, which is an account in the nominal ledger. Sage categorises each nominal code into nine different ranges, and these categories form the basis of your COA.

✔ **Nominal ledger:** The nominal ledger is an accumulation of all the nominal accounts – it's the main body of the accounting system. Each nominal account shows all the transactions posted to that specific code, so it follows that the nominal ledger represents all the transactions of the business in one place. Deep joy, I hear you say!

To find the nominal ledger, click on Nominal Codes on the Navigation bar, down the left side of the screen.

✔ **Nominal record:** Each nominal code has an individual nominal record. To create a new nominal code, open up a new nominal record and give it the new nominal code as its reference. See Chapter 3 for more details about nominal records.

Sage categorises nominal codes in a specific way, so don't change them without careful consideration. Using common sense and planning at the early stages of implementing Sage can pay huge dividends in the future. You need to correctly categorise your nominal codes in order to create meaningful reports.

Preparing reports

One of the reasons you're investing in Sage is probably so you can run reports to see how your business is doing. And your money is well spent, for Sage has many reports you can run at the click of a button. The important thing to remember is that reports are only as good as the information contained within them. The old saying 'Rubbish in, rubbish out' is never truer.

The two key financial reports every business and every accounting system uses are:

✔ **Balance sheet:** This report shows a snapshot of the business. It identifies assets and liabilities and shows how the business is funded via the capital accounts.

✔ **Profit and loss report:** This report shows the revenue and costs associated with the business for a given period and identifies whether the business is making a profit or incurring a loss.

The profit and loss and balance sheet reports are created from the information in the COA, so it's important to get the COA right.

I discuss the profit and loss report and balance sheet more fully in Chapter 18, where I also cover producing monthly accounts and the types of report you may need.

Looking at the Structure of Your COA

The COA is a list of nominal codes, divided into the following nine categories:

- ✔ Fixed Assets
- ✔ Current Assets
- ✔ Current Liabilities
- ✔ Long-term Liabilities
- ✔ Capital and Reserves
- ✔ Sales
- ✔ Purchases
- ✔ Direct Expenses
- ✔ Overhead

The first five categories form the balance sheet; the remaining categories create your profit and loss report. So the COA is a pretty important part of the system.

A look at the nominal list on the Nominal Ledger screen shows that the list runs in numerical order, with the balance sheet codes first. If you click the Chart of Accounts icon within the nominal ledger, and look at the default layout of accounts, you notice a tab for Profit and Loss and another for Balance Sheet. You can click on either of these two tabs and a preview of the report appears on the right side of the screen.

Checking out the default COA

Being a caring, sharing software developer, Sage provides a default COA for you to use, with a ready-made list of nominal codes. (You select the type of COA you want using the Active Set-up wizard, which I go through in Chapter 1.) Your COA is determined by the type of business you operate.

When you install Sage, it asks you what business type to use. I use the Limited Company business type to demonstrate Sage in this book.

Although Sage can spot if a new nominal code is outside the range of the usual COA, it can't really help with the structure of the coding system that you choose to use, so plan ahead to avoid costly mistakes.

You can also customise the default COA to suit your business. I tell you how in the 'Editing Your COA' section later in this chapter.

The COA is in the Nominal codes module. To display it, click Modules on the Menu bar and then select Nominal codes, or simply click Nominal codes from the Navigation bar down the left side of the screen.

The Navigation bar is in full view all the time you use Sage.

The opening screen for the Nominal codes module is shown in Figure 2-1. You can access the COA by clicking on the icon shown in the Nominal codes module.

Figure 2-1: Clicking on Nominal codes to get to the COA.

The Nominal codes screen shows a series of icons, one of which is the Chart of Accounts icon. You can also create and amend nominal codes from this screen, create journals, accruals, and prepayments, and run a series of nominal ledger reports.

For a better look at the Chart of Accounts screen, follow these steps:

1. Click the Chart of Accounts icon on the Nominal codes toolbar.

The Chart of Accounts window opens, which gives you a list of all the COAs you have created. At first, only the Default Layout of Accounts shows, but any subsequent COAs you create also show here.

2. **Highlight the COA you want to view and click the Edit button at the bottom of the next screen.**

   Initially, the COA you want is the Default Layout of Accounts.

   The Edit Chart of Accounts window for the Default Layout of Accounts screen opens, as in Figure 2-2. This screen shows the category types and a description in the top left of the screen, and the Category Accounts list showing the nominal codes associated with those categories outlined below. To the right of the screen, you see a preview of the profit and loss report layout.

   As you click each category type in the first box, you see that the nominal codes shown in the Category Account List below change to match the category type.

Figure 2-2:
Looking at the Edit Chart of Accounts window.

The first category is Sales, as in Figure 2-2. Since Sales is highlighted in the first box, you notice that the Category Account List below shows the high and low ranges of nominal codes within each sales category. I explain the nominal code ranges in the next two sections.

If you're not sure which nominal codes fall into the range described, you can print a complete list of nominal codes. Alternatively, you can click the number in the Low or High column and use the dropdown arrow next to the field to see which account the nominal code refers to. You can then scroll down the list of accounts that appear and view the range of codes.

To print a hard copy of the nominal list, use the following steps. The list usually consists of two or three pages, but the length depends on the number of codes you create. The more codes, the longer the list.

1. **From the Navigation bar, click Nominal codes.**

2. **Click the Print List button at the top right (third from the end) of the screen.**

   A command is sent to your printer to run off a hard copy of the existing codes.

The list of nominal codes may look rather daunting at first, but I talk you through the basics in the next sections.

Identifying balance sheet codes

The *balance sheet* is a snapshot of your business at a fixed point in time. The balance sheet identifies your company's assets and liabilities and shows how your business has been funded via the capital accounts. To achieve this snapshot, the balance sheet looks at your business's assets and liabilities, so it draws on the numbers in a range of nominal codes:

- ✔ **Fixed assets (0010–0051):** A *fixed asset* is an item likely to be held in the business for a long period of time – more than 12 months. The range of fixed-asset codes is used for transactions relating to freehold and leasehold property and other items the company plans to hold for a while. You can add other capital items, such as computer equipment, to this list.

- ✔ **Current assets (1001–1250):** A *current asset* is an item that has a lifespan of 12 months or less. You should be able to *liquidate* (turn into cash) current assets reasonably quickly. Common current assets include stock, debts owed to the business, and bank and cash items. Current assets are normally ordered in the least liquid order first, meaning items that take the longest to convert into cash appear at the top of the list. Therefore you expect to see cash, which is so liquid it runs through some people's hands like water, at the bottom of the current assets list.

- ✔ **Current liabilities (2100–2230):** *Current liabilities* are amounts the business owes, normally outstanding for less than 12 months. At the top of the list is the Creditors control account, which is basically the total owed to all suppliers. The list also includes amounts owed to HM Revenue & Customs, such as VAT and PAYE, if applicable.

✔ **Long-term liabilities (2300–2330):** *Long-term liabilities* are amounts owed by the business for a period of more than 12 months. They include long-term loans, hire-purchase agreements, and mortgages.

✔ **Capital (3000–3200):** Capital accounts show how the business is funded. These codes include share issues, reserves, and the current profit and loss balance.

Reserves is another word for earnings retained within the business – they're officially called *retained earnings.* Annual profits swell this account, and any distributions of dividends to owners of the business reduce the balance.

In order for the balance sheet to balance, the capital account includes the current-year profit, as shown in the profit and loss report.

Table 2-1 shows the range of nominal codes that form the balance sheet.

Table 2-1	Balance Sheet Nominal Codes	
Category	*Low*	*High*
Fixed Assets		
Property	0010	0019
Plant & Machinery	0020	0029
Office Equipment	0030	0039
Furniture & Fixtures	0040	0049
Motor Vehicles	0050	0059
Current Assets		
Stock	1000	1099
Debtors	1100	1199
Bank Account	1200	1209
Deposits & Cash	1210	1239
Credit Card (Debtors)	1250	1250
VAT Liability	2200	2209
Current Liabilities		
Creditors: Short Term	2100	2199
Taxation	2210	2219
Wages	2220	2299

Category	Low	High
Credit Card (Creditors)	1240	1240
Bank Account	1200	1209
VAT Liability	2200	2209
Long-term Liabilities		
Creditors: Long Term	2300	2399
Capital & Reserves		
Share Capital	3000	3099
Reserves	3100	3299

Looking at profit and loss codes

In the default set of nominal codes, all codes from 4000 onwards are profit and loss codes, which, appropriately enough, include the numbers that show how much money the business brings in and spends. The profit and loss codes include the following:

- ✔ **Sales (4000–4999):** Sales codes apply to goods or services that your business offers; they indicate how you earn your money. The 4000– range also includes income other than sales, for example royalty commissions.

  The default descriptions against the sales codes are nonsense. The names Sales type A, B, C, D and so on are not meaningful to anyone. You need to change the sales types to make them applicable to your business. If you own a card shop, for example, Sales type A may become nominal code 4000 for birthday cards, sales type B may become nominal code 4005 for get-well cards, and so on. I look at editing nominal codes in Chapter 3.

- ✔ **Purchases (5000–5299):** These codes identify material purchases and purchasing costs such as carriage, packaging, and transport insurance. *Material purchases* is a very general term for the purchase of the raw materials used to make the products the business sells. For example, flour is a material purchase for a bakery.

- ✔ **Direct expenses (6000–6999):** A *direct expense* is a cost directly associated with the product being manufactured or created by the business. Labour costs, including subcontractors, come under these codes. The codes also include expenses such as sales commissions, samples, and public relations costs that can be associated directly with the products.

- ✔ **Overheads (7000–9999):** By far the largest range of codes is *overheads*, which covers all other expenses not directly associated with making and providing the products or service. You can see the overheads subsections in Table 2-2.

Table 2-2 lists the nominal codes that form the profit and loss report.

Table 2-2	Profit and Loss Nominal Codes	
Category	*Low*	*High*
Sales Revenue		
Product Sales	4000	4099
Export Sales	4100	4199
Sales of Assets	4200	4299
Credit Charges	4400	4499
Other Sales	4900	4999
Purchases		
Purchases	5000	5099
Purchase Charges	5100	5199
Stock	5200	5299
Direct Expenses		
Labour	6000	6099
Commissions	6100	6199
Sales Promotion	6200	6299
Miscellaneous Expenses	6900	6999
Overheads		
Gross Wages	7000	7099
Rent & Rates	7100	7199
Heat, Light & Power	7200	7299
Motor Expenses	7300	7399
Travelling & Entertainment	7400	7499
Printing & Stationery	7500	7599
Professional Fees	7600	7699
Equipment Hire & Rental	7700	7799
Maintenance	7800	7899
Bank Charges & Interest	7900	7999
Depreciation	8000	8099
Bad Debts	8100	8199
General Expenses	8200	8299
Suspense & Mispostings	9998	9999

You use the suspense and mispostings nominal accounts when you can't find another suitable nominal code. Suspense and mispostings nominal accounts serve as holding pens – somewhere to post an item while you try to find a better code to post it to. At the end of each month, review the suspense and mispostings accounts and put the items in their correct locations. Unfortunately, the suspense account can become a dumping ground – try to use this account only when absolutely necessary.

Leaving gaps and mirroring codes

The ranges of codes leave plenty of gaps between the categories. For example, Sales codes start at 4000 but Purchase codes don't begin until 5000. You can fill the large gap between 4000 and 4999 with Sales codes, which provides a great deal of flexibility for a growing business.

I suggest leaving gaps of ten between each code to allow for growth, but it's entirely up to you to decide the best fit for your business.

You may consider mirroring corresponding sales and purchase codes, so the last two digits are the same for the sale and purchase of each item, as in Table 2-3, which shows the nominal codes for Jingles, a fictional card shop and party-planning company I created to serve as an example throughout this book.

Table 2-3		**Mirroring Nominal Codes**	
Nominal Code	*Description*	*Nominal Code*	*Description*
4000	Sale of greetings cards	5000	Purchase of greetings cards
4020	Sale of party balloons	5020	Purchase of party balloons
4030	Sale of party gifts	5030	Purchase of party gifts

Accommodating floating nominals

A *floating nominal* is a code that can be placed as a current asset or current liability, depending on whether the balance is a debit or a credit. For example, if your bank account is in the black, it's a current asset – but if your account is overdrawn, it shows as a current liability. Another example is the

VAT liability account, as you can sometimes get a refund from HM Revenue and Customs.

Sage automatically places floating nominals to the correct side of the balance sheet, but only if you identify the specific codes that can be treated as an asset or a liability in the Floating Nominal Accounts section on the Edit Chart of Accounts screen. Sage normally designates accounts as floating nominal codes, so you don't have to do anything.

Editing Your COA

One of the first things to consider when setting up Sage is how well the COA suits your business. Have a look at the categories and nominal codes to make sure they contain suitable descriptions for your products or services. For example, the Product Sales category doesn't suit a business that primarily provides a service. You may want to change a few categories, or you may decide to make wholesale changes, in which case it may be simpler to create an entirely new COA. The next sections tell you how to change and create COAs.

If you place a nominal code in the wrong category, you may find inaccuracies in the reports you produce. Miscodings are every accountant's nightmare. When you create new codes, be sure you know whether the code should be a balance sheet or a profit and loss item. You can usually rely on your common sense, but if you're unsure, give your accountant a quick call. Accountants don't mind answering a quick question like this, but they do mind if you mix up balance sheet and profit and loss codes and they then have the task of unpicking your mistakes.

Amending your COA

You can edit the default COA to suit your business.

In Figure 2-2 (in the earlier 'Checking out the default COA' section), the category types showed profit and loss items on the first tab and balance sheet items on the second tab. If you move your cursor down the list of categories in the first box, you notice the details in the Category Account list below change to reflect the heading names and nominal codes contained within the highlighted category types. To view the nominal code ranges in more detail, click the nominal code and then use the dropdown arrow to identify the name of the nominal code.

You can change the description of each category in the first box on the COA screen. You can also change the description of the ranges of nominal codes shown in the Category Account list. One of the first things to change is the Product Sales headings. These headings are very general descriptions and won't suit all businesses. For example, if you're a baker, you may want to change the sales types to bread sales, cake sales, and so on.

The headings in the COA show up in your profit and loss report and balance sheet (which you can preview on the right side of the COA screen), so you need to give careful consideration to which headings you want to see on your financial reports. If you don't want an extensive list of different types of sales categories on your profit and loss account, consider grouping together several nominal codes under more general headings.

After you decide on the level of detail you want to show on your reports, you're ready to amend your COA by following these steps:

1. **From the Navigation bar, click Nominal codes and then click Chart of Accounts.**

2. **Highlight Default Layout of Accounts and then click Edit.**

3. **Make any changes to headings within the category account.**

   Changes available are:

   - **Rename a heading:** Simply click the title and overtype with the new name. Jeanette, the owner of Jingles, changes Product Sales to Shop Sales.

   When you rename a heading, make sure all the nominal codes included within the renamed heading relate to the new heading. (Check out Chapter 3 for more help with this.)

   - **Insert a new heading:** To insert a line in the Category Account list, click the line below where you want to insert a line and press the F7 function key. A message comes up to say that inserting a line moves all categories down by one. Click Yes and don't panic when the codes above disappear from view. They're still there – they've just moved up. Scroll up the category accounts to see where your line has been inserted. Type the name of the new heading and then enter the range of nominal codes to which it relates.

   Figure 2-3 shows the newly created Party Fees heading for Jingles. At the moment, the new heading has only one relevant nominal code (4350 Party Organising), so this code is both the low and high range. If Jeanette wants to add more nominal codes at a later date, she can include them in the high range. If the new code was 4370, the range of nominal codes for Party Fees would be 4350–4370.

Figure 2-3:
Inserting a
new head-
ing in the
COA.

- **Delete a heading:** You can use F8 to delete a heading line, but make sure you won't want to use those nominal codes in future.

4. Click Save when you're happy with the changes you've made.

You need to go through your COA for errors, so take a look at the 'Checking Your COA' section later in this chapter.

Creating a new COA

If the existing COA doesn't suit your business at all, you may find that creating your own COA is less work than adapting the COA Sage provides. You may decide to use your existing nominal codes from your old accounting system, in which case you can customise the COA with your existing codes.

Alternatively, you may find your business has particular geographical locations or segments that you wish to report on. You can create a new COA for each segment or location, but make it specific for your business. For example, you may have an office in London and one in Edinburgh. With the creation of suitable nominal codes, you can produce a profit and loss report to the gross profit line for each office. So you group together all the sales codes associated with the London office and deduct from them all London office purchases and direct costs. This results in a London office gross profit. You can do the same exercise for the Edinburgh office with a separate COA, and then you can compare the two, to see which office was the most profitable.

Being able to analyse any further than gross profit requires an extremely complex set of nominal codes. Speak to your friendly accountant, who can assist with complicated nominal code structures.

 When you add a new COA with the purpose of producing a profit and loss report to gross profit level, be aware that you can only select the nominal codes specific to that geographical location or segment of the business. As a result, the word *partial* appears after the COA name because you haven't selected all of the nominal codes. In addition to the gross profit reports, you must always have a fully complete COA for the whole business, which you must check for errors before you run reports, as I explain in the section 'Checking Your COA' later in this chapter. Don't try to check a COA that has *partial* in the title, as Sage always brings up a list of codes that are missing.

To add a COA, follow these steps:

1. **From the Navigation bar, select the Nominal codes module and click Chart Of Accounts.**

2. **Click Add from the Chart of Accounts window.**

   The New Chart of Accounts window appears.

3. **Enter the name of your new COA and click Add.** A new Edit Chart of Accounts window opens, with the title of your new COA in the top right corner.

4. **Select each category type by clicking the Description field in the first box and then enter a description in the Category Account List box below.** Enter new headings and assign a range of codes for each heading for the Profit and Loss tab and the Balance Sheet tab.

Figure 2-4 shows a new COA called Jingles Card Shop. The Jingles business consists of two parts: One part is the card shop, which sells cards, balloons, and so on, and the other part is party-planning. To see the gross profit made on each part of the business, I created a separate COA for each segment. I selected only the nominal codes specific to the card shop and ignored any party-planning codes. Because I didn't include all the nominal codes in this COA, Sage includes the word *partial* in the title.

To get accurate reports for the whole of the business, I need to use the default COA, as this COA includes all nominal codes.

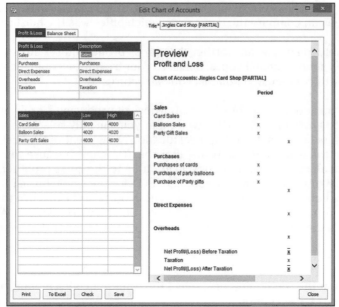

Figure 2-4:
A new COA
created for
the Jingles
Card Shop.

After you add a new COA, you can run your profit and loss report to see what information pulls through. Pay attention to the descriptions that you use in your COA, as they transfer through to your profit and loss and balance sheet reports. At this point, you can see the gross profit for each part of the business and determine what is making money or not, as the case may be.

When you edit your COA, you can use the F7 function key to insert a line and the F8 key to delete a line.

Deleting a COA

You may find that when you play around designing new COAs, you create too many variations and want to delete some of them. Follow these steps to delete a COA:

1. **Click Nominal codes and then Chart of Accounts.**

   The Chart of Accounts window opens.

2. **Highlight the COA that you want to delete and click Delete.**

3. **Click Yes to confirm that you want to delete the COA.**

   If you decide that you don't want to delete, click No and return to the main Chart of Accounts window.

If you want just one code within the range, then the code is the same in both the High and Low columns.

Checking Your COA

After you make changes to your COA, you need to ensure your COA doesn't contain any errors. If an error is present, the profit and loss or balance sheet reports may be incorrect, and a warning message flashes up every time you run these reports.

To check your COA, follow these steps:

1. Go to the Nominal codes module and click Chart of Accounts.

2. Click Edit.

3. Click Check.

If no problems are present, Sage tells you no errors were found in the COA and you can breathe a sigh of relief. However, if a little window entitled Chart of Accounts Errors appears, be prepared to take corrective action.

Previewing errors

The Chart of Accounts Errors window gives you four output options for displaying the error report:

✔ **Printer:** This sends the report directly to your printer.

✔ **Preview:** This lets you look at the errors on the screen before you decide to print or exit.

✔ **File:** This saves the report to a new location.

✔ **Email:** This lets you email the document to another person.

Usually, the best method is to preview the report first, to make sure it provides the information you expected, and then print a hard copy if you like what you see.

Make sure the option you want has a filled-in circle next to it and then click the Run button at the bottom of the pop-up screen. Figure 2-5 is a sample error report, showing that a nominal code is not represented in the chart. The missing code must be included within the nominal code ranges to stop the error report coming up.

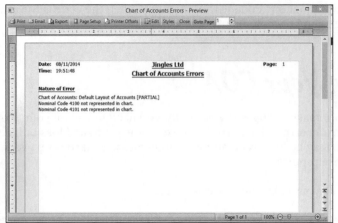

Figure 2-5:
An error
showing up
in a COA
error report.

Looking at some common errors

Whenever you add new nominal codes, the chance exists that the codes may not fit within the nominal code structure currently in place. This common oversight leads to errors within the COA.

Check the steps in the 'Amending your COA' section earlier in this chapter for advice on how to fix the errors I list here.

Other common errors include the following:

- ✔ **Overlapping ranges:** The same nominal code occurs in two different ranges and is therefore counted twice.

  For example, Jeanette, the owner of Jingles Card Shop, assigned the Sale of Cards category nominal codes from 4000 to 4199, and then assigned the Sale of Balloons category nominal codes from 4100 to 4299. The error report points out that the categories overlap between 4100 and 4199. Jeanette needs to amend the ranges so they don't overlap.

- ✔ **Enclosing one range within another range:** Assigning a range of codes within another range is a big no-no.

  For example, Jeanette assigned the Sale of Balloons category a range from 4100 to 4299, and then assigned the Sale of Party Gifts category codes from 4200 to 4250, which is within the Sale of Balloons range. She needs to fix this so she knows whether she's selling mostly balloons or mostly party gifts.

✔ **Using a floating code in one category but not in its complementary category:** You may require a floating code so that an item such as the bank account can be both a current asset and a current liability, depending on whether the account is in the black or overdrawn. If you set up a floating code in Current Assets but not in Current Liabilities or vice versa, you get an error message.

Chapter 3

Setting Up Records

. . . .

In This Chapter

▶ Choosing a quick start or step-by-step process

▶ Setting up records for customers and suppliers

▶ Registering your bank accounts

▶ Accounting for your products

▶ Depreciating your fixed assets

. . . .

*A*fter you install your Sage software, you quickly realise that the hard work is only just beginning. You now have to create the records necessary to operate your accounting system, including records for your customers, suppliers, and existing bank accounts. Depending on your business, you may also need to set up stock and project records. In this chapter I tell you how to do these things.

Choosing How to Create Your Records

Setting up records may seem a daunting task, but Sage provides at least two ways of doing things. You can use the quick way, which uses the New icon within the relevant module, or you can use the step-by-step way, which uses the Wizard icon. If you like the belt and braces approach, click the Wizard icon, as the wizard helps you complete each section of the record thoroughly. If you're a bit of a speed freak and want to get on with things as quickly as possible, and you don't mind leaving a few less important data fields blank (you can always update them later), choose the quick start option. I always use the quick start method, as my time is invariably of the essence.

Getting a quick start using the New icon

If you want a quick start, find the module you want to create a new record for and click the New icon. This opens up a new blank record, where you can start typing in the details straight away.

Having a change of view

When you create a customer or supplier record, you can choose which view you see each time you open your customers or suppliers module – flowchart or dashboard layout. The default settings within Sage have these options switched off – to look at and activate these screens, you need to do the following:

1. **From the Menu bar, click Tools.**

2. **Select Options.**

3. **Click Yes to the confirmation screen if you have other windows open.**

4. **In the Options menu, select the View tab.**

   When the Options window opens, as in Figure 3-1, uncheck the boxes in the Global settings module. Select the options you'd like to see each time you open a new record.

5. **Click OK.**

Figure 3-1:
Changing
the defaults
settings
from list to
process
maps or
dashboard
display.

Following the wizards brick by brick

Like Dorothy and friends finding their way to the Emerald City, going brick by brick or step by step can take some time, but it does get you where you need to be. Using the wizards is slower than using the New icon, as the wizards guide you through the completion of every box in each record. For example, if you're keen on keeping customers within their credit limit and offer discounts for early settlement, you may want to use the Customer wizard to guide you through setting up the intricacies of your credit control.

To awaken a wizard, click the module you want to create a new record within and then click the Wizard icon. The program takes you through a step-by-step wizard, which prompts you to dot every i and cross every t. Wizards are thorough, but using them can be time-consuming. (For more information about wizards, check out Chapter 22.)

Creating Customer and Supplier Records

Setting up customer and supplier records is essentially the same process, so I cover both in this section. Wizards can walk you through creating both types of record – just click the Wizard icon in the relevant module.

If you prefer to use the quick start method, click the New icon within Customers and a blank customer record appears, as in Figure 3-2. Several tabs appear across the top of the record:

✔ **Details:** Type the usual contact details in these fields.

Decide how you want to set up the account reference before you begin your data entry. Think carefully about this first data-entry field and the eight-digit short name you give each account. Sage recommends you use an *alphanumeric* reference – containing both letters and numbers – in case you have clients with the same name. For example, you may have the references Smith01, Smith02, and so on. Alternatively, you can use customers' initials, so the reference for Julian Smith is SmithJ, Sarah Smith becomes SmithS, and so on.

After you type in the account reference, tab through the other fields and enter the relevant information.

If you transfer from a different computer package, you may be able to import the customer records from your old system to Sage. See Chapter 19 for info on how to do this.

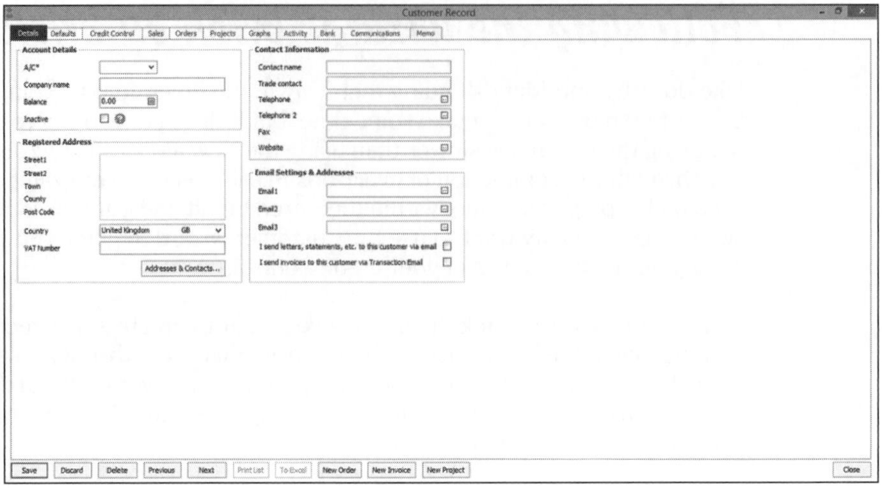

Figure 3-2:
Example
of a blank
customer
record.

✔ **Defaults:** The basic defaults are shown in each record. You can override the details for each individual record and tailor the defaults for your customers.

For example, the default nominal code is currently set at 4000, but if you have a customer for whom this code never applies, you can change the code to something more suitable. For example, Jingles may sell only balloons to one customer, so it makes sense to set the default nominal code for that customer as Sale of Balloons.

✔ **Credit Control:** You can enter your credit control details here for both customers and suppliers. For example, you can set credit limits so if a customer exceeds those limits, Sage warns you and you can take steps to get the customer's account back under control. You can note details such as credit reviews and settlement discounts to assist you in your credit control.

I suggest you tick the Terms Agreed box in the bottom left corner of the Credit Control screen. If you don't, every time you open that record, you get an audio and visual prompt saying you haven't agreed terms with this account.

✔ **Sales (customer record):** You can view a history of all invoices, credit notes, balances, receipts, and payments against this account, helping you identify trends in the customer's monthly transactions.

✔ **Purchases (supplier record):** You can view a history of all invoices, credit notes, balances, payments, and receipts applied to this supplier's account so you can see trends developing in your transactions with the supplier.

✔ **Orders:** You can see the history of all sales orders applied to this account. Double-click any of the orders to enter the details of the sales order record. You can also create a new sales invoice or a new order from this screen.

✔ **Projects:** You can view a list of all the projects associated with this customer. You can also create a new project record for the customer by clicking New Project Record (I explain this in more detail in Chapter 13).

✔ **Graphs:** Prepare to be wowed with a graphical representation of the history of your month-by-month transactions.

✔ **Activity:** I use this screen a lot. It shows a list of every transaction ever made on the selected account. You can see all the invoices and credit notes, payments, and receipts. The screen also shows the balance, amounts paid and received, and turnover for the account.

Each line on the Activity list represents a single invoice, credit note, receipt, payment, or payment on account. You can drill down into additional detail by clicking the plus sign (+) on the left side of the transaction line. You can also view the aged detail of your customer or supplier accounts, shown at the bottom of the Activity tab. Future, Current, 30 days, 60 days, 90 days, and Older buttons show values according to the age of the outstanding amounts.

✔ **Bank:** You can enter bank details on each record. This option is useful if you do a lot of online banking, particularly payment of suppliers.

✔ **Communications:** You can record details of telephone conversations with both customers and suppliers. For example, if you're making a credit control call, you can make notes of promised payments and follow-up dates for callbacks, which creates an event in your Sage Diary. This information also appears in the Task Manager.

If your business charges on a time basis, you can directly invoice a customer from the Communications tab for time spent on a phone call. See Chapter 6 for more details on this.

✔ **Memo:** You can attach electronic documents and files for all your customer and supplier records using the Document Manager function. For more details on this function, see Chapter 19. You can also make notes about your customers and suppliers, including details of phone calls.

Setting customer and supplier defaults

Whenever you create a customer or supplier record, you enter details such as the credit limit, discounts, and terms of payment. If all the same terms apply to all your customers or suppliers, you can set up this information only once so it then applies to all customer or supplier records that you create. This option can save you time, particularly at the start when you create lots of records. If terms are different for a few individual customers or suppliers, or if the terms change for some reason, you can override the defaults in individual customer or supplier records at any time.

If all your customers and suppliers are different, don't set up defaults.

If you set up Sage using the Customise your Company option (which I explain in Chapter 1), you can ignore this section.

The following steps apply to setting up customer defaults, but you can use the same process for supplier defaults:

1. **Click Settings from the Menu bar, and then click Customer Defaults (or Supplier Defaults).**

   The Customer Defaults (or Supplier Defaults) screen opens on the Record tab. Here you can enter the currency if Foreign Trader is enabled (otherwise it's greyed out) and edit the VAT code, nominal code, and any discounts applicable.

2. **Click the Statements tab if you want to change the way some of the wording shows on customer statements.** For example, when invoices are shown on statements, and the default wording is 'Goods/Services', you can change this to whatever you like – 'Fees charged', for example.

3. **Click the Ageing tab if you want to switch from Period Ageing to Calendar Monthly Ageing.**

   Period ageing sets periods of less than 30, 60, 90 days, and 120 days or more. For example, if an invoice is dated 15 January 2013, the invoice falls into the current period between 15 January and 13 February (within 30 days) and the 30-days plus period between 14 February and 14 March.

   Calendar monthly ageing means all the month's transactions are classed as outstanding on the first day of the month. For example, if the invoice is dated 15 January 2014, the invoice falls into the current period if an aged report is run between 1 January and 31 January. If the aged report is run between 1 February and 29 February, the invoice falls into Period 1, and so on.

4. **Click the Discount tab if you apply different discount percentages, depending on the value of the invoices.**

   This option applies to customer defaults only, not supplier defaults.

Deleting customer and supplier records

You may want to delete a record if you set up a duplicate account in error.

You can delete a record only if there are no transactions on the account and the account balance is zero. If neither condition is met and you try to delete an account, Sage lets you know in no uncertain terms that you can't do it.

If there are no transactions on the duplicate account, you can delete it. If you have unwittingly added transactions to the duplicate account, you can change them using the File Maintenance option, which I describe in Chapter 9. You then need to rename the duplicate account with the words Do Not Use! in the title.

To delete a record, follow these steps:

1. **Open the appropriate customer or supplier ledger and select the account you want to delete.**

2. **Click Delete.**

   When the confirmation message appears, click Yes.

Creating Your Nominal Records

Nominal records are the main body of an accounting system. They're categorised into a chart of accounts structure, which I explain in Chapter 2.

In this section, I look at how you can amend and customise the nominal codes for your own business. This might involve amending existing nominal codes, creating new ones or even deleting codes that aren't needed. I also discuss how you can search for nominal codes and, when you find what you're looking for, how to explore the details shown within each nominal record.

Exploring your nominal records

To explore your nominal records, click Nominal Codes from the Navigation bar to open up the Nominal Codes screen. Alternatively, click on Modules from the Menu bar and then click Nominal codes. You can change the way the information is presented on this screen by clicking on the List, Analyser or Graph button at the top right of the screen. Figure 3-3 shows the Analyser layout.

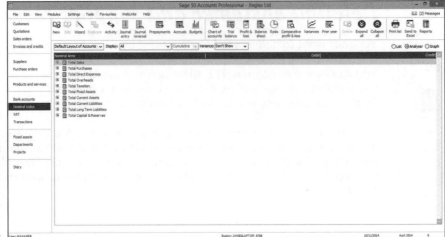

Figure 3-3:
Looking at
the nomi-
nal ledger
through the
Analyser
layout.

The main body of the screen shows the categories of the nominal codes. To see which codes lie within the categories, click the plus sign (+) next to each category. This drills down to the next level and shows the subcategories. You can click the plus sign next to a subcategory to see the actual codes that form part of that subcategory.

Alternatively, you can view all the nominal codes at a glance by following these steps:

1. **Click the List button at the top right corner of the screen.**

   The screen changes to show a list of all your nominal codes along with a description or name. After you enter your transactions, you also see Debit and Credit columns containing figures next to each nominal code.

2. **Scroll up and down the page to see the numerous codes.**

   The codes start at 0010 and finish at 9999. You may think this is an awful lot of numbers, but the numbering system has gaps.

The Graph layout shows a piechart of the nine categories of accounts within the nominal ledger – this option is colourful but not particularly useful. My preferred option is the List layout, which shows the nominal codes in their clearest format.

Renaming existing nominal records

You may want to rename some of your nominal records. For example, Sage helpfully gives you several sales type codes from A to E – but these descriptions are meaningless, so you need to change them to suit your business. For example, Jeanette, the owner of Jingles, wants to change nominal code 4000, currently designated as Sales Type A, to Sale of Greeting Cards.

Follow these steps to rename the nominal records:

1. **Click Nominal codes.**

   The list of nominal codes appears.

2. **Click one of the nominal codes and then click the Edit icon.**

3. **Type the number of the nominal code you want to change in the N/C (nominal code) box and press Enter.**

   In the Jingles example, Jeanette types in 4000.

4. **Place your cursor in the Name box and delete the current name.**

   Replace the name with the name of your new sales type.
   For Jingles, Jeanette replaces Sales Type A with the name
   `Sale of Greeting Cards`.

5. **Click Save and then click Close.**

Adding a new nominal record

When you add a new nominal record, make sure the nominal code you use fits into the correct part of the chart of accounts. Refer to Chapter 2 to see the nine different ranges of nominal codes that make up the chart of accounts.

If you want to add new codes into your range, you need to decide where you can slot the codes into your existing structure. For example, if you want to add a nominal record with a new nominal code for mobile phones, look at the profit and loss account, because mobiles phones are an expense item. Mobiles phones aren't a direct product cost, so place them in the Overhead section, close to the telephone costs for the business, around the 7500 range of nominal codes.

In the Jingles example, Jeanette wants to add a new sales nominal record, Sale of Birthday Cakes, with the new nominal code 4040.

Follow these steps to add a new nominal record:

1. **On the Navigation bar, click Nominal codes.**

2. **On the Nominal codes toolbar, click the New icon.**

3. **In the N/C box, type the new nominal code number and then tab to the Name field.**

   For Jingles, Jeanette enters the new nominal code 4040. The words `new account` pop up next to the nominal code because Sage doesn't recognise the nominal code.

4. **In the Name field, type the name of your new record.**

   For Jingles, Jeanette enters `Sale of Birthday Cakes`, as in Figure 3-4.

5. **Click Save and close the box.**

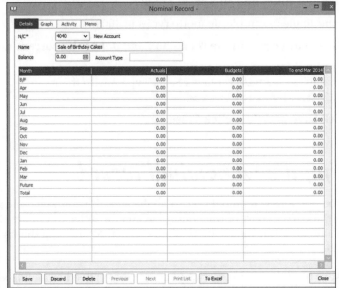

Figure 3-4:
Adding Sale of Birthday Cakes to Jingles' nominal ledger.

After you add a new nominal record, check your chart of accounts is free of errors. Refer to Chapter 2 for more on how to do this.

Looking for a nominal record

Each nominal record has its own nominal code, but not every nominal code is easy to find. Sage doesn't try to make things difficult, but it does need to slot an awful lot of codes into categories – and some codes fit into categories better than others.

I have memorised a lot of the nominal codes, but as a Sage beginner you may need some tricks to find those elusive codes.

Searching for a record alphabetically

If you know the name but not the number of a record, follow these steps to
find the record:

1. **Click Nominal codes.**

   The list of nominal codes opens. The codes appear in numerical order.

2. **Click the dark grey Name bar.**

   Sage resorts the codes into alphabetical order.

3. **Type the first letter of the record you want to find.**

   For example, if you want to find the nominal record Telephone, pressing
   T on the keyboard takes you to the first record beginning with the letter
   T, which just so happens to be Taxation. The next record is Telephone
   and Fax with the nominal code is 7550.

To see where a record sits in the overall range, sort the nominal records back
into number order by clicking the dark grey N/C (nominal code) heading and
scrolling down to the appropriate codes.

After you sort the records back into number order, if you want to get to a
specific number range again, click on one of the nominal codes and then type
the first digit of the nominal code you require. Sage takes you to the first
code starting with that number.

Finding a record numerically

If you know the approximate nominal code range but not the specific code to
use, click on Nominal codes and then click one of the nominal codes on the
list. Enter the first numerical digit in Sage. Sage scrolls down the list to the
number you specified.

In the Jingles example, Jeanette is looking for a code for mobile phones.
She thinks it will be close to the telephone codes, which are usually around
the 7500 mark. She types 7 and then scrolls down the list until she finds
Telephone and Fax at 7550. A bit further down the list she spots code 7553,
called Mobile Charges.

Looking around a nominal record

Sage offers a number of different ways to view the information contained
within a nominal record. It also provides some demonstration data. I sometimes find it helpful to explore parts of the system with dummy data already
entered.

To view the demonstration data, use the following steps:

1. **From the Menu bar, click File➪Open➪Open Demo Data.**

   Click Yes to the confirmation window that appears.

2. **Type** manager **into the Logon field.**

   No password exists, so click OK.

3. **Click Nominal codes and then click on one of the records.**

   Click the Edit icon.

4. **Type a code in the Nominal Code field and press Enter.**

   To follow this example, type 4000 to bring up the Sales North nominal record, shown in Figure 3-5.

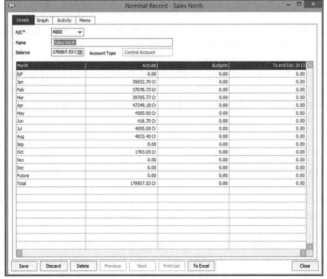

Figure 3-5:
Looking at a nominal record with Sage's demonstration data.

You may notice the following four tabs at the top of the nominal record:

✔ **Details:** This screen shows actual amounts posted to the account on a month-by-month basis and prior-year figures if they're available. You can see a column for budget figures. In the Budget field you can enter figures directly into each month for each nominal record as part of your budget-setting process. These figures then appear on the Budget report (which I tell you about in Chapter 18).

If you can't see the column for budget figures, change your budgeting method from Advanced to Standard on the Budgeting tab in Company Preferences. You can access this by clicking on Settings from the Menu toolbar and then clicking Company Preferences. For more details on advanced budgets, look at the Sage Help menu by pressing F1.

✔ **Graphs:** Using this tab, you can view a graphic format of the account information in lots of pretty colours.

✔ **Activity:** In this screens you can scroll up and down to see exactly what transactions have been posted using this nominal code. Any credit notes or journals also show here.

As 4000 is a sales code, you can see exactly which sales invoices have been posted.

✔ **Memo:** You can make notes that relate to this account. You can also attach electronic documents with the Document Manager (which I talk about in Chapter 19).

Deleting a nominal code

You can delete nominal codes that you never use to tidy up the list. For example, if you sell only one product, you may want to delete the codes associated with Sales Types B, C, D, and E.

To delete a nominal code, follow these steps:

1. **Click Nominal codes from the Navigation bar.**

2. **Click on the Nominal list screen to highlight a code and then click Edit.**

3. **In the N/C box, type the number of the code you want to delete and press Enter.**

4. **Click Delete.**

   Click Yes when the confirmation box appears.

You can delete a nominal record only if no transactions are associated with that code.

Recording Your Bank Accounts

Sage automatically gives you seven bank accounts, as shown in Figure 3-6. The accounts include an ordinary bank current account and a credit card receipt account. I suggest you review the list of bank accounts and rename

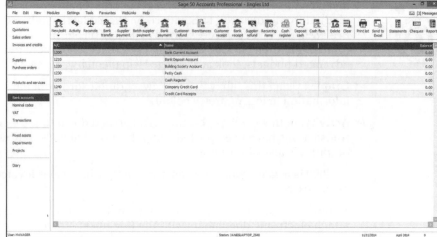

Figure 3-6:
The default
list of bank
accounts
that Sage
provides.

them, add new ones, and delete those that don't apply to your business. I tell
you how to do these tasks in the following sections.

Renaming an existing account

You probably need to rename the bank accounts that Sage gives you to suit
your business. For example, you may want to specify the name of the bank or
the type of account.

Don't create a new account if you can simply rename an existing account.
Then you don't need to amend your chart of accounts for new nominal codes.

To rename an account, follow these steps:

1. **Click Bank accounts and then highlight the bank account you want to
   edit in the list of accounts displayed.**

   Click the New/Edit icon and then click Edit.

2. **Your chosen bank record opens.**

   In the Nominal Name field, overtype the new name for your bank
   account.

3. **Click Save.**

Creating a new account

If you have a lot of bank accounts, you may need to create additional bank account records to accommodate your business needs. The simplest way to create a new bank account is as follows:

1. **From the Bank accounts module, click the New/Edit icon and select New.**

   A blank bank account record opens.

2. **Click the dropdown arrow in the Account Reference box.**

   Sage lists all the existing bank accounts and their nominal codes.

3. **Enter a new nominal code reference for your bank account in the Account Reference field.**

   Try to keep all the current accounts and deposit accounts between 1200 and 1229 and the credit card accounts between 1240 and 1249. This makes the chart of accounts more presentable.

   I used nominal code 1205 to create a new bank account for Jingles, as in Figure 3-7.

4. **Tab down to the Nominal Name field and give your new bank account a name.**

5. **From the Account Type box, use the dropdown arrow to select cash, cheque, or credit card account.**

   The default setting is cheque account.

6. **Ignore the Balance box.**

   Have a look at Chapter 4 for information on opening balances.

7. **If you operate foreign currency accounts, select a currency.**

8. **Tick No bank reconciliation if you don't want to reconcile the bank account.**

   You'll probably only choose this option for the petty cash account. You need to reconcile all accounts, including credit card accounts, to a bank or credit card statement to get a good picture of how your business is doing.

9. **Click Save and then close the record.**

   Your new bank account appears on the list of bank accounts in the main window.

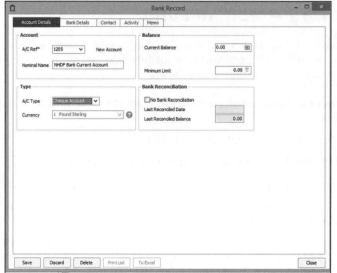

Sage also offers these alternative ways to create a new bank account:

- **Set up a new account using the wizard:** Click Bank accounts on the Navigation bar, click the New/Edit icon, and then choose Wizard from the menu options displayed. After the wizard opens, click through each screen and enter the details Sage requests.

- **Access the Bank accounts window from the Menu bar:** Click Modules and click Bank accounts, and then select the New/Edit icon.

- **Duplicate an existing account:** From the Bank accounts module, highlight the account you want to duplicate and click the New/Edit icon. Select Duplicate from the list of options given. A duplicate bank record appears. Give the account an appropriate nominal code and name, click Save, and off you go.

Deleting a bank record

To keep your bank account list tidy, you can delete any bank records you don't want to use. You can only delete a bank account record if the following conditions apply:

- The bank account has no transactions associated with it.
- The balance is zero.
- The bank account is not a control account.

Getting a handle on control accounts

Sage uses control accounts to make double-entry postings. The debtors and creditors control accounts let you see total figures for all your debtors and creditors without having to add up the individual invoices and credit notes.

To see a list of all the control accounts, click Settings and then Control Accounts on the main

toolbar. You don't need to alter these accounts because they're default accounts.

If the Debtors, Creditors, and Sales Tax or Purchase Tax control accounts have balances on them, you can't make any changes to these codes. Journal to these codes only if you're confident with your double-entry bookkeeping – otherwise, leave them to your accountant!

To delete an account that meets these conditions, highlight the bank account concerned and click Delete. Sage shows an affirmation message. Click Yes to continue or No to return to your original record.

Getting Your Product Records in Order

Planning your nominal codes is important, but planning your product records is just as crucial. The product records that you create eventually become your *product list* – a list of all your stock items. As your business grows, the number of stock items also grows, so you need to design a stock-coding system that's easy to use. You need to be able to identify a product type quickly and easily from a stock list or stock report.

Creating a product record

Sage offers three methods for creating a product record. The simplest method follows these steps.

1. **From the Navigation bar, click Products and services.**

   Alternatively from the Menu bar, click Modules and then select Products and services. Click the New icon.

   A blank product record opens, as in Figure 3-8.

2. **Enter your chosen product code.**

   Use 30 digits or fewer.

Figure 3-8:
Viewing a
blank prod-
uct record.

3. Type in a description of the product and fill in as many of the product details as you can.

In the Product field you can enter the alphanumerical barcode for your product, up to 60 characters in length.

In the default section, you may need to change the default sales nominal code and purchase nominal code. For example, a stock record for birthday cards requires a nominal code for birthday cards.

When you enter your product details, you can choose the following item types:

- **Stock Item:** A regular item of stock with a product code and description. You can give a stock item a project code and issue it to a project.

- **Non-Stock Item:** An item that isn't a usual item of stock, perhaps purchased for use within the business instead of to sell. You can't post non-stock items to a project as they aren't stock and can't be issued.

- **Service Item:** Usually a charge, for example a labour charge, that can be set up as a product code. You can't post service items to a project as they aren't physical products in stock and can't be issued.

4. When you've finished entering your product details, click Save.

Your first record is saved, and the screen goes blank, waiting for your next record.

Sage shows the following tabs for each product record:

✓ **Memo:** You can attach electronic documents to the product record or enter additional notes about the product.

✓ **BOM (Bill of Materials):** Here you can create a product from an amalgamation of other products that you have in stock. BOM is a list of products and components required to make up the main product. (See Chapter 12 for more details on this.)

✓ **Sales:** This tab shows the sales value and quantity sold month by month for that product. The Actuals column is driven from actual invoices raised. You can enter budget values and prior-year information for each month. This information lets you produce useful comparison reports for the product.

✓ **Graph:** Clicking this tab shows a graphical representation of products sold against budget and the prior year at a glance.

✓ **Activity:** Clicking this tab shows the individual transactions created for each product, for example goods in, goods out, goods transferred, or stock adjustments. You can also view the quantity of the item in stock, on order, allocated, and available.

✓ **Discount:** This tab lets you give up to five different quantity discounts per product.

✓ **Web:** Using this tab you can enter information about your web shop, including images of your product.

Sage also offers the following methods to create a product record:

✓ **Use the wizard:** Click Products and services from the Navigation bar, and then click the Wizard icon. This opens up the Product wizard, where you have several screens of information to complete. Fill in as much detail as you need. Click Next on each screen until you get to the end. Using this wizard can be quite time consuming, which is why I recommend instead using the method that I outline in the steps above.

✓ **Duplicate an existing record:** Highlight a product and then click the Duplicate icon. A duplicate record opens, where you can change the necessary fields. Click Save to save the product record.

Editing a product record

You can edit a product record at any time by double-clicking the product to bring up the Product Record screen. You can then make the necessary changes, click Save, and close the screen.

Alternatively, highlight the product record from the list of products and services and then click the Edit icon. The Product record appears for you to edit.

Deleting a product record

You can delete a product record if the record meets the following criteria:

✔ The product record has no transactions on the product activity. You need to remove any history using the Clear Stock option – see Chapter 16 for info on how to do this.

✔ The In Stock, On Order, and Allocated balances are all zero.

✔ The product is not a component of a bill of materials.

✔ The product has no outstanding transactions, such as outstanding orders.

To delete a product record, follow these steps:

1. **In the Products and services module, highlight the product you want to delete.**

2. **Click Delete.**

   An affirmation message appears. Click Yes.

Entering a project record

Creating a project record gives you a place to hold all the relevant information describing your project. Sage offers a few different ways to create a project record. The simplest way is to follow these steps:

1. **In the Navigation bar, click Projects.**

   The project main window opens, showing a list of the existing projects. If this new project is the first project, the screen is blank.

2. **Click the New icon.**

   The project record opens. Work through the following tabs:

   • **Details:** Enter your project details, including start dates, completion dates, and contact names and addresses. You must give the project a unique project reference before you save the project. You can link the project directly to a customer by clicking on the A/C Ref field in the Customer Details section and selecting the customer using the dropdown arrow; If the project is internal, leave this section blank.

- **Analysis:** Enter the price quoted for a project on this screen. All the other information falls into the look-but-don't-touch category – you can see it but you can't change it. As you create and post invoices to raise bills to your customer for the project, the billing total is updated. This tab also shows an analysis of the total budget and costs associated with the project.

- **Activity:** You can view the transactions posted against the project, such as invoices, costs, and product movements.

- **Budgets and Structure:** The Budgets tab records monies allocated to the project. The Structure tab is used to maintain a project with several phases. Both tabs are applied to the project record after you create the record. As you create the project, you apply all costs associated with it.

- **Memo:** Using the Attachments pane, you can add electronic documents or filing references to the project. You can edit the memo pad as you require. See Chapter 19 for more information on Document Manager.

3. After you enter the project details, click Save.

Your new project appears in the Projects screen.

When you create a sales order with the product code S3, you have the option to create a project for that order.

Sage also offers the following methods to create a project record:

- ✔ **Summon the Project Record wizard:** Click Projects on the Navigation bar, and then click the Wizard icon. The wizard takes you through a step-by-step process to complete the details of your project through a number of different screens – just follow the directions to set up your project record.

- ✔ **Duplicate an existing project:** Highlight a project that you want to duplicate and click the Duplicate icon. A duplicate project record appears on screen – you can amend the relevant details and save your new project record.

Setting Up Fixed Asset Records

Fixed assets are items usually held in the business for at least 12 months or more. When your business purchases a fixed asset, such as a building, a vehicle, or machinery, instead of deducting the whole expense at the time of purchase you *depreciate* the asset over the extent of its useful life. The charge to your profit and loss account is apportioned over a longer period of time – for example, you may apportion the cost of a car over a four-year period instead of charging the whole cost in the first year.

To keep track of your depreciated items, you need to set up a fixed asset record so Sage knows what items are fixed assets, over what period, and at what rate they depreciate.

To set up a fixed asset record, follow these steps:

1. **Click Fixed Assets from the Navigation bar, or click Fixed Assets from the Menu bar.**

   The main screen is blank. As you start to record your assets, the screen fills up with detail, one line per asset.

2. **Click the New icon.**

   A blank asset record appears. Use the Details tab to describe the asset and give it a reference. Enter information as necessary on the Posting tab, as in Figure 3-9:

   • Select a department, if required.

   • Use the Balance Sheet Depreciation N/C dropdown arrow to select the appropriate code. This record requires a balance sheet code, so it starts with 00. For example, Plant and Machinery Depreciation is 0021.

   • Use the Profit and Loss Depreciation dropdown arrow to select your code. Then select a profit and loss code. For example, Plant and Machinery depreciation is 8001.

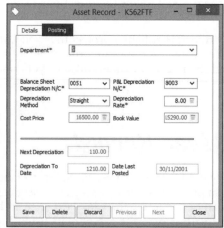

Figure 3-9: Entering information into a fixed asset record.

You may feel confused by the two codes for depreciation – one in the balance sheet and one in the profit and loss account – but Sage operates a double-entry bookkeeping system and needs two codes to post your transactions to. Be careful to select the correct codes.

- Select the Depreciation Method, usually straight line or reducing balance. If you're not sure, check with your accountant. After you select the method, you can't change back, except to write off the asset.

- Set the Depreciation Rate. The depreciation rate is the percentage rate that reduces the value of the asset. For example, if you want to depreciate a car over four years and apply the straight line method, you apportion the value of the asset equally over four years and apply a 25 per cent depreciation charge per year.

- Enter the cost price, net of VAT of the asset.

3. **Enter the current book value of the item you want to depreciate.**

   If the item is brand new, the book value is the same as the cost price. If the item has already been depreciated, the book value is cost price less depreciation. If you decide to use the reducing balance method, the book value is the value used to calculate the depreciation amount. Sage automatically updates the remaining boxes.

4. **Click Save when you're happy with the information you've entered.**

Sage posts depreciation when you run the month-end option. (For more details on running the month-end, go to Chapter 16.)

If you want to delete an asset because you sold it or it was stolen or damaged, follow these steps:

1. **Click Fixed Assets.**

   Highlight the asset you want to delete.

2. **Click Delete.**

   Click Yes to agree to the confirmation message, or click No to return to the previous menu.

Chapter 4

Recording Your Opening Balances

· ·

In This Chapter

▶ Choosing the right time to switch to Sage

▶ Getting your opening balances

▶ Recording your opening balances

▶ Checking for accuracy

· ·

*I*n this chapter I explain how to transfer the individual account balances from your previous accounting system, whether it's manual or computerised, into Sage 50 Accounts. Effectively, you take the values that make up what your business is worth on the day you swap from your old system and start using Sage. You need to set up your nominal records before you record balances, so check out Chapter 3 if you haven't done that yet.

Opening balances give you a true picture of your business's assets and liabilities to use as a starting point. If you don't enter your opening balances, you don't have accurate information about who owes you money, how much money you owe, or how much money you have in the bank. You won't even be able to reconcile your bank balance. In short, without opening balances, the information in your Sage program isn't worth the paper it's printed on.

Entering your opening balances can be a bit tricky, so make sure you're not going to be disturbed too much. After you do this, you can print an opening balance sheet to check you've entered your balances correctly.

Timing Your Switch to Sage

The best time to start with a new system is at the beginning of a financial year. You roll the closing balances from the previous year-end forward so they become your opening balances for your new year. Take advice from your accountant if you have one, as everyone's circumstances are different.

If you can't wait until the new financial year to switch to Sage and you're VAT registered, at least wait until the start of a new VAT quarter. This way, you avoid having a mixture of transactions in your old and new systems that makes reconciling your data extremely difficult.

Enter your opening balances before you start entering transactions. You can then check your accuracy by proving your opening trial balance matches your closing trial balance from your previous system. Without the clutter of day-to-day transactions, you can check much more easily.

Obtaining Your Opening Balances

Whether you transfer to Sage from a manual or computerised bookkeeping system, the process is still the same. Essentially, you transfer into Sage the balance sheet information that shows the net worth of your business.

An opening *trial balance* is a list of all account balances carried forward from the previous year-end. Your previous accounting system is your source for your trial balance. As you zero down your profit and loss items at the end of the financial year, any retained profit and loss items from the previous year now sit in your balance sheet, so an opening trial balance contains only balance sheet codes. An opening trial balance report looks quite short and shows debit and credit entries for all your balance sheet items, with grand totals at the bottom of your Debit and Credit columns.

If you start to use Sage at the beginning of a new financial year, ask your accountant to provide your opening balances.

If you transfer from a manual bookkeeping system, make sure you balance off all your individual accounts for the previous period. You may find it easier to print off a list of your newly created nominal accounts in Sage and create two columns, one for debit balances and one for credit balances. (To print a nominal list, click Nominal codes from the Navigation bar, which takes you to the Nominal codes screen, and then click the Print List icon at the top right of the screen.) You can then total each column to create an opening trial balance.

The figures contained within a trial balance are simply the accumulated value of items. For example, the Debtors control account is the combined value of all monies owed by customers at that point in time. To establish your opening balances, you need to know the specifics of which customers owe you money and what invoices are outstanding. The same applies to your suppliers: You need to see a full breakdown of who you owe money to. You obtain this information from a variety of sources. Table 4-1 shows the types of report you need from a computerised or manual system.

Table 4-1   Information Sources for Entering Opening Balances

Category	Computerised System	Manual System
Customers		
For a standard VAT system, record the transaction including VAT. For a VAT cash accounting scheme, record both the net and VAT amounts. If this figure isn't the same as your opening debtors balance, you need to investigate why.	An aged debtors report, showing a breakdown of who owed you money at the start of the year/period.	A list of customers who haven't paid at the year-end, including the amount outstanding.
Suppliers		
For a standard VAT scheme, include the VAT amount. For a VAT cash accounting scheme, show both the net and VAT amounts. If this figure isn't the same as your opening creditors balance, you need to investigate why.	An aged creditors report, showing a breakdown of who you owed money to at the start of the year/period.	A list of suppliers who you haven't paid at the year-end, along with the monies owed.
Bank		
When you start reconciling the first month's bank account, you may see cheques from the prior year clearing through the bank account. You don't need to worry about unpresented cheques and lodgements as they've already been taken into account in the previous year and are included in the opening balance for your bank account. Simply mark the items on your bank statement as being prior-year entries. Don't post the items again.	A copy of the bank statements showing the balance at the year-end and a copy of the bank reconciliation showing a list of any unpresented cheques or outstanding deposits. (Your accountant can help with this.)	A copy of the bank statements showing the balance at the year-end and a copy of the bank reconciliation showing a list of any unpresented cheques or outstanding deposits. (Your accountant can help with this.)
Products		
	A stocktake list showing the number of items in stock at the start of the year/period.	A stocktake list showing the number of items in stock at the start of the year/period.

Entering Opening Balances Using the Wizard

Sage has developed a wizard to help you magically enter your opening balances with ease. To access the wizard, click Tools and then Opening Balances from the Menu bar. The Opening Balances window opens, as shown in Figure 4-1.

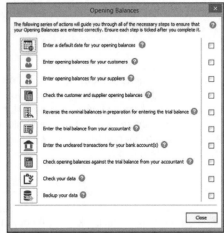

Figure 4-1: Entering your opening balances using the wizard.

The opening balances represent the financial position of your business on the day you start entering transactions into Sage. Even a new business has opening balances as the funds used to start up the business need to be accounted for – the owner's money or grant funding, for example.

In this section, I take you through the steps necessary to enter your opening balances using the wizard as your mystical guide. Click the first button on the list of icons shown in Figure 4-1 and you can begin to enter your default date.

After you perform each task, Sage puts a tick in the box next to that task. Go through the list in the given order to ensure maximum accuracy.

Entering your default date

The default date is usually the last day of the previous month, normally the day before the start of your financial year. So, if your financial year starts on 1 April 2014, your default date is 31 March 2014.

When you click the first button, a new window opens, as shown in Figure 4-2, and Sage asks you to enter your default date. If you're not sure of the default date, check with your accountant. Click Save once you're happy that the date is correct.

Figure 4-2:
Entering
your default
date.

When you enter your date, you use the last date of the prior period/year. For example, I used 31 March 2014. The system flags up a warning message saying the date is outside the financial period. Click Yes to continue.

Entering customer and supplier balances

Despite the fact that customers owe you money and you owe money to suppliers, the process for entering opening balances for both is pretty much the same, so I talk about them together in this section.

Using your aged debtors report or debtor list for customers and your aged creditors report or creditor/supplier list for suppliers, access each individual account and enter each opening balance, recording each invoice individually.

Enter your opening balances as separate invoices, as this helps with ageing the debts and affects any future reports that you run. You definitely need to enter transactions separately if you choose to use VAT cash accounting or the UK flat VAT rate (cash-based).

Whether you click the customer icon or the supplier icon, Sage presents very similar screens. Figure 4-3 shows the entry screen for entering customer opening balances.

Figure 4-3:
Entering
customer
opening
balances.

Use the dropdown arrow to select the customer for whom you have a opening balance to record and click OK. The screen displays the full account name and Sage automatically enters the default date. The reference O/Bal is used to identify the transaction, but you may wish to enter a further reference in the Ex.Ref column to identify your invoice number. You can also enter a department reference.

Notice that the word 'Invoice' already appears in the Type column. If you have credit notes to enter, use the dropdown arrow at the side of the Type column and select Credit Note instead.

Then you need to enter the gross value of the invoice. When you're happy with the details on the screen, click Save. You now see a tick against the Customer and Supplier Opening Balances line.

You need to record customer balances only if you keep customer records. If you run a shop that collects all receipts at the till and doesn't send out invoices, you don't need to keep customer records. If you send invoices to your customers, keep records for each customer and record how much each customer owes you at the start of your new accounting period with Sage.

If you used wizards to create your customer and supplier records, you've already entered your opening balances because the wizards ask for them.

Checking the customer and supplier opening balances

When you click this option, Sage opens up a Criteria Value window. If you click OK, you see a preview of your aged debtor, aged creditor, and trial balance reports. Check the system generated reports with the information that you're using to enter your opening balances. They should be the same; if not, recheck and amend all your entries until they are correct.

Reversing the nominal balances in preparation for entering the trial balance

Wow, what a mouthful! If you struggle to understand what this means, don't worry – it's an automatic process and Sage does all the hard work for you. In a nutshell, after you enter the balances for your customers and suppliers, Sage enters values into the nominal account for both debtors and creditors. When you start entering the information from the opening trial balance in the next step, you duplicate entries for debtors and creditors, but thankfully Sage intercepts at this point and reverses out the duplicated entries.

All you need to do is click the icon next to Reverse the Opening Balances. Sage asks if you want to make a backup before proceeding. (I say yes, because it's always a good idea to make a backup.) Then a new screen opens called Opening Balances Reversals, as shown in Figure 4-4.

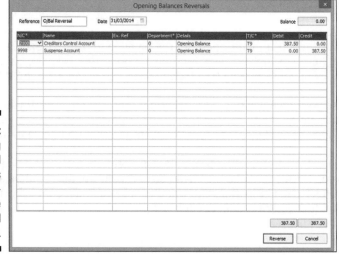

Figure 4-4: Reversing the nominal balances in preparation for the opening trial balance.

Sage has already completed the journals for you, but you can check them before clicking Reverse in the bottom right corner. If you're not happy, you can click Cancel, and Sage returns to the opening balances wizard.

When you click Reverse, Sage brings up a warning message saying that the date is prior year. Click Yes because you're entering a prior-year date. The screen then returns to the Wizard list.

It may look as if Sage hasn't actually done anything, but in reality it has. You can check on the Financials page to see evidence that Sage has posted reversing journals.

Entering the trial balance from your accountant

You may already have an opening trial balance from your accountant; if not, I recommend you ask for one. You need an opening trial balance if you traded in the previous year and you're moving your accounts from your old system to Sage.

If you're a business start-up and have no previous accounts records, you may simply want to enter the odd invoice or transaction as an opening balance. You can do this manually, as I explain in the 'Manually recording opening balances' section later in this chapter.

Click the icon next to Enter the trial balance from your accountant and the Trial Balance Entry window opens, as shown in Figure 4-5.

Using your opening trial balance, enter each item systematically into the Trial Balance Entry window.

If you use the Sage default set of nominal codes, use common sense and match the items from your opening trial balance to those of Sage. For example, Accruals in Sage has the nominal code 2109. Take the balance for Accruals from your opening trial balance and use nominal code 2109.

If you use your own existing nominal codes, enter them here. If you use your own codes, you need to choose to use a customised chart of accounts when you set up Sage – refer to Chapter 1 for company set-up information.

After you enter your opening trial balance, check that the Debits and Credits columns on both your Sage trial balance and your opening trial balance match. Check each individual entry and ensure each account is correctly entered. When you're satisfied, click Save.

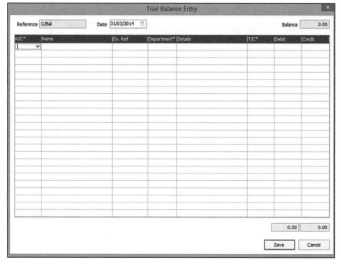

Trial Balance Entry

Figure 4-5:
Entering
your open-
ing trial
balance
from your
accountant.

You return to the Opening Balance Wizard list. A tick should now show in each completed step.

Entering the uncleared transactions for your bank account

This is where you enter items that haven't cleared your bank account. This includes cheques that you wrote before the previous year-end but haven't cleared the bank account yet, and bank receipts that you paid into the bank but haven't cleared yet.

Click the icon next to `Enter the uncleared transactions for your bank accounts` and the screen shown in Figure 4-6 opens.

Using the dropdown arrow, select the appropriate bank account. Sage pre-fills some of the columns, but you must select the type of transaction, such as Receipt or Payment. You then enter the amount and the appropriate VAT code. The amount is the Net amount if you select VAT code T1.

When you're happy with the details, click Save.

As an additional prompt, I enter the cheque number or paying-in slip refer-ence in the reference field (next to where it says O/Bal) – this extra detail makes reconciling the bank account a lot easier.

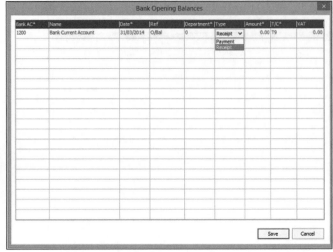

Checking opening balances against the trial balance from your accountant

When you click on the icon next to the line Enter the trial balance from your accountant, Sage opens up Criteria Box for the Trial Balance report. If you use the dropdown arrows, select the brought forward date for your trial balance report, as shown in Figure 4-7.

Click OK and your opening trial balance appears on the screen. You can print Sage's opening trial balance and double-check it against your accountant's opening trial balance.

Checking your data

Sage gives you an option to check your data to ensure everything is okay. I do this just for peace of mind.

Click the icon next to Check your data. Sage automatically runs the File Maintenance process and informs you of any errors or warnings associated with your data.

Backing up your data

Sage asks you to back up your data. When you click on the icon, Sage asks if you want to check your data. If you click No, Sage takes you straight to the backup window. Choose an appropriate filename, perhaps something referring to the backup after posting opening balances, and click OK.

That's it! You've now completed all the steps necessary to enter your opening balances.

Manually recording opening balances

As with most things in life, there's always more than one way to do things. I'm not a great fan of using wizards to enter records and data, as I find them rather cumbersome and slow to use, but many people find wizards incredibly useful. The opening balances wizard is much more useful than most wizards, however, and I believe it guides you correctly and smoothly through the whole process, letting you check details as you go along. The opening balances wizard also gives you a visual aid of your progress, as you can see at a glance which items you have already ticked off the list.

If you want to manually enter the opening balances in the old-fashioned way, here's how you do so. Depending on whether you want to enter balances for customers or suppliers, you start from different places:

- ✓ **Customers:** From the Navigation bar, click Customers, highlight the correct customer account, and click the Edit icon.
- ✓ **Suppliers:** From the Navigation bar, click Suppliers, highlight the correct supplier record, and click the Edit icon.

Then follow this process:

1. **Check you've selected the correct account and then click the OB (Opening Balance) button to the right of the Balance box.**

   The Opening Balance Setup window appears, as shown in Figure 4-8.

2. **Click the Reference field and type** opening balance.

3. **Tab to the Date field and enter the original date of the invoice or credit note.**

   Entering the original invoice date ensures the invoices are allocated to the correct period when printing aged debtors or creditors reports.

4. **Tab to the Type field and select Invoice or Credit.**

5. **Enter the invoice or credit amount in the Gross field.**

   Record the gross amount including VAT if you use standard VAT accounting. Record the net amount and VAT separately if you use the VAT cash accounting scheme.

6. **Press Enter to move to the next line if you have more transactions to enter for that customer or supplier, and then repeat Steps 2–6.**

   The system warns you that the date you've used is outside the financial year. Click Yes to continue.

7. **Click Save to accept the details you entered. Click Cancel if you aren't happy with the accuracy of your entries and want to return to the main customer record without saving.**

8. **Check your customer balance agrees with your aged debtors or customer list for customers, and with your aged creditors or supplier list for suppliers.**

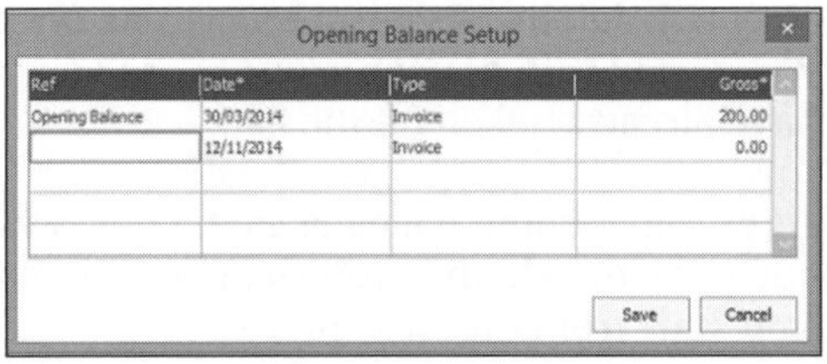

Figure 4-8:
The Opening Balance Setup window.

Ref	Date*	Type	Gross*
Opening Balance	30/03/2014	Invoice	200.00
	12/11/2014	Invoice	0.00

Manually recording opening bank balances

You need to record the opening balance for each bank account associated with your business. Use the following steps to enter opening balances for each bank account:

1. **From the Navigation bar, click Bank accounts, highlight the bank account you wish to enter an opening balance for, and click the New/Edit icon. Select the Edit option from the dropdown list that appears.**

2. **The bank record opens. Click the OB button next to the Current Balance box.**

   The Opening Balance Setup window opens. The reference automatically defaults to O/Bal (Opening Balance), which is fine – leave it as it is.

3. **Enter the date.**

   Enter the prior year's end date. For example, if you start with Sage on 1 April 2014, the date should be 31 March 2014 to ensure Sage posts this as an opening balance. The closing balance as at 31 March 2014 is the same as the opening balance as at 1 April 2014.

4. **Enter the account balance.**

   If the account is in the black, enter the account balance in the Receipt box. If the account is overdrawn, put the amount in the Payment box.

5. **Click Save when you're happy that the opening balance figure is correct.**

You may have uncleared payments or receipts already included in your bank balance shown on the opening trial balance. The best way to deal with uncleared payments is to obtain a copy of your bank reconciliation statement at the year-end and identify the items shown as unpresented cheques or outstanding paid-in items. After your bank statement arrives, mark these items on your statement as being pre-year-end transactions. When you come to reconcile your bank account in Sage, you can ignore these items as they're already included in your opening balances.

Manually recording nominal opening balances

If you're manually entering your opening balances, you've probably already entered the debtors control account, the creditors control account, and the opening bank balances, so you don't want to enter them again.

When you enter the individual opening balances on to each customer record, Sage does some double-entry bookkeeping in the background, crediting the sales account and debiting the debtors control account. When you come to enter the remaining nominal account balances from your trial balance, don't post the debtors control account total, otherwise you're double-counting. If you do post the debtors control account balance in error, you need to reverse the posting by using a nominal journal. Turn to Chapter 16 for information on journals.

If you use the opening balance wizard, Sage does the reversing journals automatically for you, so you don't need to worry about double-counting anything.

Working in a methodical manner, using your opening trial balance, enter all the remaining balances, such as fixed assets, stock, loans, and so on, using the following steps:

1. **From the Navigation bar, click Nominal codes and then click the New icon.**

2. **A blank nominal record appears. Enter the nominal code.**

   If you use the Sage default set of nominal codes, use common sense and match the items from your opening trial balance to those of Sage. For example, Accruals in Sage has the nominal code 2109. Take the balance for Accruals from your opening trial balance and use nominal code 2109.

   If you use your own existing nominal codes, enter them here. If you use your own codes, you need to use a customised chart of accounts when you set up Sage – refer to Chapter 1 for company set-up information.

3. **Click the OB button next to the Balance box.**

   The Opening Balance Setup window appears.

4. **Keep the reference as O/Bal (opening balance), and tab along to the Date field, and then enter the closing date of the prior period.**

5. **Tab to the Debit or Credit column and enter a debit or credit figure from the opening trial balance.**

6. **Click Save.**

You must use the prior year-end date as your opening balance date so the trial balance you bring forward is correct. If you inadvertently enter 1 April as your date, the figure you enter drops into the current year and not into the brought-forward category. To rectify this, enter a nominal journal to reverse the previous journal that Sage automatically posted for you. (See Chapter 16 for help with journals.) If you want to view the automatic journal that Sage has posted, click Company from the Navigation bar and then click Financials from the Links list.

Putting in opening balances for products

You need to add opening balances for products if you want to track stock items. Make sure you create product records for all the items of stock that

you wish to put an opening balance to before you try to enter opening product balances. (Refer to Chapter 3 for information on creating records.)

I use Jingles, a fictional greetings card company, in the following steps.
Jeanette, the owner, created a record with the product code Card-HB for
birthday cards. Her stocktake at the year-end showed 1,000 cards in stock.

1. **From the Navigation bar, click Products and services. Highlight the
   product you want to enter an opening balance for, and then click the
   Edit icon.**

   For Jingles, Jeanette highlights Card-HB. The product record opens.

2. **Click the OB button next to the In Stock button.**

3. **Keep the reference as O/Bal and enter the date as the prior year-end.**

4. **Enter a quantity and cost price for the item.**

   In the Jingles example, Jeanette enters 1,000 as the quantity and 50p as a
   cost price, as shown in Figure 4-9.

5. **If you're happy with the details, click Save.**

   If you're not happy, click Cancel to return to the product record and
   start again from Step 2.

   After you click Save, Sage posts an Adjustment In (AI) transaction to the
   product record, which you can see in the Activity tab. To view activity on an item, from the main screen, click the stock item you want to
   view and double-click the product to take you into the record. Click the
   Activity tab to see the adjustment posting.

Figure 4-9:
Entering
product
opening
balances.

The product opening figures don't automatically update a stock value into
your nominal ledger. Opening stock is one of the figures you enter as part of
your nominal ledger opening balances, as I explain in the section 'Manually
recording nominal opening balances' earlier in this chapter.

Checking Your Opening Balances

If you enter your opening balances manually, you need to make sure the figures are correct and agree with the opening trial balance you used to enter those figures. The best way to do this is to print your own opening trial balance from Sage and compare it with the document you've been working with. If you find discrepancies, go back and fix them.

Printing an opening trial balance

Follow these instructions to run an opening trial balance:

1. **From the Navigation bar, click Nominal codes and then click the Trial Balance icon.**

2. **Select Preview and then Run in the Print Output box.**

3. **Change the date in the Criteria Values box to Brought Forward, using the dropdown arrow.**

4. **Click OK.**

   This previews the opening trial balance.

5. **Click the Print icon to print the trial balance and check your report.**

Look for the following information on the report:

   ✔ Check the *suspense account* (the temporary account where you put problematic transactions until you determine where they properly belong) shows a zero balance.

   ✔ Check the totals on your new trial balance are the same as the totals on the trial balance from your previous system.

If you have problems with either of these balances, see the section 'Dealing with errors'.

Dealing with errors

If the suspense account doesn't have a zero balance, check you haven't entered the debtors or creditors control account twice. If you've entered something twice, turn to Chapter 16, where I tell you how to reverse the duplicated item using a nominal journal.

If your total balance doesn't match the total of your opening trial balance, make sure you entered an opening balance for each nominal code and you haven't missed anything out by mistake.

After you enter all of your opening balances and your opening trial balance matches that of your previous system, you're ready to begin entering your transactions.

Part II

Looking into Day-to-Day Functions

Head online to www.dummies.com/extras/sage50accountsuk for free online bonus content.

In this part . . .

✔ Get familiar with the day-to-day functionality of the Sage system.

✔ Find out how to go about issuing sales invoices, entering purchase invoices and doing banking transactions.

✔ Maintain and correct your transactions, which hopefully leads to correct information and good reporting!

Chapter 5

Processing Your Customer Paperwork

● ●

In This Chapter

▶ Entering sales invoices manually

▶ Posting credit notes

▶ Allocating customer receipts

▶ Getting rid of invoices and credit notes

● ●

*I*n this chapter I show you how to process the sales invoices for your company. If you want to process invoices created manually or from another system, such as Microsoft Word, this is the chapter for you. Alternatively, if you prefer to produce your sales invoices directly from Sage, check out Chapter 6.

Posting Batch Entry Invoices

Don't you just groan when you see a huge pile of invoices that you need to enter? Sage can help you speed your way through those invoices by letting you post batches of invoices. In other words, you can enter several invoices on the same screen and post them all at the same time as a batch on to the system – *post* simply means enter information into an account.

You can use this method to record sales invoices raised from a system other than Sage. For example, you can issue invoices with Microsoft Word and then enter the invoices on to Sage by using batch entry.

You can enter any number of invoices in one sitting. For example, if you have 20 invoices to process for the day, you can enter them all on to one screen and then check the total of the batch to ensure accuracy. Larger companies often process large quantities of invoices in a number of smaller batches, making processing a much more manageable task.

You can enter one invoice per line on your Batch Entry screen, but if you have an invoice where the value needs to be split into two different nominal codes, you need to use two lines for that one invoice.

When you have a whole batch of invoices in front of you, follow these steps:

1. **Click Customer and then click the Batch Invoice icon.**

   The Batch Customer Invoices screen appears.

2. **Click the A/C (Account) field and use the dropdown arrow to select the correct customer account for the invoice.**

3. **Enter the invoice date.**

   Sage automatically enters the system date, which is usually the current day's date. Make sure you change this date to the one on the invoice.

4. **Enter the invoice number in the Ref (Reference) field.**

   Every invoice needs a unique number derived from a sequential system.

5. **Add any additional references in the Ex.Ref field.**

   You can choose to leave this field blank or enter order numbers or other references.

6. **Change the nominal code, if necessary, in the N/C (Nominal Code) field.**

   This field automatically defaults to 4000, unless you changed the nominal default code on the Default tab of your customer record.

7. **Click the department for your invoice.**

   You can leave this field blank if you don't have any departments set up. If, on the other hand, you want to be able to analyse information from different offices or divisions within the company, setting up departments is the way to go. To set up departments, from the Navigation bar click Departments. Click the department number and then click the Edit icon. This opens up the Department Record window, where you enter the department details. Click Save.

8. **If you use projects, click the dropdown Project Ref arrow to select the appropriate project.**

   You can leave this field blank if you don't use projects.

9. **Describe what the invoice is for in the Details field.**

10. **Enter the amount net of VAT in the Net field.**

11. **Choose the tax code applicable for this invoice in the T/C (Tax Code) field.**

   Some common VAT codes include the following:

   - T0: Zero-rated transactions.
   - T1: Standard rate 20 per cent.
   - T2: Exempt transactions.
   - T4: Sales to VAT-registered customers in the European Community (EC).
   - T5: Lower VAT rate at 5 per cent.
   - T7: Zero-rated purchases from suppliers in the EC.
   - T8: Standard-rated purchases from suppliers in the EC.
   - T9: Transactions not involving VAT, for example journal entries.

   The system updates the VAT field according to the tax code you choose.

   Make sure the VAT Sage calculates is the same as the amount on the invoice. Sometimes Sage rounds up the VAT, and you may find you have a penny difference. If this happens, overwrite the VAT amount in Sage so the amounts match.

12. **Perform a quick check of the total value of the invoices you're about to post.**

   To check the value:

   - Add up the gross value of the pile of invoices you entered.
   - Check this total against the total on your Batch Entry screen in the top right corner of your Sage screen.
   - If the totals are different, check each line on your Batch Entry screen against the invoices.

13. **Click Save when the totals in Step 12 are the same.**

   To speed up the entry of invoices, you can use the function keys. To see how the F6, F7, and F8 keys can help you, have a quick look at Chapter 22.

Creating Credit Notes

A *credit note* is the opposite of an invoice. Instead of charging the customer, as you do with an invoice, you refund money to a customer through a credit note. Posting a credit note reverses or cancels an invoice you entered previously.

You use credit notes for a number of different reasons. For example, you may need to cancel an invoice because you sent the wrong product or the customer returned the goods.

To ensure you raise the credit note correctly, you must identify which invoice you want to correct. You need to know the invoice number, the date the invoice was raised, and the nominal code the invoice was posted to. It's important to use the same nominal code on your credit note as on your invoice. This way, the double-entry bookkeeping posts the entries in the correct nominal codes and you don't find odd balances in your accounts.

You can produce credit notes from the Invoicing module that I describe in Chapter 6. If you're not invoicing directly from Sage, you must use the batch-entry method for processing them, which is what I describe here.

To enter a credit note, follow these steps:

1. **Click Customer and then the Batch Credit icon.**

   Note the font colour changes from black to red. This feature is useful, as the Credit Note screen looks identical to the Invoice screen. You won't be the first person to merrily continue entering credit notes rather than invoices.

2. **Select the account you wish to enter the credit note against.**

3. **Change the date in the Date field if necessary.**

   Unless today's date is acceptable, remember to use your desired date for raising the credit note.

4. **Put the credit number in the Credit No field.**

   Use a unique sequential numbering system for your credit notes. Some people prefer to have a separate numbering system for credit notes, but others just use the next available invoice number. The method you choose doesn't matter, as long as you're consistent.

5. **Enter any additional references in the Ex.Ref field.**

   This step isn't necessary if you don't have any further references.

6. **Make sure the nominal code (N/C) is the same as the invoice you're trying to reverse.**

7. **Select the department the original invoice was posted to.**

8. **Select the project the original invoice was posted to in the Project Ref field.**

   This step isn't necessary if you're not using projects.

9. Use the Details field to record the specifics of the credit note.

Type something like `Credit note against Invoice No. 123.` If possible, add a description to explain why the credit is necessary – the goods were faulty, for example.

10. Enter the Net, Tax Code, and VAT.

If you're completely refunding the invoice, these three values are the same as on the original invoice. Otherwise you need to apportion the net amount and allow the VAT to recalculate.

11. Click Save when you're happy with the information you've entered.

Sage posts the credit note: It debits the sales account and credits the debtors control account.

You can check to see if the credit has been posted properly by viewing the Activity screen for the nominal code you used – see Figure 5-1 for an example. You can see the original invoice being posted to the sales nominal code as a credit and then the credit note showing the debit in the nominal code at a later date. If you've written a description in the Detail field linking the credit note to the invoice, it comes in useful here.

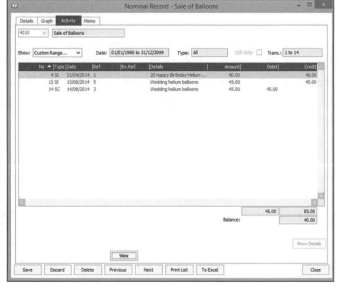

Figure 5-1:
A credit note and invoice on the Activity screen for nominal code 4010.

Registering Payments from Your Customers

Ideally, when a customer sends you a cheque you also receive a *remittance advice slip*. This slip identifies which invoices the customer is paying with the cheque sent in. You then pay the cheque into the bank, using a *paying-in slip,* which is kept for your accounting records.

To match the cheque to the correct invoices, follow this procedure:

1. **From the Navigation bar, click Customers and then click the Customer receipt icon.**

2. **Select the account you wish to post the receipt against by using the dropdown arrow.**

   As soon as you open an account, Sage displays all outstanding items for that customer on the main body of the screen. The first column shows the transaction number and the second column displays the transaction type: *SI* indicates a sales invoice, and *SC* indicates a sales credit.

   The top part of the Customer Receipt screen is split into three sections. The first column identifies the bank account, the second column shows the customer details, and the third column shows the receipt details.

   Figure 5-2 shows a list of two outstanding invoices and a credit note on the Balloon Madness account – a Jingles Card Shop customer.

3. **Enter the date the money was received in the Receipt Details column.**

   If you're recording a cheque paid into the bank, type the date from the paying-in slip.

4. **Tab past the Amount field without entering an amount.**

5. **Type BACS (Bankers' Automated Clearing Services) in the Reference field if the customer pays the invoice automatically, or type the paying-in slip reference if the customer pays by cheque.**

6. **To allocate a receipt against a specific invoice, click the receipt column on the line of the invoice that you want to allocate the receipt against.**

7. **Click the Pay in Full button at the bottom of the screen.**

   The top right box (the Amount field you ignored in Step 4) now shows the amount of the invoice paid. In the Jingles example in Figure 5-3, the amount shows £52.87, which is the total of the first invoice.

8. **Click Save at the lower left of the screen if you're happy that the receipt amount is correct.**

   If things aren't right, click Discard. A confirmation button appears. Click Yes to clear your data, ready to start again.

   After you click Save, the screen returns to the original Customer Receipt screen ready for your next customer receipt.

9. **Click Close to finish after you enter all your receipts.**

Figure 5-2:
Outstanding items on a customer's account.

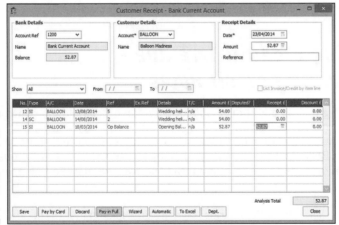

Figure 5-3:
A customer receipt after clicking the Pay in Full button.

You need to enter and save each receipt individually.

If you want to see what's happened in your Customer account, click the Activity tab. Figure 5-4 shows the Activity tab for Jingles' customer Balloon Madness. The sales receipt shows on the account. However, two unallocated items still remain on this account – these are the items with asterisks against them. In the next section, I show you how to allocate credit notes to invoices rather than payments to invoices.

Figure 5-4:
The Activity
tab for
Balloon
Madness.

Giving credit where due – allocating credit notes

Allocating means matching a specific invoice to a specific payment or credit note. As well as knowing how to allocate a payment specifically to an invoice, you also need to know how to allocate a credit note against an invoice. Because a credit note is usually raised to cancel the whole or part of an invoice, it stands to reason that the two are matched off against one another.

In Figure 5-4, two of the entries have an asterisk against them. The asterisk means the item is unallocated or unmatched. The two unallocated items are sales invoice 5 and credit note 2CR. You can tell they should be allocated against each other because the description on the credit note refers to invoice 5.

The steps you follow to allocate a credit note are almost identical to allocating a customer receipt:

1. **From the Navigation bar, click Customers and then click the Customer Receipt icon.**

2. **Select the customer account you need to allocate the credit note to.**

3. **Put the date of the credit note in the Date field.**

   In the example, the date is 14 August 2014.

4. **Tab past the Amount field and the Reference field, down to the Credit Note line. With the cursor sitting in the Receipt column on the Credit Note line, click Pay in Full.**

   Figure 5-5 shows the Balloon Madness account with a –£54 balance in the Analysis Total field in the bottom right corner. This indicates the credit note value is ready to allocate against the invoice.

5. **Click the Receipt column on the line that has the invoice you wish to allocate against. Then either click Pay in Full or, if the credit note is less than the value of the invoice, manually enter the value of the credit note you're allocating.**

   The Analysis Total now reduces to zero.

6. **Click Save if you're happy that you've allocated the correct amount against the invoice.**

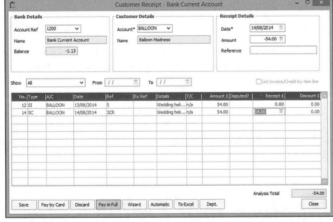

Figure 5-5:
Allocating
a credit
note to a
customer
invoice.

The Customer Activity tab for Balloon Madness now shows a zero balance outstanding, as all invoices have either been allocated against a credit note or been paid. A small letter *p* against a balance on an account means that the account is part paid or part allocated.

Recording payments on account

You may receive payment from a customer that you can't match to a specific invoice. For example, a customer may inadvertently pay an invoice twice or forget to include the remittance advice slip so you're not sure which invoice to allocate the payment to.

You can still enter the receipt on to your customer account, but you may not be able to allocate it against a specific invoice.

To enter the receipt, follow these steps:

1. **From the Navigation bar, select Customers and then click the Customer Receipt icon.**

   Select the customer account.

2. **Enter the date of the receipt in the Date field.**

3. **Enter the amount received in the Amount field.**

4. **Note in the Reference field why the payment isn't allocated against an invoice.**

   For example, if you think the customer has duplicated a payment, type `duplication`.

5. **Click Save.**

6. **Click Yes after you see the message saying there's an unallocated balance and asking if you want to post this payment on account.**

The Customer Activity screen shows a payment on account as transaction type SA. In the event of a customer overpaying, you may find the account now has a negative balance. To rectify this, you can send the customer a cheque or leave the balance on account and wait until you start raising more invoices to net this off against.

Deleting Invoices and Credit Notes

The traditional accounting method for reversing an invoice is to create a credit note for the same amount. However, Sage has made it even easier to sort out such problems: You simply delete the invoice. That way, you don't have to raise the credit note or allocate it to the invoice. You maintain an audit trail, as any deleted items still show and are highlighted in red, so your accountant can always see what you've been up to.

Clicking on Transactions from the Navigation bar lets you look at the details of any transaction and edit or delete the transaction. See Chapter 9 for details on deleting transactions.

Chapter 6

Invoicing Your Customers

*Y*ou can generate invoices directly from your Sage accounting software, which means you can streamline your paperwork process by printing invoices quickly – and even directly from sales orders if you use Sage Accounts Professional. You end up with more time to make more money for your business – or more time to take a break from making money for your business.

Sage is an integrated system, so when you produce a sales invoice, the system automatically updates the nominal ledger and the customer account, along with products and projects if you use those options.

Deciding on an Invoice Type

Depending on the type of business you run, you probably issue mainly one of two types of invoice:

- ✔ **Product invoices:** Used for businesses that sell physical items – cards, widgets, and so on. A manufacturing company issues product invoices, using product codes.

- ✔ **Service invoices:** Used for businesses that don't sell tangible products but provide a service to their clients.

A business that sells physical products may need to generate a service invoice occasionally. For example, Manufacturers of Widgets might service some of the products they manufacture, and the engineer's time is charged using a service invoice. However, a business that provides services rarely needs to send a product invoice. For example, a consultant charges for the time spent providing a service but usually doesn't need to issue product invoices.

If you need to send invoices with both service details and product items on the same invoice, you need to have Sage Accounts Professional, otherwise you have to send one invoice for service items and another invoice for product items. For example, a car repair centre needs product invoices for the sale of parts and service invoices to show the labour costs for servicing vehicles.

Creating Invoices

You create product and service invoices in much the same way, so I combine the two methods in this section and simply highlight the differences between the two as I go along.

Before you start your product invoices, make sure you set up your product records, which I explain in Chapter 3.

To create your invoice, from the Navigation bar, click Invoices and credits. Click the New Invoice icon and the Product Invoice screen comes up, as shown in Figure 6-1. The next sections cover the four tabs on the Product Invoice screen.

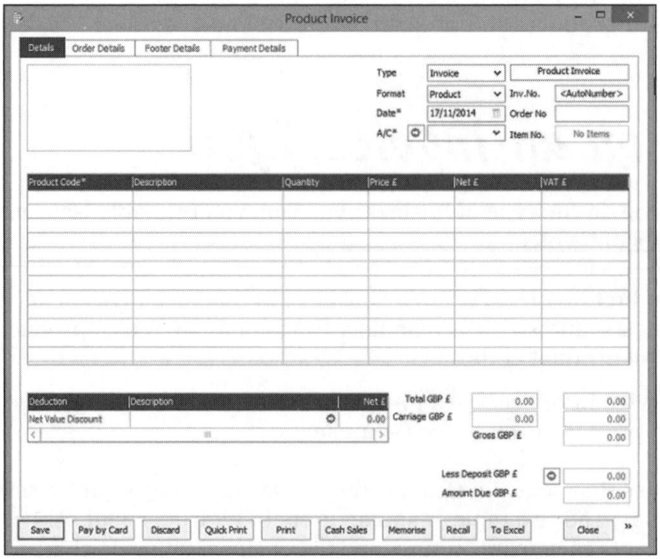

Figure 6-1: Creating a blank product invoice.

Issuing a proforma invoice

A *proforma invoice* is an invoice supplied in advance of the goods or services being provided. This document is a more formal and detailed version of a quote.

You create a proforma in the same way as a sales invoice. However, after you receive payment for a proforma, you need to convert it to an actual invoice. To do this, open up the proforma and change the Type field from Proforma to Invoice using the dropdown arrow in the top right corner of the screen. You can then update the record.

A proforma invoice isn't a valid VAT invoice and can't be used in your VAT return.

Putting in the details

The Invoice screen opens with the Details tab, where the default invoice type is for a product invoice, as indicated in the top right corner of the screen. Starting in that corner, you can set the following options for your invoice:

- ✔ **Type:** Use the dropdown arrow if you want to change from an invoice to a proforma invoice. If you use the Professional version of Sage, refer to the nearby sidebar 'Issuing a proforma invoice'.

- ✔ **Format:** You can choose a product or service invoice. In the Professional version, you can produce invoices that include both elements. The nearby sidebar 'Mixing product and service invoices' tells you how to do this.

- ✔ **Date:** The date automatically defaults to today's date, so change the date if necessary.

- ✔ **Account:** Select your customer account using the dropdown arrow.

- ✔ **Invoice Number:** The `<Autonumber>` notation here indicates that Sage automatically numbers your invoices. It starts with number 1 and automatically increases by one for each subsequent invoice. If you want to start with a different number, click Settings from the Menu bar and then Invoice/Order Defaults and select the Options tab.

- ✔ **Order Number:** You can enter your own order number or leave it blank. However, if you use Sage Professional and generated the invoice using Sales Order Processing, an order number automatically appears within this box.

- ✔ **Item Number:** This shows the item line of the invoice that the cursor is currently sitting on.

- ✔ **Rate:** This field appears in Professional versions of Sage when you enable the Foreign Trader facility, which I explain in Chapter 14.

Mixing product and service invoices

If you use the Professional version of Sage, you can produce invoices that include both products and services. Start by raising a product invoice and then when you want to raise a service charge, select the S3 special product code. The Edit Item line for a service invoice opens. Follow the steps in the later section 'Selecting service invoices' for details on how to complete this transaction.

You can process all other info, including order, footer (see the 'Getting down to the footer details' section later in this chapter for more on footers), and payment details, in the normal manner.

You can save the invoice and print it whenever you decide. If you're not happy with the invoice contents, click Discard to clear your entries and start again.

Even though you've saved the invoice, you can still make changes and resave it.

Getting to the main attraction

The main body of the invoice has the most differences between product invoices and services invoices. As you would expect from a product invoice, you must select the product code, which in turn comes up with the product description and a quantity field. A service invoice doesn't require these items and instead has a details field.

Producing product invoices

Enter the following fields to create a product invoice:

✔ **Product Code:** Normally you set up product codes within product records. You can type in the relevant product code directly or use the dropdown arrow.

You may encounter instances where a regular everyday product code isn't suitable and you need a special product code, such as the following:

- **M Message Line:** Use this to add extra lines of description or to make comments about the products.

- **S1 Special Product Item Tax Chargeable:** Use this for product items that are standard VAT rated and don't have their own product code.

- **S2 Special Product Item Zero Rated:** Use this code for zero-rated items that don't have their own product code.

- **S3 Special Service Items Tax Chargeable:** Use this code when you want to add service items to product invoices and sales orders. It uses the standard VAT code.

If your S1–S3 codes don't appear in your dropdown list, click Settings in the main toolbar and select Customer Invoice/Order Defaults. Tick the Show Special Product Codes invoicing box.

✔ **Description:** The product description displays automatically from the product record, but you can overwrite it if necessary. You can also click F3 to edit the item line and add any one-off product details or comments.

✔ **Quantity:** Enter the number of items you're invoicing. Sage automatically shows *1* if a quantity is in stock or *0* if no items are in stock. If you don't have enough stock for the quantity you enter, Sage issues a warning – it's difficult (not to mention illegal) to charge people without delivering the product, so pay attention to the warning.

✔ **Price:** The unit price for the product record appears here, but you can change this if you need to.

Selecting service invoices

A service invoice has fewer columns in the main body than a product invoice.

After you enter the header details for your invoice (customer details, date, and so on), you need to add the details of the service provided:

✔ **Details:** You can expand the information entered in the Details field by using the F3 key. This function lets you add additional information to the invoice detail. You can only use F3 after you enter some information into the Details field.

✔ **Amount:** You can enter the amount using the Edit Item Line window that appeared if you used the F3 key in the Details field. Alternatively, if you didn't need to use the F3 key for additional details, add only one line of detail on the main screen and then tab across to the Amount column and enter the amount there.

Figure 6-2 shows what happens after Jeanette from Jingles inserted the detail Hire of Clown for Party into the Details field. As soon as you type in the description, press F3 and the edit box appears. Sage duplicates the words typed into both the Description and the Details fields.

You can now apply the number of hours worked and enter the unit price. You can also check the nominal code is one that you want to use or adjust it where necessary. In the Jingles case, Jeanette chooses to change the nominal code from 4000 for Sale of Cards (the default nominal code) to a more suitable code, such as Party Organising. Because Party Organising isn't an existing code, she needs to create a new nominal code. Refer to Chapter 3 to see how to create new nominal codes.

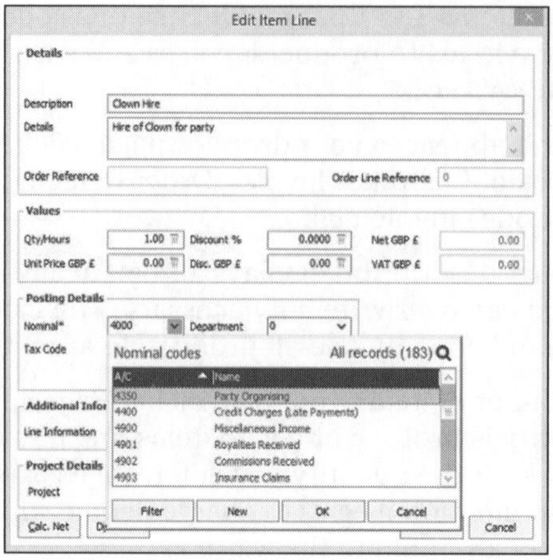

Figure 6-2:
Using the F3
function key
to expand
the details
of the ser-
vice invoice.

After you enter the details on the main body of the invoice, you can work
through the following, which are the same for both product and service
invoices:

- ✔ **Net:** This is an automatic calculation, which applies any discount
  attached to the customer account. You can change the discount by
  using the F3 key.

  An additional Discount and Discount Percentage column shows if you
  selected this option within Invoice/Order defaults. Click the Discount
  tab and tick the Show Discount on Main Invoice/Order box.

- ✔ **VAT:** Sage automatically calculates this column. You can edit this
  column only if you selected the Item VAT Amendable box on the VAT
  tab of Company Preferences on the main toolbar.

- ✔ **Total:** Sage totals the invoice, showing net, VAT, and any carriage
  charges applied.

- ✔ **Deposit:** This feature has a smart link – a little grey arrow that takes
  you to the Payment tab of the invoice so you can record any deposits
  received against the invoice.

- ✔ **Deduction:** This lets you provide a net value discount on the Details tab
  of your invoice (see below). You can use the deduction feature to offer
  seasonal discount promotions and one-off offers.

- ✔ **Net Value Discount:** Clicking the dropdown arrow in the Description box
  reveals an Edit Item line, where you can enter information referring to
  the discount and a discount value. If you press Tab, Sage automatically
  calculates the percentage discount. If you enter a discount percentage,
  the value is calculated for you.

Editing the service invoice with the F3 key

When you press F3 from the Description line of an invoice, an edit box appears where you can amend some of the detail of your invoice. The nominal code, tax code, and department all appear in the posting details in this edit box. The details shown are defaults. You can amend the tax and nominal codes for each item line on the invoice by using the dropdown list. Alternatively, if you want to use the same nominal code and tax code for all lines of the invoice, you can click the Footer Details tab of the invoice and enter the appropriate codes in the Global section. The new codes overwrite any codes used on an individual line of the invoice.

Filling in the order details

You can use the Order Details tab to fill in details of where the goods are delivered and who took the order. You can also add up to three lines of text. If the customer tells you the order can be left outside by the chicken shed, this is the place to share that information.

Getting down to the footer details

You can enter carriage terms, settlement terms, and global details in the Footer Details tab:

- ✔ **Carriage Terms:** You may want to assign postal or courier costs to the invoice. You can set up specific nominal codes to charge carriage costs. If you set up departments, use the dropdown list to select the appropriate department. You can also add the consignment number and courier details and track your parcel by accessing the courier's website.

  To set up a courier on your Footer Details tab, click Help from the main toolbar. Using the Contents and Index option, type in `couriers` to see how to add a new courier.

- ✔ **Settlement Terms:** You may already see some information in these boxes if you entered the details on the customer record. For example, you can enter how long an early settlement discount applies for, and what discount percentage is applied. It also shows you the total value of the invoice.

- ✔ **Global:** This section lets you apply global terms to the whole of the invoice or credit note. If you choose to do this, only one line is added to the audit trail, although carriage is always shown as a separate line.

You can apply one nominal code to the whole invoice. If you do this, you can also enter details (using no more than 60 characters) to accompany the posting to the nominal ledger.

The same global effect can be applied to your tax code and your departments.

 ✔ **Tax Analysis:** The tax analysis for each product item appears at the bottom of the Footer Details tab. The list shows a breakdown of all the VAT into the separate VAT codes (assuming you haven't used the Global Tax option).

Going over payment details

In Accounts Plus and Accounts Professional, you can record a payment directly to your sales invoice by clicking on the Payment details tab. You can enter details of deposits already received, make a payment on account if you don't want to allocate the payment to a specific invoice, or allocate the money to a specific invoice.

If you enter a deposit, Sage updates the details of the deposit on the Details tab of your invoice.

If you click Payment Already Received, Sage displays the deposit but doesn't post a receipt transaction. You don't want to double-count the deposit receipt if it's already been posted. After you're happy with the detail on your invoice, click Save to keep a copy of it on the Invoice list. If you're not happy with your invoice, click Discard.

Checking your profit on a product invoice

You can check the profit you've made on each invoice. This is a nifty little device, but treat this feature with a little caution, as it only compares the sales price of your product with the unit cost price – at least it gives you an idea of whether you're making any money.

Preparing credit notes

You prepare credit notes in a very similar way to product and service invoices. The screens look exactly the same, but after you type in the details of the credit note, the font becomes red. From the Navigation bar, click on Invoices and

credits and then choose the New Credit icon. Update your credit notes in the same way as you do invoices. If you don't, the credit notes aren't updated to the nominal ledger.

To check your profit, follow these steps:

1. **From the Navigation bar, click Invoices and credits to view a list of invoices.**

2. **Double-click the invoice you want to check. At the bottom of the screen, click the small chevron next to Close and select Profit.**

   Sage calculates the profit using the information you entered in your product record. It simply displays the difference between the sales price and the cost price. If either of these fields isn't completed in the product record, the calculation doesn't work.

   Sage gives you a profit value in pounds sterling and the profit percentage.

3. **Click Close to return to your invoice.**

   Alternatively, you can print the information.

Remembering that Communication is Key

Communication and credit control are key to the success of any business. With this is mind, Sage lets you record details of telephone calls, emails, letters, meetings, record follow-up actions via the Communications tab of each customer record. This function is particularly useful if you're a credit controller, as it can record follow-up phone calls to customers. Sage makes diary entries to remind you of your future tasks.

From the Navigation bar, click on Diary, which lets you access and view any appointments or follow-up calls made via the Communications screen.

Invoicing from a phone call

This option lets you charge your client when you talk to them on the phone. For service businesses that bill by their time, this service is essential. For example, if you're a solicitor, you may need to charge clients for the time you spend on the phone with them. So, before you pick up the phone, follow these steps:

1. **From the Navigation bar, choose Customers, highlight the customer of your choice, and click the Edit icon.**

   This opens up the customer's record.

2. **Click the Communications tab and click New at the bottom of the screen.**

(continued)

(continued)

The Customer Communications History window appears.

3. **Enter the topic or client in the Subject field and then dial the phone number. When the call is answered, click Start on the Telephone Timer.**

The system automatically starts recording the duration of the call. You can type notes in the Communication Results part of the screen. When you've finished the call, click Stop on the Telephone Timer.

4. **Click Invoice to raise an invoice for the time spent on the phone call.**

A Communication Invoice Details box appears, which lets you enter the hourly rates, nominal codes, departments, and VAT

details. Any notes from the Communication Results field pull through to the Details To Invoice field, where you can edit them as necessary. The time of the phone call is recorded in the Invoice Details box.

If you simply want to record details of the phone call without billing for it, skip this step.

5. **Click Save when you're happy with the details. A confirmation message appears. Click Yes to raise the invoice and then click Save again to return to the customer record.**

The invoice now appears on the Invoice List. Click Customers and credits from the Navigation bar to view it.

Managing Your Invoice List

After you save an invoice, it appears on your Invoice List and you can then do all sorts of business-like things with the invoice.

Printing invoices

As soon as you save your invoice, you can print it. If you still have the invoice open in front of you, simply click Print. The Layouts window opens, which initially opens on the Favourites tab. Select Layouts and the right side of the window displays the different report options, as shown in Figure 6-3. When you scroll down the screen and highlight your chosen report, some floating icons appear, giving you the options of previewing, printing, exporting, exporting to Excel, and emailing the document.

If you haven't got the invoice open in front of you, click Invoices and credits from the Navigation bar to display a list of all the invoices and credit notes that have been raised (in chronological order). Highlight the invoice you want to print from the list, click the Print icon to open the Layout window, select Layouts as before, choose the appropriate report required, and click the floating print icon.

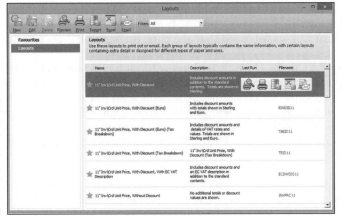

Figure 6-3:
Choosing
the layout
before you
print your
invoice.

The layout choices are pretty self-explanatory: You choose a layout based on paper size and whether the customer is offered a discount.

You can preview the invoice before you print to make sure the details are correct. Click the floating preview icon to load the invoice on to the screen. If you're happy with what you see, you can print the invoice directly from this screen or choose to email it directly to the customer.

You can print the invoice without previewing it, but I always check to ensure I'm happy with the details. You can edit or change an invoice at any point before you send it to the customer and update the ledger.

You can print off a number of invoices at the same time by highlighting all the invoices you want to print and clicking Print. Then select your desired invoice layout.

You can choose an invoice layout as a favourite by clicking the star at the side of the report when you select an invoice layout. This copies the invoice to the Favourite screen, which is the first screen to open when you click the Print icon. This saves you time scrolling through all the layouts each time you print.

After you print an invoice, the Printed column on the Invoice List has the word Yes in it. You can reprint at any time, but you can easily identify which invoices have already been printed.

Using Quick Print

Sage has a feature called Quick Print that lets you select a default print layout and print items with a single click. The Quick Print icon sits alongside the Print icon when you view the list of invoices.

This is a quick way of printing invoices, particularly if you want to select more than one invoice. Be aware, though, that you won't see a preview of the invoice before it prints, so you need to make sure you select the correct layout.

If you try to use the Quick Print icon without having set up the default layout, a warning message appears and Sage asks if you want to set up the default now. If you know which report layout you want to use, click Yes. Sage then directs you to the Layout window, where you can click the appropriate layout. Highlight the invoice layout that you require and click OK. The report now prints. Be aware that you don't get the opportunity to preview this invoice.

Another way of setting up your default Quick Print invoice layout is to click Settings, followed by Invoice/Order defaults, and then click the Quick Print tab. Here, you can select the default print layouts for Invoices, Quotations for invoices, Sales Orders, Purchase Orders, and Quotations for Sales Orders.

Updating ledgers

When you're 100 per cent happy with your invoices, you're ready to *update ledgers*, a process that posts the invoice to both the nominal ledger and the customer ledger.

You can update invoices individually or in batches. First, check to see which invoices have been updated and printed already. To find out the status of each invoice, work through these steps:

1. **From the Navigation bar, click on Invoices and credits to view the Invoice List.**

2. **Look at the last two columns – the Posted and Printed columns.**

   The word Yes indicates whether an invoice has already been printed or posted.

To update the invoices:

1. **Highlight the invoices you want to update.**

2. **Click Update Ledgers.**

   The Update Ledger box opens and you have the opportunity to print, preview, or send to file. You may want to leave Preview highlighted, so after you click OK you can view all the invoices you've updated. You can print this report if you want to, but it isn't really necessary. Notice the main screen now has a Yes against that invoice in the Posted column.

Deleting invoices

Deleting invoices and credit notes is easy, but be aware that if you've already posted the invoice to the nominal ledger, deleting the invoice or credit note doesn't reverse the posting in the ledger.

To delete an invoice or credit note:

1. **From the Navigation bar, select Invoices and credits to open up the Invoice List.**

   Select the required invoice or credit note from the Invoice list.

2. **Click the Delete icon.**

   An affirmation message appears. Click Yes to continue or No to exit.

Saving Time while You Ask for Money

When you create invoices, it's useful to know about some of the time-saving features that you can use. I explain some of these features in this section.

Duplicating existing invoices

If you need to send the same invoice details to a number of different clients, this function is very useful. From the Invoice List, highlight an existing invoice and click the Duplicate icon at the top of the screen. The system produces an exact replica of the original, but you can edit the details, such as the date and the customer's name. Check all the details of the invoice before saving and amend where necessary.

When you duplicate an invoice, Sage replicates the details but gives the invoice a new sequential number, so you have an accurate audit trail.

Repeating recurring transactions

This feature is useful if you invoice for the same product or service on a recurring basis. After you set up your recurring transaction, you can continue to process the invoice in the same way.

To set up a recurring sales invoice, follow these steps:

1. **From the Navigation bar, click Invoices and credits and then click New Invoice.**

2. **Enter your invoice details as shown in the earlier section 'Creating Invoices'.**

3. **Click Memorise.**

   The Memorise box appears and Sage asks you to provide the following:

   • Reference and description for your recurring item.

   • Frequency – is it every day, week, or month, and when does it start and finish?

   • Last processed – for ongoing recurring transactions, the date shown is the date the invoice was last processed.

4. **To save your recurring transaction and return to the invoice, click Save. To exit without saving, click Cancel.**

   When you click Save, a copy of the new invoice shows on your invoice list.

 Every time you open Sage, it asks if you want to post your recurring entries. Choose Yes if you want to post the transaction, or choose No if you don't want to post the transaction. You can turn this reminder off by clicking Settings⇨Company⇨Preferences⇨Parameter tab and then selecting the No Recurring Entries at Startup checkbox.

To process the transactions, follow these steps:

1. **From the Invoice list, select the Recurring Items icon.**

   The Memorised and Recurring Entries box appears.

2. **Click the item you want to process and click Process.**

   The Process Recurring Entries box appears and asks you what date you want to process transactions up to. After you put your date in, Sage lists all the items included. Make sure all the transactions you want to process have a green tick in the box next to them. If you don't want to include a transaction, make sure the box doesn't have a tick in it.

   If you clear a tick from the Process Recurring Entries box and then click Process, the system asks Do you wish to update the last posted date for excluded transactions? Select No if you want to post transactions at a later date. If you want to exclude a transaction because you don't want to put it through this month, click Yes.

3. Click Process.

Sage processes the recurring items and says Processing Complete.

4. Click Cancel to return to the Invoice List screen.

Using defaults

You may have invoices and credit notes with similar items or characteristics, and you can enter defaults for them. For example, you may want to assign carriage costs to all your customers.

To access the defaults, within Customers, scroll down the Links list and click Invoice/Order Defaults. To adjust carriage defaults, click Footer Details.

For help with other invoice defaults, select Help from the main toolbar, click Contents and Index, and select Invoices followed by Defaults.

Chapter 7

Dealing with Paperwork from Your Suppliers

- -

In This Chapter

▶ Getting and posting bills

▶ Entering credit notes

▶ Recording supplier payments

▶ Sending remittance advice notes

- -

*Y*ou probably receive lots of invoices from your suppliers, so you need to put systems in place to help you easily locate those invoices if required. Sometimes Sage contains enough detail to answer a query about an invoice, but on some occasions you may need to pull the actual invoice out of the file.

As you process each invoice, Sage allocates it a sequential number. Use this sequential number as a reference, so you can always track down an invoice quickly and easily.

Receiving and Posting Invoices

You need a good system for capturing all the purchase invoices that come into your business, so you pay your bills on time and you can continue doing business. Two steps are involved in making sure this gets done: Receiving the invoices properly and posting the invoices.

Setting up your receiving system

Send all invoices to one person or department (depending on the size of the business). You don't want lots of different people receiving your invoices, as more people means more chance of invoices getting misplaced or entered incorrectly.

Enter invoices on to the accounting system as soon as possible after you receive them so the liability is recorded in the business accounts. Depending on the size of the business, you may want to make a copy of the invoice: Keep one copy within the Accounts department and send the other copy to the person who requested the goods so they can check the details for accuracy and authorise the invoice for payment.

Posting invoices

The term *posting* doesn't mean putting the invoice into a letterbox. In accounting terms, *posting* means processing an invoice to the nominal ledger. I talk about the nominal ledger in Chapter 2.

You can post a number of invoices in one sitting. If you have large quanti-ties of invoices to process, separate them into smaller batches and total the values of each batch so you can check those same values against Sage to ensure you haven't made any mistakes.

If you use Sage Accounts Professional, you have two different ways of posting invoices:

- ✔ If you receive an invoice as a result of raising a purchase order, you can update your order details and Sage automatically posts the invoice. See Chapter 11 for more information about processing purchase orders.

- ✔ If you don't have an order for your invoice, you need to use the Batch Entry screen to process your invoice, which I describe below.

Sort the invoices into date order before separating them into batches. This ensures you enter the invoices in chronological order, which helps when you view them on screen.

To enter a batch, follow these steps:

1. **From the Navigation bar, click Suppliers and then click on the Batch Invoice icon.**

   This brings up the Batch Suppliers Invoice box.

2. **Select the correct supplier account for the invoice.**

   When you have several items on an invoice, enter each item from the invoice separately on the Batch screen as you may need to give each item a different nominal code. You can use the same supplier account, date, and reference so that Sage can group those items together.

3. **Put the invoice date in the Date field.**

   Sage automatically defaults to today's date, so you may need to over-type the invoice date. If you don't, Sage won't age the invoice correctly and you'll have a distorted view of the transaction on your aged creditors reports.

4. **Enter your sequential number in the Ref (Reference) field.**

   Your *invoice reference number* is the number order in which you file your invoices. I usually give each invoice a sequential number and mark this in pen at the top right corner of the invoice. I then use the Ref field to enter this number into Sage.

5. **Add details in the Ex.Ref field.**

   You can add more references here or leave this field blank. I always enter the supplier's own invoice number here, as it acts as a secondary means of identification. This is important when you need to retrieve an invoice from your filing system. Having an additional reference particularly helps if you have invoices from a supplier with the same value.

6. **Select the nominal code in the N/C field using the dropdown arrow, otherwise Sage uses the default code 5000.**

7. **Click the department applicable for your invoice in the Dept field.**

   You can leave this field blank if you don't have any departments set up.

8. **Click the dropdown Project Ref arrow to select the appropriate project.**

9. **Enter the Cost code if you're using project costing.**

   See Chapter 13 for further details on project costing.

10. **Enter information describing what the invoice is for in the Details field.**

    Put as much detail as you can here. In addition to entering the supplier's invoice number in the Ex Ref field, I also enter the supplier's invoice number and the description in the Details column. You can then identify the invoice quickly using the supplier's number. If you need to contact the supplier about an invoice, it helps to use the supplier's reference numbers.

    I use both the Ex.Ref field and the Details columns for the supplier's invoice number, because different reports sometimes include one but not the other. This is a bit belt and braces, but experience has taught me this system works.

11. **Enter the amount net of VAT in the Net field.**

12. **Choose the tax code applicable for this invoice in the T/C (Tax Code) field.**

    Depending on the tax code, Sage updates the VAT field.

    Make sure the VAT that Sage calculates is the same as the amount on the invoice. Sometimes Sage rounds up the VAT, and you need to overwrite the amount in Sage to match the VAT on the invoice.

13. **Repeat Steps 2–12 for each invoice in your batch.**

14. **Check the total of your batch of invoices matches the total in the right corner of the Batch Entry screen, as in Figure** 7-1.

    If the totals match, click Save. Doing this check confirms you've entered accurate data. When you click Save, Sage posts the invoices to the nominal ledger, posting a debit to the Cost account and a credit to the Creditors control account.

Check out Chapter 22 to see how using the function keys speeds up the batch-entry process.

After you post your supplier invoices, you can view them on the Supplier Activity screen, which is split into two parts. The top part has one line entry for each transaction (in other words, all the individual lines of each invoice are grouped together), and the bottom part has the detail of each transaction. Clicking an invoice highlights it in blue, and the bottom part of the screen shows each line entry of that invoice.

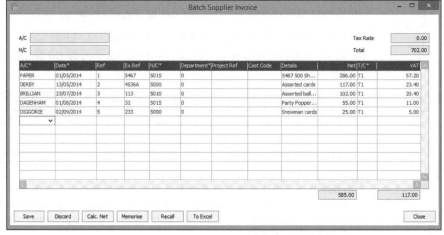

Figure 7-1:
A batch of
purchase
invoices
entered
on to Sage
before
posting.

Memorising and recalling batch invoices and credit notes

You can use the Memorise and Recall functions in Sage Accounts Plus and Professional versions to save you entering the same information again and again. For example, if you regularly buy the same product from the same supplier, you can use the Memorise function to save time when ordering the product.

Another great function is memorising a batch of invoices that you're in the middle of sorting out so you can come back and amend them later. You can save the batch, go away and check some details, and then come back, recall the batch, make the amendments, and post.

To memorise a batch of invoices from within the Batch Entry screen, click Memorise, add a filename for the batch, and click Save. To recall a batch of invoices, click Recall from within the Batch Entry screen, select the appropriate file, and click Open.

Getting Credit

Credit notes are raised for a variety of reasons. You may have received faulty goods, or the goods may be the wrong colour, for example. The supplier assumes you've already posted the original invoice supplied with these goods and sends a credit note to reduce the amount you owe. The credit note may completely reverse the value of the original invoice or partially credit the invoice.

Processing a credit note is much the same as processing an invoice, so follow the steps in the earlier section 'Posting invoices', paying special attention to the following points:

✔ **From the Navigation bar, click Suppliers, click the Batch Credit icon, and select the account to enter the credit note against.**

The screen looks very similar to that of the Invoice screen, but the font colour is red rather than black to alert you to the fact that you're processing a credit note.

✔ **Remember to change the date, unless today's date is acceptable.**

✔ **Enter a credit number instead of a reference number.**

Use a unique sequential numbering system for your credit notes. Some people have a separate numbering system for credit notes, but others just use the next available invoice number.

✔ **Make sure the nominal code (N/C) is the same as the invoice you're reversing.**

This ensures the correct cost code is reduced in value.

✔ **Put some notation in the Details field.**

I suggest you type something like `Credit note against Invoice No. 123` plus a description of why it's necessary.

✔ **If the credit note is reversing just part of an invoice, apportion the Net and VAT amounts.**

When you click Save, Sage posts the credit note, crediting the Purchase account and debiting the Creditors control account.

You can check to see if everything is posted by viewing the Activity screen for the nominal code you used. The Jingles example in Figure 7-2 shows the Activity screen for nominal code 5000. You can see transaction number 23, the purchase of get-well cards (debiting code 5000), and transaction 29, the credit note (crediting the nominal record). The Activity screen shows the original invoice posted to the purchase nominal code as a debit and then the credit note showing at a later date, crediting the nominal code. Here's where having a description in the Details field linking the credit note to the invoice comes in handy.

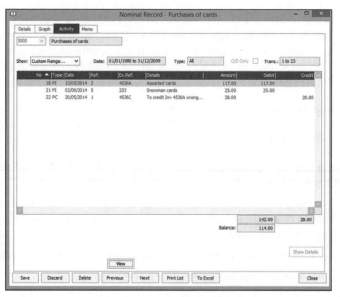

Figure 7-2:
The nominal code Activity screen showing a credit note posted for the purchase of cards.

Allocating a Credit Note

You allocate credit notes in the same way as you make payments. You need to allocate a credit note specifically against an invoice.

You can tell if something hasn't been allocated if a transaction in the Supplier Activity screen has an asterisk against it.

To allocate a credit note, follow these steps:

1. **From the Navigation bar, click Suppliers and then click Supplier Payment.**

2. **Select the account you require.**

   All outstanding transactions are shown.

3. **Enter the date, usually the date of the credit note.**

4. **In the Payment column, click Pay in Full Against the Credit Note.**

   Doing so puts a negative value in the Analysis total at the bottom right side of the screen.

5. **Move up to the invoice that you wish to allocate the credit note to, and type in the value of the credit note.**

   The Analysis total becomes zero.

6. **Click Save.**

   Saving posts the allocation, as shown in Figure 7-3.

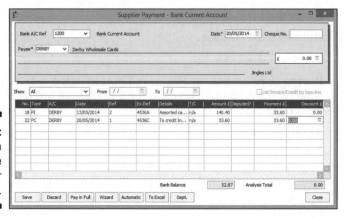

Figure 7-3: Allocating a credit note to a supplier invoice.

Paying Your Suppliers

When you process the payments for your supplier, you can still use the Supplier module. In previous versions of Sage, you had to use the Bank module – you can still do this, but you now have the option to make your payment using the Supplier module:

1. **From the Navigation bar, select Suppliers and then click the Supplier Payment icon**

   A screen that looks a bit like a cheque book opens up.

2. **Check that the Bank A/C Ref field shows the correct account.**

   This field automatically defaults to account 1200, which is usually the bank current account. If this isn't the account you wish to use, select the appropriate account.

3. **Enter the supplier name or use the dropdown arrow to select the payee.**

   As soon as you select an account, Sage brings up a list of outstanding transactions for that account.

4. **Enter the payment date in the Date field.**

   Usually you use the date on your cheque stub or the date of the direct debit or other form of payment.

5. **Record the cheque number or method of payment in the Cheque No. field.**

   Type DD for direct debit, BP for bank payment, or any other short description to help identify the transaction when you reconcile your bank account.

6. **Click the Payment column.**

   You have several options here:

   - **Paying in full:** Click the Pay in Full button at the bottom of the screen. The amount appears in the £ box at the top of the screen, as in Figure 7-4.

     If you have a discount for early payment, enter the discount amount in the Discount column. Sage calculates the amount you owe and shows this value in the £ box and in the Payment column.

   - **Paying part of an invoice:** Enter the amount you wish to pay against the invoice. The amount shows up in the £ box at the top of the screen.

- **Making a payment on account:** Enter the amount you wish to pay in the £ box.

  You may find you need to make a payment against a supplier account but can't specify an invoice to allocate the payment to. You can make a payment to the supplier account without matching it to a specific invoice.

7. **Click Save.**

   If you make full or partial payments to an invoice, the payment posts to that invoice in the supplier account.

   If you make a payment on account, Sage gives you a confirmation message, asking `There is an unallocated cheque balance of £x. Do you want to post this as a payment on account?` Click Yes to accept or No to cancel.

Figure 7-4:
A happy supplier, paid in full.

Printing a Remittance Advice Note

You may want to print a remittance advice note to accompany your cheque. A *remittance advice note* tells your supplier which invoices you're paying. Alternatively, you can just make a note of the invoice numbers on a compliments slip.

If you select Always Create a Remittance in your Bank defaults, the system automatically stores a remittance for you. When I loaded my version of Sage, this default was already set, but you can change it by clicking Settings from the Menu bar then Bank Defaults. If you uncheck the Always Create a Remittance box, Sage creates a new Create Remittance button on your Payment screen. You can then selectively create remittances.

To print a remittance from the Bank module, click Remittance. Sage lists all the remittances generated, whether manually or automatically (depending on how you set your defaults). Highlight the remittances you want to print, or select the date range if you have several, and click Print. You can preview the remittances or send them straight to your printer.

You can choose from four different remittance advice layouts, depending on your paper size. When you print preview a report, you see a beautifully formatted document – but if you try to print this on plain paper, it looks awful. None of the formatting prints well on normal paper – for good printing, you need to buy preprinted Sage paper, which does look very professional.

Chapter 8

Recording Your Bank Entries

*I*f you're the sort of person who likes checking your bank accounts and keeping track of spending on the company credit card, this chapter is for you. In this chapter I show you how to process bank payments and receipts that aren't related to sales invoices or purchase invoices. I look at processing credit card transactions and deal with petty cash – one of the bookkeeping jobs that can be a real pain in the backside if you don't do it properly.

I also show you how you to transfer money between bank accounts – perhaps to take advantage of earning some extra interest (every little helps!). As many businesses often have a lot of banking transactions, I show you ways to speed up the processing by using recurring entries.

Understanding the Different Types of Bank Account

Clicking Bank accounts from the Navigation bar shows you the default bank accounts that Sage provides, including the following:

✔ **Bank accounts:** These include current, deposit, and building society accounts.

✔ **Cash accounts:** These include a petty cash account.

> ✔ **Credit card accounts:** These include a credit card receipts account in case you receive customer payments via credit card.

You can add new bank accounts, rename existing accounts, and delete accounts you don't need – refer to Chapter 3 to find out how.

In the following sections, I show the account number or range of numbers Sage assigns to each account. These account numbers are the same as the nominal code for that bank account.

Keeping up with current (1200) and deposit (1210) accounts

The Bank Current account is the default bank account in Sage that automatically pops up when you enter a bank transaction. You can choose another account if the Bank Current account isn't the right one for your transaction.

Most people use a current account for the majority of their transactions, although you may have additional bank accounts for different areas of your business. If you have surplus cash that you want to earn a bit of interest on, you may have a deposit account and then transfer surplus cash between the current account and the deposit account to take advantage of higher rates of interest. I talk about transferring money between accounts in the 'Transferring Funds between Accounts' section later in this chapter.

Many companies regularly transfer funds to a separate deposit account from their current account to accumulate enough money to pay their VAT bills or PAYE.

Change the name of the Bank Current account to that of your own business current account. If you have more than one business current account, include the account number within the bank account name – for example, Barclays Current Account 24672376. To add or amend bank accounts, check out Chapter 3.

Sage's deposit account functions in the same way as the current account. You can make transfers between the deposit and current accounts in Sage.

Sage also includes a building society account, although not many businesses actually have one of those.

Counting the petty cash (1230) account

You use the petty cash account for cash stored somewhere other than a bank or building society – a strong box or safe in the office, perhaps.

You can operate the petty cash account in the same way as a normal bank account, although most people don't choose to reconcile it as you don't have bank statements to reconcile to.

You can transfer funds into the petty cash account from any of the other Sage bank accounts and make payments accordingly. I give further details in the later section 'Dealing with Petty Cash'.

Handling your cash register (1235)

Sage offers a separate bank account to handle your cash register transactions. You may want to use this function to record receipts of cash and card payments. This type of transaction allows the sale, supply, and payment to happen at the same time. A cash register sale can include details of the sale and the method of payment used (cash, cheque, or card), the price, and any VAT.

The default cash register bank account is automatically set at 1235. Check your Cash Register settings in your Bank Default menu. From the Menu bar, click Settings and then Bank Defaults. Here, you can select the sales nominal code for your Cash Register takings, which automatically defaults to 4000 (you can change this). When using a cash register account, you may find discrepancies exist between the account and actual takings. If so, use the Discrepancy account to balance the books – the default code is 8206 (which you can change). The account has a tickbox to confirm whether your cash takings include VAT.

For further help in using the Cash Register function within Sage, click Help on the main toolbar and select Contents and Index. Click the Search tab and type `recording cash till takings`. Sage offers a list of helpful reports.

Managing the company credit card (1240) and credit card receipts (1250)

You can set up a bank account for each individual credit card and manage these accounts as normal bank accounts – reconciling them, for example, with your credit card statements. See the 'Paying the Credit Card Bill' section later in this chapter for further details about the mechanics of processing credit card transactions.

If you accept payment by credit card, keep a separate bank account for these transactions. You deposit batches of credit card vouchers into your account in the same way that you deposit cheques. Use the Customer option if you receive money against a customer invoice. The credit card company then deposits the real cash into your nominated bank account, and you can make a transfer between that and the Credit Card Receipts account. You receive a statement detailing all the transactions, including a service charge, which can be reconciled.

Tracking Bank Deposits and Payments

Sage helps you keep track of how much money you put in the bank with the Bank module. Sage also keeps tabs on any bank payments you make, such as wages, interest charges, loan payments, and dividend payments.

For both types of transaction, start from the Navigation bar and click Bank accounts. This opens up the Bank module:

- ✔ For receipts, click the Bank Receipt icon.
- ✔ For payments, click the Bank Payment icon.

In both cases, a new window appears. Although the receipt and payment screens are different, they ask you for the same basic information. Use the Tab key to move across the screen and enter the details Sage asks for:

- ✔ **Bank:** Select the correct bank account using the dropdown arrows. Sage automatically defaults to account 1200, which is normally the Bank Current account.
- ✔ **Date:** Sage defaults to today's date, so make sure you change this detail to match the date of the transaction.
- ✔ **Reference (Ref):** If you have a cheque number, payslip reference, or BACS reference, enter it here as it proves very useful when you come to reconcile your bank account.

  When you make a payment, be aware that the reference you enter appears on the audit trail in the Reference (Ref) column for that transaction. Use notation you can understand, such as DD for direct debit or SO for standing order. If you paid by cheque, enter the cheque number.

- ✔ **Nominal Code (N/C):** Using the dropdown arrow, select the appropriate nominal code. You can create a new nominal code here if you need to.

✔ **Dept:** Enter the department using the dropdown arrow. Ignore this field if you don't use departments.

✔ **Project Ref:** Enter your project reference here. When the transaction is saved, Sage updates the project activity and analysis information. If you make a payment, enter the relevant cost code.

✔ **Details:** Record any details that may help you with reconciling your account or identifying the transaction.

✔ **Net:** Enter the net amount of the transaction before VAT. If you aren't VAT registered, put the gross amount here and tax code T0, or T9 if you don't want it to appear on a VAT Return report.

If you only have the gross amount of your receipts or a payment, you can enter this number and then click Calc Net at the bottom of the Bank Payments/Receipts box. Provided the tax code is set correctly, Sage calculates the net and VAT amounts for you.

✔ **Tax Code (T/C):** Use the dropdown arrow to select the appropriate tax code.

✔ **Tax:** Sage calculates the amount of VAT for the transaction based on the net amount and the tax code selected.

Whatever your business type, all businesses receive monies that have nothing to do with their customers, such as bank interest and grants. Post these payments using the Bank Receipts option.

You can continue to enter receipts or payments in a batch. Figure 8-1 shows a Payment Batch Entry screen. As you enter new transactions, the total in the bottom right corner of the screen increases. Check the batch total you calculated against the total Sage reached in the Total box in the top right of the screen.

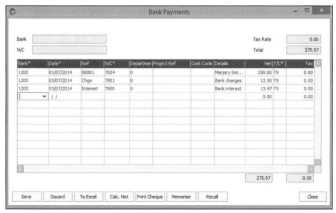

Figure 8-1:
A Payment
Batch Entry
screen.

Using a template to avoid tedium

If you regularly record the same types of receipt and payment, such as regular receipts of bank interest or regular payments of interest charges, you can set up a template and load it whenever you need to. You can change the date and any values or additional information as necessary without having to enter tedious details such as the nominal code and tax information. A template not only saves you time but also reduces the possibility of errors.

To use the Memorise option for a batch of bank receipts or payments, enter the transactions as normal and then click the Memorise button at the bottom of the screen. Select the directory where you want to save your template and enter a filename. (If you're making payments, Sage defaults to an invoices directory, but you can browse to find a more suitable alternative.) Click Save to preserve the template (otherwise, click Cancel) and then click Close.

To recall the template, click Recall from the Bank Receipts or Bank Payments window and choose the directory where you saved the template. Click Open to load the appropriate template. Make any changes necessary and then click Save.

The boxes at the top of the screen show which bank account the receipt is going to, the nominal code, and the tax rate. You can also see A Total box that subtotals all the lines of information in the batch.

When you're happy that the details on the screen are correct, click Save at the lower left of the screen to post payments to the appropriate nominal accounts and bank accounts. If you aren't happy with the information on your Batch Entry screen, click Discard to clear the information. To exit the Payment Batch Entry screen, click Close.

Transferring Funds between Accounts

Just as big banks move money around, you may occasionally want to move money from one account to another. For example, when you pay off your company credit card each month, you make a payment from your current account to your credit card account. You can create a bank transfer between the two accounts to process this transaction easily.

To process a bank transfer, follow these steps:

1. **From the Navigation bar, click Bank accounts and then click the Bank Transfer icon.**

   The Bank Transfer window opens.

2. **Select the bank account you want to transfer the money from, using the dropdown arrow.**

3. **Select the account you want to transfer the money to, using the drop-down arrow.**

4. **Complete the information on screen:**

   - **Date:** Enter the date of the transaction. You need to overtype this, as the system uses today's date.

   - **Reference (Ref):** Enter a reference relating to the transaction.

   - **Description:** You have up to 60 characters to describe the transaction.

   - **Dept:** Select a department, if applicable.

   - **Amount:** Enter the amount of the transaction.

   - **Exchange Rate:** Only use this if you have Sage Accounts Professional and set up a foreign exchange rate as I explain in Chapter 14.

5. **Click Save if you're happy with the information you entered.**

   Sage updates both bank accounts. If you aren't happy, click Discard to clear the screen clear.

6. **Click Close to exit the Bank Transfer screen.**

Repeating Recurring Entries

Designating recurring entries is extremely useful. Doing so speeds up the processing of data and saves time because you enter the information only once, at the set-up stage, and then process all future transactions with the click of a button. You don't have to re-enter the full details of those transactions again.

You can treat many different transactions as recurring items, although they're typically direct debits and standing orders. In the next sections I explain the different types of recurring transaction you can set up.

Going for consistency with your bank entries

You probably make regular payments into and out of your current and credit card accounts and transfer money between accounts on a monthly basis. To set up any of these transaction types as recurring, follow the steps below.

1. **From the Navigation bar, click Bank accounts and then click the Recurring Items icon.**

   The Recurring items window opens.

2. **Click Add to open the Add/Edit Recurring Entry box.**

   Fill in the Recurring Entry From/To section. The information Sage asks for includes:

   - **Bank A/C:** Select the bank account the transaction is coming from or going to.
   - **Nominal Code:** Enter the nominal code for the transaction.

3. **Enter details of the recurring entry.**

   These details include:

   - **Transaction Type:** Choose from Bank/Cash/Credit Card Payment, Bank/Cash/Credit Card Receipts, and Bank/Cash/Credit Card Transfer.
   - **Transaction Ref:** Enter a reference here. Note that Sage already uses DD/SO (direct debit/standing order), which may be sufficient for you, but you can change it as necessary.
   - **Transaction Details:** Enter details of the transaction. In the example in Figure 8-2, I set up a recurring building insurance payment.
   - **Dept:** Enter a department, if applicable.

4. **Determine posting frequency.**

   Make selections about frequency:

   - **Every:** Enter the posting frequency here – for example, daily, monthly, weekly, or yearly.
   - **Total required postings:** If you know the exact number of postings you need to make, enter the number here. The finish date automatically updates.
   - **Start date:** This is the date you want the recurring entry to start. The system automatically defaults to today's date, but you can overtype it with the correct date.
   - **Finish date:** If you haven't updated the total number of postings, leave this date blank. This means the recurring entry continues until you choose to suspend posting or delete the recurring entry.
   - **Last posted:** This shows the date of the last posting made. You can't change this date.

- **Suspend posting?** Tick this box if you don't wish to continue posting the recurring entry. You can untick the box after you decide to resume posting.

5. **Type in the posting amount.**

   Break down the amount as follows:

   - **Net Amount:** Enter the net amount of the transaction.

   - **Tax Code:** Select the appropriate tax code, using the dropdown arrow.

   - **VAT:** This displays the VAT amount, determined by the net amount and tax code selected.

6. **To save the recurring entry, click OK. To exit without saving, click Cancel.**

Figure 8-2:
Creating
a recur-
ring bank
payment.

To view existing recurring entries, from the Bank module on the Navigation bar, click Recurring List on the Links list or click the Recurring icon in the Bank module.

Repeating customer and supplier payments

If a customer pays you or you pay your suppliers regularly, you can set up recurring payments, particularly if the amount's the same each time (although it doesn't have to be):

1. **From the Navigation bar, click Bank accounts and then click the Recurring Items icon.**

2. **In the Recurring items window, click Add.**

   Fill in the following information:

   - **Transaction Type:** Select Customer Payment On Account for a customer payment or Supplier Payment On Account for a supplier payment. Notice the Recurring Entry To/From box changes to accept the Bank A/C and Customer or Supplier A/C details.

   - **Bank Account:** Select the account you want to deposit the payment into, or the account that you want to pay a supplier payment from.

   - **Customer/Supplier Account:** Choose the relevant account using the dropdown arrow.

   - **Transaction Ref:** Enter a reference for your recurring transaction here.

   - **Department:** Select a department, if required.

3. **Select the posting frequencies as in Step 5 in the section 'Going for consistency with your bank entries'.**

4. **Enter the posting amount.**

5. **If you're happy with the information supplied on the screen, click OK to save the recurring entry.**

   If you click Cancel, Sage asks if you want to save the changes. Click No to return to the main screen.

If you use this method to post payments on account to both suppliers and customers, allocate the receipts or payments to the specific invoices as a separate exercise. I don't tend to use this type of recurring option very often because it's quicker to process directly to the invoice in one step: it takes two steps to process a payment on account and then allocate that payment. But every business has different needs and different sets of circumstances, so this recurring option may appeal to you.

Making regular journal entries – if you dare

This option is useful if you have to make an adjustment to the accounts where only a journal is possible. For example, if you make regular payments on a loan, you can set up the payment as a journal and record both the payment and the interest (the specific journal depends on how the loan has been set up).

Only use a journal if you're confident with double-entry bookkeeping. If you aren't competent with your bookkeeping, this is dangerous territory. (I offer a brief explanation of double-entry bookkeeping in Chapter 16.)

To make a regular journal entry, follow these steps:

1. **From the Navigation bar, click on Bank accounts and choose the Recurring Transactions icon.**

   In the recurring transactions window, click Add. The Add/Edit Recurring Entry box appears.

   Although you enter your debit and credit transactions separately, you need to ensure your journal entries balance, otherwise you get an error message. For every debit entry, you need to make a credit entry of the same amount.

2. **Enter the transaction information in the boxes.**

   You need to enter the following details:

   • **Transaction Type:** Select either Journal Debit or Journal Credit.

   • **Nominal Code:** Using the dropdown arrow, select the nominal account to use. The name of the nominal account appears in the box next to the code selected.

3. **Complete the transaction details, posting frequency, and amounts fields, as in Steps 4–6 in the section 'Going for consistency with your bank entries'.**

4. **Click OK if you're happy with the journal details, or click Cancel if you don't like the changes.**

Your newly created recurring entry now appears on the Recurring list.

Processing and posting recurring entries

After you set up recurring entries, every time you start up Sage, it asks if you want to process your recurring entries. Generally, you need to answer No at this stage, as processing your recurring entries in a controlled manner is better.

You can turn off this reminder by selecting the No Recurring Entries At Start Up checkbox in the Parameters tab of Company Preferences (click Settings and then Company Preferences).

You normally process your recurring entries just before you reconcile your bank account so they're ready and waiting to be reconciled. To process your recurring transactions, you need to do the following:

1. **From the Navigation bar, click Bank accounts and then click Recurring Items icon.**

   The Recurring Entries window opens.

2. **Select the entry you wish to post and click Process.**

   The Process Recurring Entries box displays the message `Show recurring entries up to:`.

3. **Enter the date you want to process recurring entries up to.**

   Normally, use the month-end date. For example, to reconcile the bank account to 30 April 2014, type that date.

   After you enter the date, Sage shows you the recurring entries due to be posted up to the chosen date.

4. **Click Post.**

Sage doesn't post recurring entries with a zero value. Cancel the Posting screen and go back and edit the recurring entry so that a value is entered or choose to suspend the item. Also, Sage won't process recurring entries if there are no balancing debits and credits, so ensure you post your recurring journal entries correctly.

Dealing with Petty Cash

Petty cash, funds kept in the office for incidental expenses, is often an absolute pain to administer. Normally a company has a petty cash tin containing a small amount of cash and stuffed full of receipts. As members of staff are given money from the petty cash fund, they exchange the money with a receipt. If you count up the amount of cash and receipts, the total of both should equal the value of the petty cash float. Unfortunately, some people request £20 from petty cash to buy some stationery, pop the receipt in the tin, but forget to return the change. In the following sections I help you keep the petty cash tin in order.

Funding petty cash

Normally, you write out a cheque for petty cash or take the cash out of the bank and put the cash in the petty cash tin. To account for this arrangement within Sage, you can easily show this transaction as a bank transfer.

To do a bank transfer, follow the instructions in the 'Transferring Funds between Accounts' section earlier in this chapter. Make sure the Bank Current account is selected as the *account from* and the Petty Cash account is selected as the *account to*. If you write a cheque for petty cash, you can use the cheque number as a reference.

Making payments from the tin

Make one person solely responsible for the petty cash tin. They can then ensure that if someone returns and doesn't have the correct change and receipts, at the very least an IOU goes in the tin for the money owed. That individual must get the money returned to the tin as soon as possible.

When a payment is made from the petty cash tin, make sure a receipt replaces the money or use a petty cash voucher to record where the money has been spent. This ensures all payments are recorded correctly and should also ensure that the petty cash tin balances to the agreed float amount.

To record a payment made from petty cash in Sage, follow the instructions for bank payments in the section 'Tracking Bank Deposits and Payments', but select the Petty Cash account instead of the Bank Current account.

Reconciling the petty cash tin

Periodically, you need to reconcile the petty cash tin. The best time to do this is when you decide to top it up. To reconcile the petty cash tin, follow these steps:

1. **Extract all the petty cash receipts, batch them up, and total them.**

2. **Give this batch a unique reference number, such as PC01.**

   You can then use PC02 for the next batch, PC03 for the next, and so on. You can use this reference in the Reference field for recording the petty cash bank payments.

3. **Count the remaining petty cash.**

   The sum of the actual cash added to the total from Step 1 should equal the petty cash float.

If the petty cash float doesn't balance, check to see if anyone is holding back any petty cash receipts or if anyone has been given cash to do something and hasn't returned all the change or the receipt.

4. **Write a cheque for cash for the value of the receipts and use this to top up the petty cash float.**

This method is known as the *Imprest system* – you only replenish what you've spent.

Paying the Credit Card Bill

Many businesses use credit cards as a convenient way to purchase goods and services. Just like other financial accounts, you need to include credit card payments in the monthly processing of transactions.

Making payments

After you receive a credit card statement, you need to match up the invoices and receipts with the statement:

- ✔ **Invoices:** If you paid a supplier using your credit card, you probably received an invoice, which you entered and filed away. To process this payment, select the Credit Card bank account and then click the Supplier icon. Make sure you insert a reference to the method of payment somewhere. For example, in the Cheque No. field use the reference *CC* for credit card. Alternatively, use a unique reference number for each credit card statement, particularly if several employees have their own credit cards. In this case, give the statement sheet for each individual its own unique reference number, such as *CC001*. This makes it easier to find the supporting papers for a transaction.

- ✔ **Receipts:** If you have a till receipt rather than a proper invoice for something purchased using the company credit card, attach the receipt to the credit card statement and record the transaction as a bank payment. Make sure you select the Credit Card account as the account from which the payment is to be made. Also, make sure you're careful with the VAT element of the payment, as the amount of VAT attributable to a transaction isn't always obvious.

Reconciling the credit card statement

After you enter all the transactions from the credit card statement on to Sage, you're in a position to reconcile the Credit Card account in the same way as a normal bank statement. (In Chapter 15 I talk about reconciling your bank account.)

When you enter the credit card statement balance, it should be a negative figure because it's money that you owe the credit card company.

The statement is usually paid via a direct debit from your bank account on a monthly basis. You can treat this as a bank transfer between the Bank Current account and the Credit Card account, which I describe in the section 'Transferring Funds between Accounts' earlier in this chapter. You can reconcile the statement in the same way as any other bank account. Provided you enter all the transactions and set the statement balance to a negative figure, you can't go too far wrong.

Chapter 9

Maintaining and Correcting Entries

. . . .

In This Chapter

▶ Locating transactions

▶ Doing file maintenance

▶ Searching for records

▶ Performing backup and restore routines

. . . .

*E*veryone makes mistakes. Sage understands this and makes it very easy for you to correct your errors. You can completely delete an item, change elements of a transaction such as the date or tax code, or find an item to double-check something.

In this chapter, I show you how to make changes to your data and correct any mistakes you find.

Finding Ways to Find Transactions

To amend or delete a transaction, you need to know the transaction number and then locate the transaction.

To find a transaction, you use the Transactions module:

1. Using the Navigation bar, click Transactions.

2. Click the Find button at the top of the screen.

   This brings up the Find box, as in Figure 9-1, which you use to find the transaction.

3. Enter details into the boxes.

Tell Sage what to find and where to look:

- **Find:** The information you enter here depends on what the Search In field shows. For example, in Figure 9-1, the Search In field reads `Transaction Number`, so the entry in this field should be a `transaction number`.

- **Search In:** A dropdown box gives you different variables to search with. The default variable is Transaction Number, but you can also choose Account Reference, Reference, Details, Date, Net Amount, Bank Account Reference, Nominal Account Reference, Ex Reference, Tax Amount, Amount Paid, Date Reconciled, and Late Entry Date.

- **Match:** You don't have to search using the exact data. You can also select how close a match you can make:

  Selecting Any finds all transactions that contain the details you entered anywhere in the field you're searching on. For example, if you're searching for an account reference and you enter RED, Sage finds references such as RED, REDMOND, and CALLRED.

  Selecting Whole finds the transaction that contains the exact details you enter in the Find What field. In our example, when you search for account references, it brings up the RED account transactions.

  Selecting Start finds all transactions beginning with the details you enter. In the example, Sage finds transactions beginning with RED, such as RED and REDMOND, but it doesn't find CALLRED.

- **Case sensitive:** Tick this box if you want Sage to find transactions that contain exactly the same upper- and lower-case letters as those in the Find What field.

4. Click Find First.

If Sage finds a transaction, it highlights it in blue. If this isn't the transaction you want, click Find Next. You may need to cancel the Find box to see the transaction properly.

If Sage finds no transactions, it tells you. Click OK to return to the Find window so you can enter new search details.

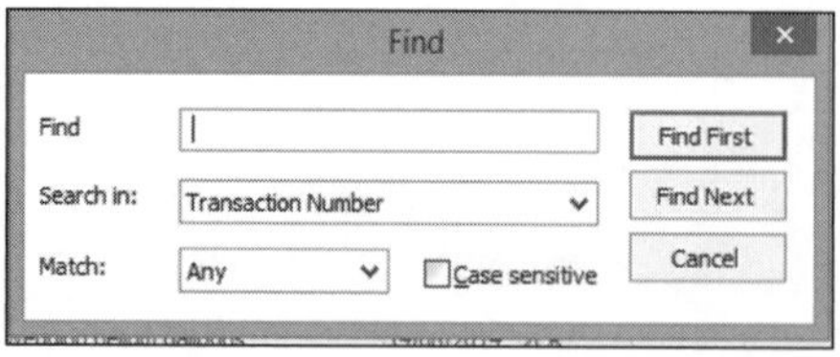

Figure 9-1:
The Find
box.

Searching For Records

You can search for records using the Filter button in the Customers, Suppliers, Nominal Codes, Invoices and Credits, Products and Services, Projects, Sales and Purchase Orders, Departments, and Transactions modules. The Search button is simply another method of tracing transactions.

I tend to search from the Transactions module, as Sage performs a search on all the transactions from this module. If you search from the other modules, Sage limits the search solely to the information in that one module – which may be precisely what you want to do, in which case, choose that specific option.

To perform a search from Transactions, follow these steps:

1. **From the Navigation bar, click Transactions and then click the Filter button.**

   The Filter box opens.

2. **Choose the variables to perform the search.**

   Your choices are:

   - **Join:** From the Join dropdown list, choose the Where option, which is the only option available. (Sage doesn't explain the connection between Join and Where, and I can't either. It's just one of Sage's mysteries.)

   - **Field:** Click the Field column and select the variable you want to search by. In Figure 9-2, Total Amount Paid is selected.

   - **Condition:** Click the Condition column and choose a condition, such as is equal to or is greater than.

   - **Value:** Enter the value you want to search for.

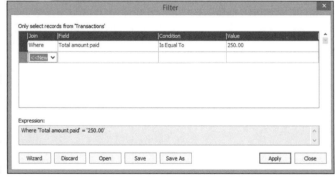

Figure 9-2: Searching for – and finding – £250.

You can enter *wildcards,* which are special characters to represent a line of text or an individual character. For more help with wildcards, in the Search box click F1, the Help function key.

Figure 9-2 shows a search for a transaction for the amount £250.

3. Click Apply.

Sage identifies all transactions that meet the conditions you selected. If Sage can't find a transaction, nothing comes up.

4. Close the Filter box to view the transactions that Sage finds.

You can click the Edit icon to view the transaction in more detail.

You can save a search so you can find records with the same criteria later. Just follow the first two steps in the preceding list and then click Save instead of Apply. Enter a suitable filename and then click Save again. To access this saved file, open the Search box, click Open, and select the chosen file.

After you use the Find facility, you can return back to viewing all transactions by clicking the icon next to the filter button.

Making Corrections

Sage makes corrections to the individual transactions themselves, so identifying the precise transaction that you want to correct is important. To make a correction to a transaction, you can delete the whole transaction or correct a part of the transaction. Just follow these steps:

1. From the Navigation bar, click on Transactions.

The screen shows you a list of all your transactions, listed in transaction number order.

2. Find the transaction you want to correct.

You can click Find or use the up and down arrows to scroll through the data.

3. Choose how to make the correction.

You have two options:

- **Edit:** This option opens a new window showing the details of the transaction. In Figure 9-3 I've chosen a bank payment. The windows differ slightly, depending on the transaction type. On the first screen, any item in black type can be changed. Click the Edit button to change greyed-out items. You then have the option of changing most other parts of the data. Make your changes and click Save. Sage asks `Do you wish to post these changes?`. Click Yes to save or No to return to the original screen. Click Close and then Yes to return to the Corrections screen. Click Close again to return to the Transactions screen.

- **Delete:** If you know you want to delete an item, highlight it and click the Delete Item icon. The Deleting Transactions window appears. You can click the View button to see more of the transaction. If you definitely want to delete it, click Delete. A confirmation message appears asking if you wish to delete the transaction. Click Yes to continue the deletion or No to take you back to the Deleting Transactions window. You can then click Close to return to the Corrections screen and then Close again to go back to the Transactions screen.

Figure 9-3:
Editing
a bank
payment.

All actions you take are recorded in the audit trail, so your accountant can see how many corrections you've made. From an audit point of view, transactions need to be traceable even if you've made mistakes. Unfortunately, any deletions or changes to data are highlighted in red on the audit trail, so if you make wholesale changes to your data they stick out like a sore thumb.

You can't correct journal entries by editing or deleting. Instead, you must use a reversing journal from within the Nominal Ledger module, which I explain in Chapter 16.

Checking and Maintaining Your Files

In this section I help you explore the file maintenance options. From the Menu bar, click File and then Maintenance. A Sage warning message opens saying that you must close all windows before proceeding. Click Yes. The File Maintenance box appears, as shown in Figure 9-4.

The File Maintenance screen may look a little daunting, but you probably need to use only the Error Checking option regularly. I go through each function in the following sections.

Checking errors

The Error Checking facility lets you check your data to make sure it's not corrupt. If your computer switches off in the middle of using Sage, I recommend you use this facility. If Sage closes without being shut down properly, your data may be corrupted.

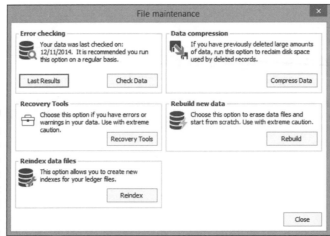

Figure 9-4:
File maintenance options let you check and correct your data.

To check no errors are present, perform an Error Checking routine, following these steps:

1. **From the Menu bar, click File and then Maintenance.**

2. **Click Check Data in the Error Checking section of the File Maintenance window.**

   The system checks each file. If no problems are evident, Sage gives you a message confirming there are no problems to report.

3. **Click OK to return to the File Maintenance screen.**

4. **Click Close to exit the File Maintenance Problems Report window and then Close again to exit the File Maintenance screen.**

Interpreting messages

If Sage finds any problems with your data, it shows a box with several tabs that you can click for more information:

✔ **Comments:** These messages tell you your data may have inconsistencies. The Comments tab shows you which accounts you need to look at. Comments are usually insignificant and don't require data correction.

✔ **Warnings:** These messages alert you to problems that may require further investigation.

✔ **Errors:** An Error message indicates a problem with the data. You can fix errors in Sage, but I recommend you make a backup before you do so. If you find errors in your data, I recommend you restore your data back to a point where you know it was fine. I help you do this in the section 'Restoring Data' section later in this chapter. Clicking 'How to fix errors and warnings in your Sage data' takes you to a Sage website that guides you through resolving any errors or warnings in your data.

Fixing data

You can correct most data problems showing errors by using the Fix option. However, correcting errors can be a complex task. If you're uncertain about the consequences of running the Fix option, I recommend you seek help from Sage Customer Support.

Re-indexing data

Sage recommends using the Re-indexing option only under the guidance of Sage Customer Support. When Sage recommends this course of action, it's usually pretty serious! I've never had to use this option myself, so I can only emphasise what Sage says: Contact Sage Customer Support if you need to re-index your data.

Compressing data

Compressing data files is pretty serious stuff and outside the scope of this book. Briefly, this function constructs a new set of data files and removes deleted records, thereby reducing the file sizes. The files are compressed to create more disk space. As the compression procedure is irreversible, you need to backup your data first, just in case any problems occur.

Rebuilding data

You need to tread carefully when using this part of the system because you can end up wiping all the data off your machine. I suggest you make a backup before you rebuild your data, so you can restore everything fairly easily if necessary.

You can choose to create new data files for all or part of the Sage Accounts system.

Click the Rebuild button to open the Rebuild Data Files window, with all the boxes ticked. A tick indicates that you don't want to create new data files for that part of the system. Removing the ticks tells Sage which parts of your software you want to create new data files for.

If you type `rebuild data files` into the Sage Help menu, Sage guides you through the process. However, I suggest you have Sage Customer Support on standby, just in case anything goes wrong, so they can talk you through the steps.

Use the Rebuild tool with extreme caution and always make a backup of your data before you attempt to use this function.

Backing Up Data

Performing regular backup routines is extremely important. If your data becomes corrupt or you need to reinstall Sage for whatever reason, you then have a backup that you can restore on to your computer, letting you continue working with the least amount of disruption.

To back up your data, follow these steps:

1. **From the Menu bar, click File and then Backup.**

   A message asks if you want to check your data. Sage recommends you check your data, which normally takes a matter of seconds, depending on how may records you have. Click Yes to check or No to continue with the backup.

2. **Make adjustments on the Backup window that comes up.**

   The Backup window contains three tabs:

   • **Backup Company:** This displays the filename SageAccts, followed by your company name, today's date, and the .001 file extension, as in Figure 9-5.

   You can change the filename to one that has meaning for your business. For example, the filename `Jingles accounts end of day 2014-11-23.001` indicates a backup of Jingles' data at close of business on 23 November 2014.

   Choose a location that you can find easily if you need to restore the data. Use the Browse button to change the location if you're not happy with the location Sage chooses.

   • **Advanced Options:** This lets you choose how much you back up. For example, you can include only data, or data plus reports, templates, and so on. At the very least, I suggest you back up your data files.

   • **Previous Backups:** This lets you see previous backups.

3. **Click OK.**

   Sage starts the backup. When the process is complete, you receive a confirmation message saying the backup was successful.

Give each backup a different name. Sage makes this easy by adding the date to the filename, but if you perform more than one backup in a day, you have to change the name slightly or a backup with the same name overwrites the first set of data.

Take backups at the end of every day, at least. If you process a large amount of data, you may want to back up more often. Many people use a different removable drive for each day of the week, naming the backup disk Monday, Tuesday, Wednesday, and so on. You can then restore information back to any day in your current week.

Figure 9-5:
The Sage
Backup
screen.

Scheduling Backups

Sage lets you schedule your data backups at a time to suit you, using the new Sage Accounts Backup Manager.

Follow these steps to schedule your backups:

1. From the Menu bar, click File and then Schedule backup.

The Sage Accounts Backup Manager window opens on the Overview screen. Here you can see who is logged on, when the last backup was done, and whether there are any problems to report on the data, as in Figure 9-6.

2. Click the Settings option to amend the backup details.

Here you can change the backup times, the file types that you want to back up, and the backup location, as in Figure 9-7.

3. On the Settings tab, click Save when you're happy with the backup details.

Close the Overview screen using the cross in the right-hand corner of the box.

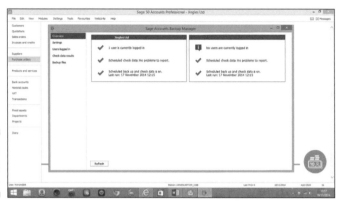

Figure 9-6:
Backing
up data.

Figure 9-7:
Checking
what data to
backup.

Restoring Data

When you restore data, you erase the current data on the computer and replace it with data from your backup files. Ideally, you won't need to ever do this – but in case you do, follow these steps:

1. **From the Menu bar, click File and then Restore.**

   Sage tells you that it can't run this function without closing windows. Click Yes to show the Restore window.

2. **Click Browse and select the file that you want to restore.**

3. Click OK.

A message appears saying you're about to restore and the process overwrites any data currently on the computer. Click Yes to continue or No to exit.

After you successfully restore your data, use the Error Checking facility in the File Maintenance screen to check for errors, as I explain in the earlier section 'Checking errors'.

Part III
Functions for Plus and Professional Users

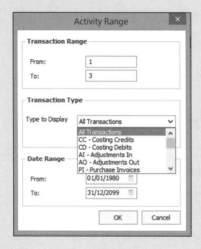

Go to www.dummies.com/extras/sage50accountsuk for free online bonus content.

In this part . . .

✔ Take day-to-day transactions to the next level with Sage 50 Accounts Plus or Professional versions.

✔ Get to grips with sales and purchase order processing.

✔ Understand stock control functions.

✔ Deal with project costings and foreign currency.

Chapter 10

Processing Sales Orders

. . . .

. . . .

Sales orders occur when a customer requests some of your goods or services. In this chapter, I walk you through the steps for processing a sales order, from the moment a quote is confirmed through to allocating and despatching the stock, and then issuing an invoice to the customer.

Sales order processing is available only if you have Sage Accounts Professional. If you don't have this version of Sage, feel free to skip most of this chapter – though the bit on quotations also applies to Sage Accounts Plus, so you may want to read this section.

Giving a Quote

I don't mean recording your words for the enlightenment of the masses. In the business sense, a *quotation* is what you prepare when a potential customer asks for a price for a product or service that you offer. You can create a quotation within Sage that you can ultimately convert into an order if the customer accepts your price.

Amending your invoice and order defaults

If you use Accounts Plus, you don't have Sales Order Processing as an option but you can still double-check the invoice and order defaults to ensure the quotations you raise can convert to sales invoices. Follow the instructions outlined here, but make sure that in Step 2 you set the `Convert Quotes To` field to Invoice.

If you use Accounts Professional, you also need to amend the invoice and order defaults. For example, you can tell Sage what number you want invoices and orders to start from – especially useful if you're continuing on from a previous system. Click the Options tab of the Invoice/Order defaults to make these changes in Sage.

To amend your invoice and order defaults, follow these steps:

1. **From the Menu bar, click Settings and then Invoice/Order Defaults.**

2. **On the General tab, set the Convert Quotes To field to Sales Orders.**

3. **Click OK to accept your changes.**

Creating a quotation

After you check your defaults, you can create a quotation by following these steps:

1. **From the Navigation bar, click Quotations.**

   The Quotation window opens.

2. **Click the New icon.**

   The Product Quote SOP window opens, which looks very similar to the Product Invoicing screen.

3. **Enter the account for which you want to create a quotation by using the dropdown arrows.**

   You can add an expiry date if you want.

4. **Enter the rest of the quotation details, including the product code and quantity.**

   In Figure 10-1 I show a sample quotation for Jingles.

5. **When you're happy with your quotation details, click Save.**

   The quotation is saved to the Quotations list.

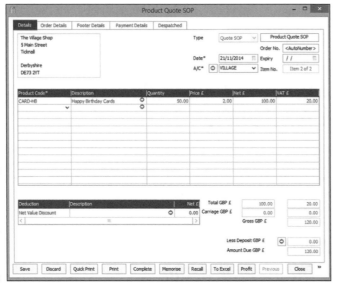

Figure 10-1:
A quotation
Jingles
created for
the village
shop.

You can access the Quotations list by clicking Quotations on the Navigation bar. If you want to edit the details of any quote, highlight the quote you want to edit, click the Edit icon, make the necessary amendments, and click Save.

Sage can list quotations using the following status categories. Generally speaking, the status of the quote is assigned automatically, unless another company gets the business, in which case you have to amend the status yourself.

- ✔ **All quotes:** Sage displays all quotations of any category.

- ✔ **Quotes won:** Sage displays all quotations that you've won. Sage automatically shows a quotation as won when you convert the quote to an order or invoice. Or manually highlight the quote you want to convert to won and click the Mark as Won icon.

- ✔ **Quotes lost:** Sage displays all quotations that you've lost. You can amend a quote by clicking the Mark as Lost icon.

- ✔ **Open quotes:** Sage displays all quotations that haven't passed their expiry dates.

- ✔ **Expired quotes:** Sage displays all quotations that have expired. A quotation expires after it's been open for a period longer than your specified expiry date. You can reopen an expired quotation by changing the expiry date.

You can change the status of a quote by highlighting and right-clicking a quote from the Quotations list. Use the Set As options to change the status of a quote to open, won, or lost.

Allocating and amending stock for a quote

You can allocate stock to an open quotation. To allocate stock, simply select the quotation and click Allocate Stock and then click Yes to confirm. If you want to amend the allocation of stock, select the quotation and click Amend Allocations. You can now the amount of stock allocated.

Converting a quotation to an invoice or order

Depending on your invoice and order default settings, you can convert your quotation to an invoice or an order. I use the example of an order in the sample steps throughout the rest of this chapter.

If you want to convert a quotation to an invoice instead of an order, set your Invoice/Order defaults to Convert quotes to an invoice and then follow the same steps as described in this chapter. You can look at the new invoice on your Invoice list by clicking on the Invoices and credits link on the Navigation bar.

From the Quotations list, select the quote you want to convert and click Mark as Won. Sage asks if you're sure you want to convert the selected quote, so click Yes.

The status of the quote changes to won and the quotation type becomes an order. Sage also creates a sales order in the Sales Order list.

Creating a Sales Order

You can create a sales order by converting a quotation, as I describe in the previous section. You can then access the new sales order by clicking Sales orders on the Navigation bar, highlighting the order, and clicking the Edit icon.

Alternatively, you can create a new sales order by clicking Sales orders from the Navigation bar and then clicking the New icon. The Product Sales Order window opens, which consists of the following six tabs:

- ✔ **Details:** This screen lets you enter the main sales order details, including customer, dates, items ordered, and prices.

- ✔ **Order Details:** In this screen you can amend the delivery details and add any notes about the order.

- ✔ **Footer Details:** You can use this tab to enter information about carriage and courier charges, settlement terms, and discounts.

- ✔ **Payment Details:** You can record a payments on this tab, including details of deposits already received and payments on account.

- ✔ **Despatched:** This tab shows the order status and details of any goods despatched notes. It only updates after you record a delivery of goods.

    A *goods despatched note* (GDN) is essentially the paperwork assigned to stock as it's despatched to your customers. The GDN shows the date the goods were despatched, the customer the goods were sent to, and details of the products, quantity ordered, and quantity despatched. I talk about GDNs in more detail in the section 'Using goods despatched notes'.

    The main body of the Despatched tab shows the GDN number, the customer's GDN, and the date the goods were despatched. It also shows *Y* for yes if you've printed the GDN and *N* for no if you haven't printed. The Despatched tab also contains the following information:

    - • **Order Status:** The status of the order appears here automatically. It may be full, part, or cancelled – or it may be blank, which means the order is complete or has no stock allocated to it.

    - • **Despatch:** This box shows the despatch status of the order and can be part or complete. If no items have been despatched for the order, the box is blank.

    - • **Invoice Status:** This box contains *Y* for yes if you've raised an invoice for the order, or *N* for no if you haven't raised an invoice.

    - • **Complete:** This box shows *Y* for yes if the order is complete, or *N* for no if the order isn't complete.

    - • **Due Date:** You can enter an estimated despatch date here. If the sales order is complete, you can't amend this field.

- **Intrastat:** This box only appears if Intrastat reporting is enabled in the Invoice/Order defaults. The box displays the Intrastat declarations status of the order. *Intrastat* is a system for collecting statistics on the movement of goods between member states of the European Union. (I address Intrastat more fully in Chapter 17.)

✔ **Invoices:** This tab shows which invoices are raised against an order. If you want to see the full details of an invoice, double-click the invoice from the list.

Entering the sales order details

You can create a sales order from a quotation, but if you want to create a sales order without creating a quotation first, follow these steps:

1. **From the Navigation bar, click Sales orders.**

   The Sales order screen opens. Click the New icon to open the Details tab for a product sales order.

2. **Enter the header details.**

   Sage asks you to select or provide information:

   - **Type:** Use the dropdown arrow to select Sales Order or Proforma Sales Order.

   - **Order Number:** Sage automatically assigns each order a sequential number after the order has been saved. The first order is number 1, the next number 2, and so on. If you want to start from a different number, change the number on the Options tab on Invoice/Order defaults.

   - **Date:** Enter the date of the order. The system defaults to the current day's date, unless you change it.

   - **Invoice Reference:** When you update your sales order to match an existing invoice, the last invoice number relating to the sales order appears.

   - **Account:** Enter the customer account reference here.

   - **Item Number:** This is the number of the item currently highlighted on the order. For example, if there are five item lines, and the cursor is currently on the second line, the box says `Item 2 of 5`.

3. **Complete the main body of the order by entering the product items you've sold.**

   Enter the basic information about the products:

- **Product Code:** Use the dropdown arrow to select the product code required. If you don't have a specific product code to use, you can use a special product code. (See Chapter 6 for more details on special product codes.)

- **Description:** This field automatically updates when you select a product code. You can edit the description by pressing F3. (Refer to Chapter 6 to find out more about using the F3 button.)

- **Quantity:** Enter the quantity of stock the customer has ordered.

- **Price:** The unit price from the product record appears here.

- **Discount:** The customer's discount for the item displays here. A discount appears only if it's been selected within the Invoice/Order defaults. You can apply discounts from the Discounts tab on the Invoice/Order defaults. Find this on the Links list within Customers.

- **Discount percentage:** This shows the percentage discount that the customer receives.

- **Net:** The net amount is calculated automatically. You can't change this value.

- **VAT:** The VAT amount calculates automatically. You can't change the value.

- **Total:** The order is totalled at the bottom, showing the net value, carriage charges if they're applicable, the amount of VAT, and the gross amount.

- **Deposit:** This new feature has a smart link to the Payment tab of the order, allowing you to record any deposits received against the order.

- **Deduction:** Here, Net Value Discount offers a drilldown arrow in the Description box, which, when clicked, reveals an Edit Item line. You can enter information referring to the discount and a discount value, and then press Tab – Sage then automatically calculates the percentage discount. If you enter a discount percentage, Sage calculates the value instead.

4. **Click the Order Details tab to add a delivery address or any notes to the order.**

   Sage pulls some information from the customer record, such as telephone number and contact. A Sales Order Status section shows if stock's been allocated to the order and the delivery status of the goods. You can enter an estimated despatch date for the sales order if required.

5. **Click the Footer Details tab to add carriage details.**

The information requested includes assignment numbers and courier details:

- **Carriage terms:** You may want to assign carriage costs to the order if it involves postal or courier costs. You can set up specific nominal codes for charging the carriage costs. If you've set up departments, use the dropdown list to select the appropriate department. You can also add the consignment number and courier details and track your parcel by accessing the courier's website.

To find out how to set up a courier record, click Help from the main toolbar on your Footer Details tab. Use the Contents and Index option and type `couriers`.

- **Settlement Terms:** Some information may already be present in these boxes, depending on what details you entered on your customer record. You can enter the number of days during which an early settlement discount applies and see the discount percentage applied. Settlement terms also shows you the total value of the invoice.

- **Global:** This section lets you apply global terms to the whole order. If you use this option, only one line is added to the audit trail. Carriage is always shown as a separate line.

    You can apply a global nominal code to the whole order. This global code is posted to the nominal ledger when you update the invoice that Sage eventually generates from the order. You can enter global details to accompany the posting to the nominal ledger. This information appears on all reports that show the Details field. Up to 60 characters are available for you to use.

    You can also apply the same global option to your tax code and your departments.

- **Tax Analysis:** The tax analysis for each product item is shown at the bottom of the Footer tab. The list shows a breakdown of all the VAT into the separate VAT codes (assuming you haven't used the Global Tax option).

6. **Click Save when you're happy with the details you've entered.**

The Sales Order screen reverts to a blank order. Sage has saved your order, which now shows on the Sales Order list. You can find the Sales Order list when you click on Sales orders on the Navigation bar.

Dealing with cash sales

Some orders are completed at point of sale, particularly if you have over-the-counter sales. The customer pays for the goods and takes them away immediately. You can receive payment for cash sales online by using the Sage Pay wizard. (Type Sage Pay into the Sage Help facility to find out more.)

Instead of manually completing each element of the sales order lifecycle from stock allocation through to ledger update, you can automate the whole process by choosing the cash sales option when you create the sales order.

To activate the cash sales option, enter the sales order details as in Steps 1–5 in the section 'Entering the sales order details'. Then click the Cash Sales button at the bottom of the order on the Details tab. A confirmation message asks if you wish to complete this order as a cash sale. Click Yes to continue or No to return to the order. If you click Yes, the Layout window opens, expecting you to select your chosen despatch note layout. When you highlight the layout you require, the floating icons appear and you can choose to preview, print, export, export to Excel, or email the despatch note. The system completes all stock allocations, creates an invoice, and creates a bank transaction for the receipt of cash.

You must have sufficient stock levels to satisfy the whole order unless you set Sage to allow negative stock values, in which case the order goes through regardless of stock levels.

You can limit the order paperwork produced for a cash sale to only those documents that you actually need. To select the documents that you need for a cash sale, follow these steps:

1. **From the Menu bar, click Settings, select Invoice/Order defaults, and click the Cash Sales tab.**

2. **Select the documents you want to generate for a cash sale.**

    You can choose sales order, goods despatched note, or sales invoice.

3. **Add a message to the invoice if you like.**

    The default message is currently Cash Sale - paid in full, as in Figure 10-2. If you prefer, you can untick the box so the message doesn't print.

4. **Use the dropdown arrow to select the default cash sales bank account you want the value of the cash sale applied to.**

5. **To save your changes click OK, or to exit without saving click Cancel.**

To complete the order, Sage generates the order and allocates a sales receipt to it.

Figure 10-2:
The Cash
Sales
screen.

Editing your order

If you want to change something after you create an order, you can easily amend the details as follows:

1. **From the Navigation bar, click Sales orders.**

   The Sales order list opens.

2. **Select the sales order you want to amend and click the Edit icon at the top of the screen.**

3. **Make your changes.**

   When you're happy with the order, click Save.

Putting sales orders on hold

You may find you need to put an order on hold while you check out the credit status of a new customer or see if you have enough stock. To temporarily halt an order, follow these steps:

1. **From the Navigation bar, click Sales orders.**

2. **Select the sales order you want to put on hold and click Amend allocations.**

3. **From the Amend Allocations screen, click Off Order.**

   The Order Status window appears.

4. **Click Held and then OK.**

5. **Close the Amend Allocations screen.**

   You return to the Sales Order Processing screen, where you can see that the status of the order is now held.

If you want to take the order off hold, highlight the order, click Amend Allocations, and then click Order. Close the Amend Allocations screen.

Duplicating a sales order

You can copy the details from an existing order into a new order. I use this time-saving device a lot when processing data. To duplicate a sales order, follow these steps:

1. **From the Navigation bar, click Sales orders.**

2. **Select the sales order you want to copy from the Sales Order Processing screen.**

3. **Click the Duplicate icon.**

   A new sales order opens that's an exact copy of the previous order. Notice it has a heading showing that it's a duplicate order. After you save the duplicated order, it acquires an order number of its own.

4. **Check the details of the order are correct and amend any parts where necessary.**

5. **To save the new order, click Save.**

   Sage asks you if you want to allocate stock now or later. If you choose Allocate Now, Sage automatically allocates the stock and then returns you to a blank sales order screen. Click Close to go to the Sales order list, where you can see your new order, with the word `full` in the Allocated column.

Printing the order

The print facility lets you print as many copies of the order as you want. Follow these steps to print an order:

1. **From the Navigation bar, click Sales orders.**

2. **Select the sales order you want to print by highlighting the order on the list.**

   Click the Print icon.

3. **The Layout window opens.**

   If you've already selected a favourite report layout, the layout appears in the first screen – otherwise click Layout and choose the layout you want. Use the floating icons to choose the output method – preview, print, export, export to Excel, or email. Preview the report first to ensure the details are correct and you're happy with the layout

   To make a layout a favourite, click the star icon next to the report layout you like. This copies the layout to your favourites page.

4. **Click Print to print the report.**

   The Print window opens. Click OK if you're happy to continue printing the order.

Allocating Stock to an Order

After you save your sales order, Sage asks if you want to allocate stock now or later. If the order has already been despatched and you've completed the order, Sage automatically allocates the goods for you. In the next sections I describe how to apportion stock automatically and manually.

Going on automatic

Sage automatically allocates as much stock as possible to your orders, so the amount of *free stock* (stock available to fulfil orders) decreases and the amount of *allocated stock* (items earmarked for specific orders) increases.

To allocate stock automatically, follow these steps:

1. **From the Navigation bar, click Sales orders.**

   Highlight the order you want to allocate stock to, and then click Allocate Stock.

2. **Click Yes when Sage asks if you want to allocate all stock to the order.**

   If you don't have enough stock to allocate to the order, Sage lets you know.

   The Sales Order Processing window reappears, and the order shows the word `full` in the Allocated column. If there isn't enough stock to allocate to the order, the column reads `part`.

Assigning stock yourself

Allocating stock manually gives you greater control over your stock. For example, if you have two orders, each for ten boxes of cards, but you have only ten boxes in total, you can manually allocate five boxes of cards to each order and tell each customer that the balance of the order is to follow.

To manually allocate stock, follow these steps:

1. **From the Navigation bar, click Sales orders.**

2. **Highlight the order and click Amend Allocations in the Sales Order Processing screen.**

3. **In the Amend Allocations screen, manually add the number of units to allocate to the order.**

4. **To save your changes, click Close.**

   The word `part` shows in the Allocated column against the order.

Sage reduces the amount of free stock and increases the amount of allocated stock in the same way that it does if you automatically allocate stock. Figure 10-3 shows a partially allocated order.

Amending the allocation of stock

If you've allocated stock to an order but haven't actually despatched the order, you can still amend the order and reallocate stock. To do this, select the sales order from the Sales Order list and click Amend Allocations. You can then change the amount of stock you've allocated to that order.

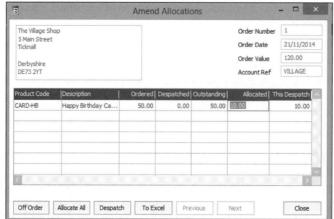

Figure 10-3:
The results
of allocating
stock for
part of an
order.

Using the shortfall generator

Sage lets you know if you don't have enough stock to fulfil all the orders
raised. To check your stocks, select the orders from the Sales Order list and
click the Shortfall icon on the Sales Order Processing toolbar. The Shortfall
Generator window shows a list of any products that have a stock level less
than the quantity required for the order, as I show in Figure 10-4. If you click
Create Order, you can generate a purchase order for the specific products
you're running short of.

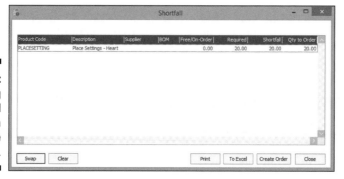

Figure 10-4:
Predicting
a shortfall
in stock is a
handy Sage
tool.

Despatching Orders

After you allocate the stock to the order, you can despatch the goods using one of the four methods Sage offers. I explain each of these methods in the next sections.

Completing an order

You complete your order once the goods are ready to be sent to the customer. Sage allocates stock to the order and marks the order as being despatched. To complete an order, follow these steps:

1. **Highlight the order from the Sales Order list, click the Edit icon to view the order, and then click the Complete button at the bottom of the Details tab.**

2. **A confirmation window asks whether you want to complete the order in full.**

   Click Yes to continue. Sage tells you if an order can't be completed, for example because you have insufficient stock, and then lets you amend the order accordingly.

3. **Another confirmation message asks if you want to create an invoice, update your stock, and record a despatch note for the selected order.**

   If you only want to print a despatch note at this stage, click No; otherwise click Yes.

4. **A third confirmation window asks if you want to print out the goods delivery note (GDN).**

   Choose whether to print now or later.

5. **A final confirmation message asks if you want to print out your sales order.**

   Select Yes or No. Sage then marks your order as complete or part complete.

Using goods despatched notes

Using a GDN automatically records the goods you despatch and provides maximum traceability because you can view all the GDNs on the Despatch tab for each order.

Before you use GDNs, you need to set up your GDN options in the Options tab of Invoice/Order defaults. You have the following choices:

✔ **Generate for all despatches:** This is the default option. Sage gives you the choice of printing a GDN now or later.

✔ **Prompt at each despatch:** Sage prompts you each time you record a despatch as to whether you want to generate a GDN now or later. If you don't generate the GDN, Sage doesn't store the GDN in the Despatched tab of the Sales Order, so you can't view or print the note later.

✔ **Do not generate:** If you select this option, Sage updates your sales order and your stock level but doesn't produce a GDN.

Sage issues a GDN depending on the default options you select. You can raise a GDN by clicking the Despatch button, or you can click the GDN button – I outline both methods in the next sections.

Using the despatch facility

You can use the Despatch facility to record complete deliveries of orders to your customers. Follow these steps:

1. **From the Navigation bar, click Sales orders.**

2. **Select the orders from the Sales Order Processing screen and click Despatch Orders.**

   Then follow Steps 3–5 from the earlier section 'Completing an order'.

   Sage generates a GDN if this option is selected in your defaults, creates a product invoice, and updates the stock level for each product on the order.

Recording a despatch manually

If you don't despatch the whole order, you can manually record the delivery of the stock you do send. Follow these steps to use the Amend Allocations facility to record complete or part despatches:

1. **From the Sales Order Processing window, click Amend Allocations.**

2. **Edit the quantity shown in the This Despatch column in the Amend Allocations window.**

3. **Click Despatch to update the product records.**

A prompt message asks if you want to create invoice details, update stock, and record the despatch for the previous order, as in Figure 10-5. Choose one of the following answers:

- **No:** This prints a delivery note only (according to the options chosen).

- **Cancel:** This returns you to the Allocations screen, which you can close if you want.

- **Yes:** This lets you continue with the despatch of the goods. For more details, see Step 3 in the earlier section 'Completing an order'.

After you complete the despatch process, you return to the Sales Order List, where you can see that Sage has amended the status to part despatched.

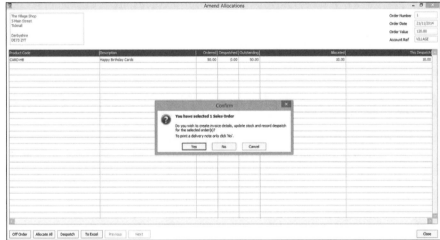

Figure 10-5: Recording a part despatch of an order.

Invoicing Your Customers

After you allocate and despatch all stock relating to your order, you need to print the invoices created from your order and update the ledgers to complete your sales order cycle.

When you despatch an order, Sage automatically generates a product invoice for each order or partial order. Sage also updates your stock levels at the same time.

You can check that Sage has raised an invoice by looking at the Invoice tab for your order to see the invoice number. You can view and print the invoice from the Invoice tab. If you've already selected a default print layout, you can use the Quick Print option. Alternatively, you can print the invoice by using the following method:

1. **From the Navigation bar, click Invoices and credits.**

   The Invoice list appears.

2. **Choose the invoice you want to print.**

3. **Click Print and select the layout you prefer.**

   When the invoice layout window opens, it may show your favourite layout. If not, choose a layout and click Print from the floating icons. Alternatively, select the Quick Print option if you've already selected a default print layout.

When you're ready to update your invoices, from Customers, click the Invoice list. Select the invoices you want to post and then click the Update Ledgers icon, following the instructions on screen. Sage posts the invoices to the sales and nominal ledgers.

Deleting and Cancelling Sales Orders

You can delete cancelled or completed orders, and you can also cancel orders before fulfilling them. To free up disk space on your computer, you can remove fulfilled or cancelled orders by compressing your data.

Before you delete any orders, I suggest you back up your data in case you change your mind and need to restore the data later. I cover backing up in Chapter 9.

Deleting an order

To delete an order, follow these steps:

1. **From the Navigation bar, click Sales orders.**

   The Sales Order List appears.

2. **Select the order you want to delete and click the Delete icon.**

   A confirmation message asks you to confirm that you want to delete.

When you delete an order, Sage deletes any GDNs associated with the order. Make sure you don't need the GDN information before you delete the order.

3. To continue deleting the order, click Yes.

Cancelling an order

You can cancel an unfulfilled sales order. After you cancel an order, it remains on the Sales Order list, but its status changes to cancelled. Any stock that was allocated to that order reverts to free stock again. To cancel a sales order, follow these steps:

1. From the Navigation bar, click Sales Orders.

The Sales order list appears.

2. Select the order you want to cancel and then click Amend Allocations.

3. Click Off Order when the Amend Allocations window appears.

The Order Status window appears.

4. To cancel your order, click Cancel Order.

Click OK to confirm the cancellation, or click Cancel if you decide you don't want to cancel the order.

When you cancel a sales order, the Off Order button changes to Order. If you want to put a cancelled order back on order, click the Order button from the Amend Allocations window.

When you cancel an order, Sage cancels all the items in the order. If you want to cancel only a specific item on an order, choose the Edit icon from the Sales Order Processing window. Delete the unwanted item from the order, or press the F8 key to delete specific lines on the order.

Chapter 11

Processing Purchase Orders

- -

- -

*I*f you have Accounts Professional, Sage helps you process your purchase orders. If you don't have this version of Sage, you can skip this chapter.

You raise purchase orders for goods that you place on order with your suppliers. The purchase order processing (POP) system is directly linked to other parts of Sage: The system updates stock records and project records if you use these functions of Sage.

In this chapter, I cover the various stages that a purchase order goes through.

Creating, Changing, and Copying a Purchase Order

When you order supplies, materials, widgets, or similar, you need to create a paper trail – or at least an electronic trail – that you can send to your supplier to tell them what you need, how much of it you need, when you need it, and for what price. This paper trail is called a *purchase order,* or PO. Sage Accounts Professional has the perfect process for conveying this information.

Creating a purchase order

Creating a purchase order in Sage consists of completing the information Sage requests in four tabs:

1. **From the Navigation bar, click Purchase orders.**

   A window appears listing all of the purchase orders. Click the New icon to open a blank purchase order.

2. **Fill in the information requested in the Details tab.**

   Sage asks you for the following basic information:

   - **Order Number:** Sage automatically issues each order a sequential number, although you don't see the number until you save the order.

     Sage gives the first order number 1, the next number 2, and so on. If you want to start from a different number, change the number on the Options tab on Invoice/Order defaults, which you can find by clicking Settings on the Menu bar.

   - **Date:** Enter the date of the order. Keep in mind that Sage defaults to the current day's date, unless you change it.

   - **Account:** Enter the supplier account reference here.

   - **Project Reference:** You see this reference only if you switch on Project Costing. Use the dropdown arrow to link the order with a specific project if you want to do so.

   - **Cost Code:** This code only appears if you switch on Project Costing. You can use the dropdown arrow to select an appropriate cost code.

   - **Reference:** You can enter an additional reference here.

   - **Item Number:** This field shows the number of the item currently highlighted on the order. For example, if you have five item lines and the cursor is currently on the second line, the box says `Item 2 of 5`.

   - **Rate:** The rate appears only if you enabled the Foreign Currency option.

3. **Complete the main body of the order.**

   List the details of the product items that you want to purchase:

   - **Product Code:** Using the dropdown arrow, select the product code you require. If you don't have a specific product code to use, you can use a special product code. See Chapter 6 for more details on special product codes.

- **Description:** The description updates automatically when you select a product code. However, you can edit the description by pressing the F3 key.

- **Quantity:** Enter the quantity of stock that you want to order.

- **Price:** The unit price from the product record appears here.

- **Net:** This amount calculates automatically – you can't change this value.

- **VAT:** This amount calculates automatically – you can't change the value.

- **Total:** The order total appears at the bottom, showing net, VAT, and any carriage charges applied.

4. **Click the Order Details tab to add a delivery address or any notes to the order.**

   Sages pulls certain information from the supplier record, such as the supplier's telephone number and contact information.

5. **Click the Footer Details tab to add carriage details.**

   You can include assignment numbers and courier details here:

   - **Carriage Terms:** You may want to assign postal or courier costs to the order. You can set up specific nominal codes for the carriage costs to be charged to. If you set up departments, use the drop-down list to select the appropriate department. You can also add the consignment number and courier details and track your parcel by accessing the courier's website.

     Click Help from the main toolbar to set up a courier on your Footer Details tab. Using the Contents and Index option, type `couriers` to find out how to enter the appropriate details.

   - **Settlement Terms:** Some information may already be present in these boxes, depending on what details you entered on your supplier record. You can enter the number of days during which an early settlement discount applies, see what discount percentage is applied, and see the total value of the invoice.

   - **Tax Analysis:** The tax analysis for each product item appears at the bottom of the Footer Details tab. The list shows a breakdown of all the VAT into separate VAT codes.

6. **Click Save to preserve the order.**

   Sage asks `Do you want to place this order On Order now?` Click either Order Now or Order Later.

If you click Order Now, Sage asks if you want to print the order. If you click Yes, the Layout window opens so you can choose a report layout. You can create a favourite report layout by clicking on the star, which turns orange, at the side of the chosen report. This copies the layout and places it on the Favourites tab.

If you don't select a favourite layout, click on the Layout tab and select one of the series of report layouts listed on the right hand side of the screen. As you scroll down the list, a floating set of icons offers you options to preview, print, export, export to Excel, or email the report directly to your supplier. If you choose to print, your report prints out. Then click the cross in the right corner of the Layout window to close it. The Purchase Order screen then shows a blank order, but Sage has saved your order and is ready for the next one.

If you click Order Later, the Purchase Order screen goes blank, waiting for you to enter a new order. The order shows on the Purchase Order List, which you can view from the Links pane.

After you close the Purchase Order screen, you can view a copy of your order on the Purchase Order list.

Editing your order

If you want to change something after you create your order, you can easily amend the details as follows:

1. **From the Navigation bar, click Purchase orders.**

   This opens a window showing a list of all your purchase orders.

2. **Select the purchase order that you want to amend and click the Edit icon at the top of the screen.**

   You can then amend any part of the order.

3. **Click Save when you finish editing the purchase order.**

I recommend you amend details only if you haven't already placed the order On Order, otherwise you may experience stock problems when products arrive and don't match what you need. Sage gives you a warning message telling you the order is already On Order, and it may affect the status of the order if you change anything.

Duplicating a purchase order

You can copy an existing order with the same details as those you want to enter for a new order. I use this feature a lot when processing orders, as it speeds up the entry time. To use the duplication feature, follow these steps:

1. **From the Navigation bar, click Purchase orders.**

   A window appears listing all your purchase orders.

2. **Select the purchase order you want to copy and click the Duplicate icon.**

   An exact copy of the previous order opens, as in Figure 11-1. Notice the heading proclaims it's a duplicate of the original purchase order.

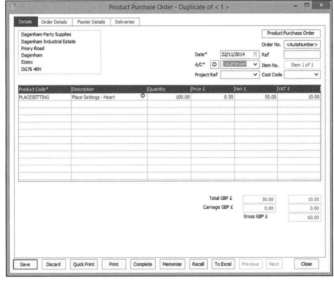

Figure 11-1:
Cloning a purchase order is easy and helpful.

3. **Check the details of the order are correct and change anything that needs to be different.**

4. **To save the new purchase order, click Save.**

5. **To close the order and return to the main purchase orders screen, click Close.**

   The Purchase Order list appears, showing the new order.

Placing the Goods on Order

After you create a purchase order and are ready to send it to your supplier, you need to put it on order with Sage.

In the following sections, I assume you clicked Order Later rather than Order Now when you saved your purchase order. You can check to see the status of your order by checking the Purchase Order List. If the On Order column is blank, you need to place the order on Sage.

Ordering via the conventional method

In the following steps, you change the status of the order to on order and update your on-order stock levels for the appropriate product codes:

1. **From the Navigation bar, click Purchase orders.**

2. **Select the purchase order you want to place on order by clicking the Place Orders icon in the POP screen.**

   A confirmation message appears, asking if you want to print the order. Click Yes if you want to print it, or No if you want to continue without printing.

3. **To place the goods on order, click Yes when Sage asks if you want to place all selected items on order.**

   The POP window reappears, showing the status of the order as on order.

When the goods come in, you can now receive them properly.

The On Order status column on the Purchase Order List is now updated to reflect the status of the new order that you placed.

Manually placing goods on order

An alternative method of placing your goods on order lets you view the order again before you place it on order. If you want to double-check the items on the order, follow these steps:

1. **Select the order from the Purchase Order list.**

2. **Click the Amend Deliveries icon.**

You see all the product records contained within your order, one line per product, as in Figure 11-2.

3. **To put your purchase order on order, click Order.**

The full order quantity appears in the This Delivery column. In Figure 11-2, the This Delivery column is currently zero – but as soon as you place the goods on order, the value changes.

4. **Click Close to return to the POP window.**

The purchase order now shows on order.

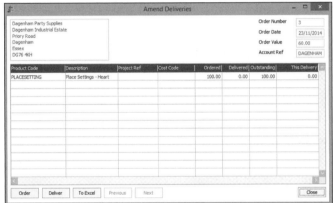

Figure 11-2:
Manually placing goods on order lets you check the order beforehand.

Completing Your Purchase Order

Completing your order is necessary only if you've already received your goods. The process of completing your order means that Sage saves the order, completes the order, and records the delivery of stock immediately.

If the order is linked to a project, Sage automatically allocates the goods to the project and then applies the costs. Sage applies actual costs at different stages, depending on the type of item ordered:

✔ **Stock item:** Sage applies actual costs when the stock item is issued to the project.

✔ **Non-stock or service item:** Sage applies actual costs when the invoice is recorded for the purchase order.

To complete your order, follow these steps:

1. **From the Navigation bar, click Purchase orders.**

   The list of purchase orders appears.

2. **From the Purchase orders window, select the order you want to complete and click the Edit icon.**

   An information window opens confirming the current order status. Click OK to take you to the Details screen of the order.

3. **Click Complete at the bottom of the screen and then click Yes when you get the confirmation message saying you've selected to complete the order in full.**

   Click Yes to continue.

4. **Click Yes again when another confirmation message asks if you want to update stock and record delivery of the order.**

   Sage generates a goods received note and asks if you want to print it now or later. Make your choice and then decide whether to print the purchase order as well.

5. **Close the Purchase Order screen.**

   The screen returns to the Purchase Order list and the status of your order shows as complete.

If you look on the Deliveries tab of your order, you see that Sage has generated a goods received note (GRN). You can view or print the GRN from this screen.

Printing Your Purchase Order

You can print or spool a copy of one or more purchase orders so you can send them out to suppliers or keep a hard copy for your records.

Print spooling is the process of transferring data to a temporary holding place known as a *buffer*, usually an area on a disk. The printer can pull the data off the buffer when required, leaving you free to carry out other computer tasks while the printing goes on in the background.

Printing purchase orders in batches makes sense, if only because you can put a wodge of the correct stationery in the printer.

To print a batch of purchase orders, follow these steps:

1. **From the Navigation bar, click Purchase orders.**

   A list of purchase orders opens.

2. **Select the purchase orders that you want to print and click Print icon.**

   You can choose Quick Print if you've chosen a default print layout.

3. **From the Layout list box, select the layout you require for your purchase orders.**

   Sage presents you with a multitude of layouts. Alternatively, you can choose to email the purchase order.

4. **Select the output you require from the floating list of icons.**

   You can choose to print, preview, export, or email.

   - **Print:** Choosing this option opens the Print window. Select the pages you want to print and change your printer settings if required. You can print orders as many times as you like.

   - **Print Preview:** The Print Preview window shows the first purchase order in the batch. If you're happy with the preview, you can send the order directly to the printer by choosing the Print option from the File menu.

   - **Export:** You can either Export to Excel or Export. If you click Export, the Save As window appears. Select a directory to store the file in and enter a filename. If you choose Export to Excel, a new Excel file is created with the details of the purchase order.

   - **Email:** This opens your email system, where you can send the purchase order as an attachment. Just follow the prompts on the screen.

Getting the Goods In

After you send a purchase order, you typically receive the goods. (If you don't, you need to pursue the issue with the supplier!) When the goods arrive, you need to book them into Sage.

If you placed the order for a project and completed the purchase order as I described in the earlier sections in this chapter, Sage automatically records the stock as delivered and allocates it to the proper project.

In the following sections, I cover three alternative ways of recording the delivery of goods.

Using goods received notes

Goods received notes (GRNs) are a quick and easy way to record the delivery of stock. GRNs let you record deliveries against more than one order at the same time. Sage keeps a record of all GRNs raised against each order. You can view and print these GRNs by going to the Deliveries tab of each order.

Setting GRN defaults

To adjust the settings for GRNs, follow these steps:

1. **From Settings on the Menu bar, click Invoice/Order defaults and then click the Options tab.**

2. **Amend the default setting for GRNs using the dropdown arrow.**

   Your options are:

   - **Generate for all received:** This is the default option. Sage generates a GRN for each delivery but gives you the option to print now or later.

   - **Prompt at each received:** Each time you record a delivery, Sage asks whether to generate a GRN. If you choose not to generate the GRN, Sage doesn't store a copy of it so you can't view or print the GRN later.

   - **Do not generate:** Sage updates the purchase order and stock levels but doesn't produce a GRN. The GRN option doesn't appear on the Purchase Order Processing toolbar.

3. **Click OK.**

Generating the GRNs

If you selected the Do Not Generate GRNs option, ignore this section, as the GRN icon doesn't appear on your toolbar. If you want to process your GRNs, then read on:

1. **From the Navigation bar, click Purchase orders.**

   Select the order you want to raise a GRN for.

2. **Click Received Notes.**

   The Received Notes window opens. You can use the GRN option only if the status of the goods is on order.

3. **Enter the date and supplier information in the boxes provided.**

   As soon as Sage identifies the supplier, all the outstanding items from the selected purchase order appear, as in Figure 11-3. You may want to enter the supplier's GRN, if you have it.

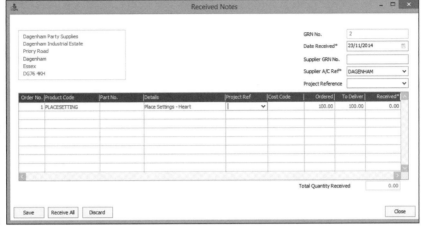

Figure 11-3:
Entering
your goods
received
information.

4. Check the details.

If the delivery is all there, click Receive All. If not all of your order was delivered, enter the actual quantities received in the Received column. The Received column changes from zero to the value of the items received.

5. To save the goods received information, click Save.

A message appears saying A goods received note has been generated for this order and stored under the Deliveries tab of the order. You can print this goods received note now, or continue processing and print it from the Deliveries tab of the order. You can tick the Do Not Show This Message Again box so you don't see this message every time.

If you don't want to save the goods received information, click Discard.

6. To return to the Purchase Order Processing window, click Close.

The status of the order changes to complete on the Purchase Order list, or to part if you received less than your full order.

Accepting delivery of everything

If everything on your purchase order comes in, you can use the Deliver function to record that, as long as you've already placed the purchase order on order, as I explain in the earlier section 'Placing the Goods On Order'.

To accept delivery, follow these steps:

1. **From the Navigation bar, click Purchase orders.**

2. **From the Purchase orders window, select the order you want to process and click Receive Deliveries.**

   Sage asks if you want to update stock and record delivery of the items. Click Yes to continue. Depending on which GRN options you selected (see 'Setting GRN defaults' earlier in this chapter), Sage may ask whether you want to print a GRN. Print as required. The Purchase Order window then reappears, showing the status of the order as complete.

Taking in part of an order

You can use the Amend Deliveries facility to manually record delivery of a complete or partial order. Here you can check the order line by line against what you have received instead of automatically updating and recording stock. Also, you can choose to process part or complete deliveries instead of being forced to record complete deliveries only.

Before you can amend your order, you must place it on order.

To use the Amend tool, work through the following steps:

1. **From the Navigation bar, click Purchase orders.**

2. **Highlight the order you want to change and then click Amend Deliveries.**

   The Amend Deliveries window appears, showing the full order quantity in the This Delivery column.

3. **To record a partial delivery, amend the actual quantity received in the This Delivery column.**

   If you want to record a complete delivery, move to Step 4 without amending the This Delivery column.

4. **Click Deliver to update the product records with the new delivery information.**

   A confirmation message appears asking if you want to update the stock and record delivery of the items. Click Yes to continue or No to return to the Amend Deliveries screen.

   Depending on the GRN options you chose, Sage may ask you to print your GRN.

5. **Click Close to return to the Purchase Order list.**

   If you received a partial order, the Purchase Order window shows the new status of the order as part.

Creating an Invoice from an Order

As part of the lifecycle of the purchase order process, ultimately you want to match the invoice received from the supplier to the order that you raised in Sage. Sage lets you do this by converting the purchase order to an invoice by using the Update icon. This icon lets you mirror the information from the invoice received from the supplier. You save time by doing this, as you don't have to type in all the supplier invoice details, because you entered most of them at the order stage.

The purchase order has a Posted column. If the Posted column is blank, the order hasn't been posted to the purchase ledger. If the order's been updated, you see a Y in the column. When the order is updated, it posts to the purchase ledger and the nominal ledger.

You can update part-delivered orders. Each part creates its own invoice, so you may have more than one invoice relating to the same order.

To create a purchase invoice for a partially or fully delivered order, follow these steps:

1. **From the Navigation bar, click Purchase orders.**

2. **Highlight the order(s) against which you want to raise an invoice and click Update Ledgers.**

   If you've enabled transaction email and linked the selected orders to a supplier record that's marked I send orders to this supplier electronically, a prompt appears asking you whether you want to send the orders now.

   The Purchase Order Update window opens.

3. **Edit any of the details shown in the Purchase Order Update window by highlighting the lines you want to change and clicking Edit.**

   Make any changes you require.

4. **Click Save. If you decide no changes are necessary, click Close.**

5. **Select the components of the order that you want to update and click Update.**

   The Batch Supplier window appears, showing the details of your purchase invoice.

6. **Match the actual invoice received from your supplier with the details on the Batch Supplier window.**

   You need to add the supplier's invoice number in the Ex.Ref field or the Details field. You also need to enter your sequential number for your purchase invoice in the Ref field. You can overtype the order number that automatically pulls through in the Ref field.

When you file your purchase invoices, you can attach a copy of the printed order to the back of the invoice.

7. **To update the purchase ledger and create an invoice from the details, click Save.**

An information message appears about Project references – answer yes or no as appropriate. If you click Yes to continue, Sage processes the information and returns you to the Purchase Order list. The Purchase Order list now shows a Y in the Posted column for the invoice you just updated.

Deleting, Cancelling, and Reinstating Orders

Sage knows the realities of the business world and accommodates them and human foibles too – sometimes you need to delete or cancel an order, and sometimes you think you need to cancel a purchase order only to find out that you need it after all.

Deleting orders

You can delete purchase orders from the Purchase Order list. If you try to delete an order that isn't complete or cancelled, Sage issues a warning message asking if you really want to delete it.

When Sage deletes a purchase order, it also deletes any associated GRNs – so if you need to keep copies of GRNs, take copies before you delete the order.

After you delete the purchase orders, you can use the Compress Files facility in File Maintenance to remove deleted orders from the data files and make the unused disk space available.

To delete purchase orders, follow these steps:

1. **Take a backup of your data in case things go pear-shaped and you need to restore a clean set of data.**

I cover backups in detail in Chapter 9.

2. **From the Navigation bar, click Purchase orders and select the order you want to delete.**

3. **Click the Delete icon at the top of the screen.**

   A confirmation box appears asking you to confirm that you want to delete the items highlighted. Click Yes to continue or No to halt the process.

Cancelling orders

With Sage, you have the ability to cancel orders. Just follow these steps:

1. **From the Purchase Order List, select the order you want to cancel and click Amend Deliveries.**

   The Amend Deliveries window appears, showing the details of the order, with one line per product.

2. **Click Off Order.**

   Clicking the Off Order button cancels the whole order. If you want to cancel one line from an order, choose the Edit icon from the Purchase Order List window and delete the required row from the order by using the F8 key.

   The status of the PO needs to be on order before you can cancel it. Otherwise when you click Amend Deliveries, the Off Order button isn't available.

3. **To return to the Purchase Order list, click Close.**

   The status of the order shows as cancelled.

Putting a cancelled order back on order

If you change your mind and decide that you want to reinstate a previously cancelled order, follow these steps:

1. **From the Purchase Order List, select the order you want to place back on order.**

   Click Amend Deliveries.

2. **Click Order in the Amend Deliveries window.**

   The button changes to Off Order.

3. **Exit the Amend Deliveries window by clicking Close.**

   The status of the order now shows as on order.

Chapter 12

Keeping Track of Your Products

- -

In This Chapter

▶ Recording a stocktake

▶ Building a bill of materials

▶ Processing stock returns

▶ Assigning stock

- -

A lot of business money is often tied up in stock. Having proper control over your stock procedures makes good business sense. In this chapter, I give you the tools to manage your stock.

I cover recording a stocktake, which you can do with any version of Sage, in this chapter. I also explore the added features available only in the SagePlus and Professional versions.

Taking Stock

Every business should undertake a stocktake periodically – once a year at the very least – so the year-end accounts show an accurate stock position. However, actually carrying out a stocktake can prove a logistical nightmare, particularly if you have a vast array of products.

Usually, recording a stocktake is best undertaken when the factory or office is closed for normal business. Many a time I've rolled out of bed on a Saturday to help do a stocktake. Sage doesn't allow you the luxury of a weekend lie-in, but it does help you organise your company's stock methodically.

Before you run the Stock Take option in Sage, run one of the Sage stocktake reports to assist you with the physical stock count. I show an example of one of the Stock Take Report (by Stock Category) in Figure 12-1 – and you can see that Sage helpfully provides the quantity of stock as recorded in Sage followed by a blank box, where you can record the actual stock quantity.

Figure 12-1:
Running a
stocktake
report.

> Date: 24/11/2014   **Jingles Ltd**   Page: 1
> Time: 17:35:48   **Stock Take Report (by Stock Category)**
>
> Stock Code From: Stock Category From: 1
> Stock Code To: ZZZZZZZZZZZZZZZZZZ   Stock Category To: 999
>
> **Stock Category**   1
>
> | Stock Code | Description | Unit Of Sale | Location | Quantity In Stock (from System) | Actual Quantity In Stock |
> |---|---|---|---|---|---|
> | BALLOONSLILAC | Lilac Balloons | | | 20.00 | |
> | CARD-HB | Happy Birthday Cards | | | 930.00 | |
> | PLACESETTING | Place Settings - Heart | | | 180.00 | |
> | | | Total Stock Quantities for Category | 1 | 1,130.00 | |
> | | | Total Stock Quantities for All Categories | | 1,130.00 | |

WARNING!

You can't run a stocktake for service or non-stock items.

After you complete your physical stocktake, you can adjust the data in Sage if there are any stock differences by following these steps:

1. **On the Navigation bar, click Products and services.**

   The screen opens with a list of existing products.

2. **Select the products you want to amend the stock for and click the Stock Take icon.**

   Using the drop down arrow in the Stock management window, select each product where you need to make a stock adjustment and amend the quantities in the Actual column. This calculates an adjustment figure in the Adjustment column, as in Figure 12-2.

   If you want to select all products for the stocktake, click Swap from the Products list page, and then click the Stocktake icon. All the products then appear.

3. **When you're happy with your stock adjustments, click Post Stock Take.**

   Close the Stock Management Window. Sage displays the new stock quantities on the product main screen. You can see the adjustments by selecting a product and clicking the Activity icon. Any adjustments contain the default STOCK TAKE reference. The adjustments shown have an AI (Adjustments In) or AO (Adjustments Out) transaction.

   You can keep a copy of the changes before posting by clicking Memorise and entering a filename where you want to save the information before clicking Save. To open the file later, click Recall and select the appropriate file.

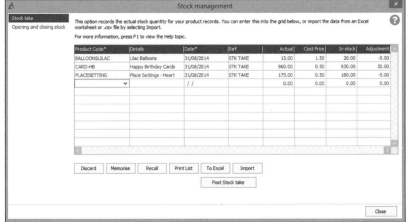

Figure 12-2:
Showing
stocktake
adjustments
for Jingles
Ltd.

Importing your stocktake

If you have lots of stock records, you can import your stock information if you have the information saved in Excel or CSV (Comma Separated Values) format.

Some stocktake reports help you prepare your stock information in these formats, so take a look to see whether one of the standard Sage reports meets your requirements.

To import the stock, do the following:

1. **From the Navigation bar, click Products and services and then click the Stock Take icon.**

2. **Select the appropriate product records and click Import.**

3. **Select the file type you want to import and click Next.**

4. **If the data you want to import doesn't include a headings row, clear the** `First Row Contains Headings` **checkbox and then click Next.**

5. **Use the field mappings page to link your imported file fields to the correct Sage fields.**

6. **Complete the imported field column and choose the relevant field from the dropdown lists provided.**

7. **When all the required fields have been mapped, click Next.**

   Click Import and then Close.

8. **Click Post Stock Take and then Close.**

Adjusting stock levels

Sage helps you adjust stock levels. For example, you may need to return some goods to stock without generating a credit note – a *stock in* movement – or record the fact that you sent some stock as samples to potential customers – a *stock out* movement. As you don't process credit notes or sales orders with these movements, you need to change the stock numbers manually to reflect the movement in stock.

To make a stock adjustment, follow these steps:

1. **From the Products and services window, select the product you want to make an adjustment to.**

   Click the Adjustments In icon to put stock back into your stores, or click the Adjustments Out icon to remove items.

   The Stock Adjustment In or Stock Adjustment Out window appears, depending on which adjustment you chose.

2. **Enter the adjustment details, using one line per product.**

   Entering a reason for the adjustment in the Details column is a good idea. You have 60 spaces to enter a description. The cost price and sale price automatically appear from the stock record.

3. **To save the details entered, click Save.**

   The stock is automatically adjusted.

If you want to check on stock, highlight the product and click the Activity icon. You can see a history of all stock movements for that product item.

Checking stock activity

You can look at a product's activity and view stock movements. The Activity screen records all movement of stock in and out and written off. (I talk about writing off stock in the section 'Processing Stock Returns' later in this chapter.) You can also look at allocated stock, stock on order, the quantity in stock, and the quantity available.

You can also use the Activity screen to view the precise sales orders and purchase orders responsible for the goods in and out. Click the little grey and white arrow next to the Goods In/Out description, and Sage shows you the order and its current status.

To check product activity, follow these steps:

1. **From Products and services, select the product you want to view.**

2. **Click the Activity icon.**

   The Activity screen opens, showing all movements of stock.

3. **You can print a list of activities, or click Close to exit this screen.**

   You return to the Products list.

Using the stock shortfall facility

You can use the shortfall facility to see if your stock levels have fallen below the reorder levels you set in your product records. If you use Accounts Professional, you can automatically create a purchase order for those items.

In Figure 12-3 I show a shortfall report for Jingles, generated because the reorder level for Heart Place settings is set at 200 units and the place settings in stock have fallen below that level. Clicking the Create Order button at the bottom right of the screen produces a purchase order for the supplier of those cards.

If you have a number of products on your shortfall list, sort the list into supplier order by clicking the top of the Supplier column. Print the list so you can place orders methodically with each supplier.

If you always buy the same products from the same suppliers, you can enter the supplier reference in the appropriate field within the product record, making it easier to place orders. You then select all the products with the same supplier reference and place a bulk order. The Create Order button in Accounts Professional lets you do this automatically.

Figure 12-3:
In Accounts Professional you can generate a purchase order from a shortfall report.

To create a product shortfall list, follow these steps:

1. **From Products and services, click the Swap icon.**

   All your product records are highlighted.

2. **Click the Shortfall icon.**

   The Product Shortfall Generator window opens, showing a list of all items that have fallen below the reorder level.

   If you use Accounts Professional, you can automatically create a purchase order from this screen by highlighting the products showing a shortfall and then clicking Create Order.

3. **Click Print List and use the output as a basis for creating your orders.**

4. **Click Close to exit this report.**

You can tell if a product has fallen below its reorder level as the product details display in red rather than black on the main Product and services window.

Understanding a Bill of Materials

A *bill of materials* (BOM) is a list of products used to make up another product – the component parts of the main product. You set up each component as a separate product record and link them all together with a BOM. The various levels of component have different names.

As an example, I use a Magic Party product that our fictional card shop Jingles offers. The *product assembly*, or the list of components that make up the Jingles Magic Party product, includes the following elements:

- ✔ A magician
- ✔ A box of tricks
- ✔ A wizard-themed party dishes pack

Each of these three items is a *subassembly* of the product assembly – it may be an individual component (such as the magician) or a group of components that together form the main product assembly, for example the box of tricks.

The box of tricks subassembly contains the following *components*, which are the individual items that form an assembly when grouped together:

- ✔ A pack of cards
- ✔ Six feather dusters

✔ Six silk scarves

✔ A box of party poppers

✔ A bag of balloons

The BOM shows the levels of components and subassemblies, and the number of assemblies or subassemblies to which each component belongs – known as the *link*.

Creating a bill of materials

Creating a BOM is a relatively simple process – a bit like making a shopping list. You essentially create a new product, the BOM, from other products that you hold in stock. You create a product record for the new product and then use the BOM tab on the product record to build up the list of products required to make it.

To set up a BOM, follow these steps:

1. **From the Navigation bar, click Products and services.**

   Highlight the product record you want to create a BOM for and click the Edit icon to open the Product Record screen.

2. **Click the BOM tab on the top of the screen.**

   A blank BOM information table appears.

3. **Enter the product code and quantity required of each item needed for the BOM:**

   • **Product Code:** Select the product items required for your main product.

   • **Assembly Level:** This field shows how many levels of components and subassemblies are below this component. Sage automatically generates this number.

   • **Link Level:** This is the number of assemblies or subassemblies to which this component belongs. Each product can be a component of more than one assembly or subassembly. Sage automatically creates a link count for each component on the BOM.

   • **Available to Makeup:** This field shows the number of units that can be made with the current stock levels.

   Figure 12-4 shows the BOM for the Jingles Magic Party's components, which include a box of tricks, a magician, and a party dishes pack.

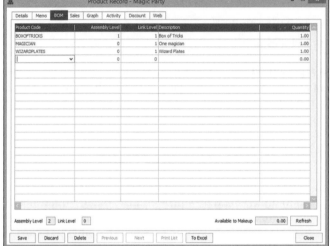

Figure 12-4:
Jeanette
has created
a BOM for
a Jingles
Magic
Party.

Before Jeanette sets up a BOM for the Jingles Magic Party, she needs to determine the subcomponents. She decides upon a magician, a box of tricks, and a party dishes pack. She has to set up a product record for each of these subcomponents before she can select the subcomponents for her Magic Party BOM. As she sets up the Box of Tricks product record, she can click the BOM tab and select the list of products required to make a box of tricks. She does the same exercise for the party dishes product record and lists the component parts on the BOM tab.

After the subassemblies are set up, Jeanette clicks the BOM tab for the Magic Party and selects the relevant subassemblies. As soon as she enters Box of Tricks, the assembly level becomes *1* rather than *0*. The number 1 indicates that Box of Tricks is a subassembly of the main assembly. The magician remains as assembly level 0 because it has no further subcomponents.

Checking stock availability for a BOM

You can use the Check bill of materials icon to see if you have enough stock available to assemble the main product. Follow these steps to check your stock availability:

1. **From Products and services, highlight the product you want to check and then click the Check bill of materials icon.**

   The Check Bill of Materials window appears.

2. **From the Product Code dropdown list, select the code of the assembly you want to check and click OK.**

   The description of the assembly appears in a text box. You can't edit this information.

3. **In the Quantity box, select the number of assemblies you want to make and click Check.**

   If you don't have enough of an item of stock, a message appears stating how many assemblies you need to get. Click OK to find out what items you need to order. If you have enough components in stock, a confirmation message appears to tell you.

   You can create a purchase order automatically by selecting the items you're short of and clicking Create Order.

4. **To print a list of items required, click Print.**

Figure 12-5 shows the component parts required for a Jingles Magic Party. Sage states that no components are in stock and gives a list of products that Jeanette needs to order.

The Check BOM screen only shows product items, not service items. If a BOM includes a service as well as products, you must deal with the service element separately.

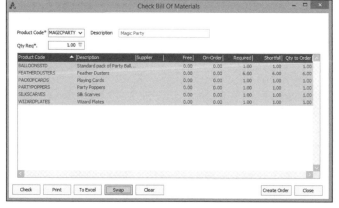

Figure 12-5: Checking component parts for a Jingles Magic Party.

Transferring stock for a BOM

You can use the product transfer function to increase the quantity of product assemblies in stock by using components currently in stock. In the Jingles example, to get a Magic Party into stock, Jeanette needs to transfer the Magic Party components and the party itself into stock.

When you use the product transfer facility, Sage automatically calculates the cost of the product assembly by adding together the costs of the component parts.

To complete a product transfer, follow these steps:

1. **From Products and services, click the Stock Transfer icon.**

   The Stock Transfer screen appears.

2. **Insert the details for each transfer in the lines provided, using one line per transfer.**

   Each transfer must involve a product assembly. In the Jingles example, Jeanette selects a Magic Party and a box of tricks. She enters a quantity of 1 and Sage transfers the necessary component parts into those items of stock, as in Figure 12-6.

3. **When you're happy with the information, click Save – if not, click Discard to cancel.**

   Click Close to exit the Stock Transfer screen.

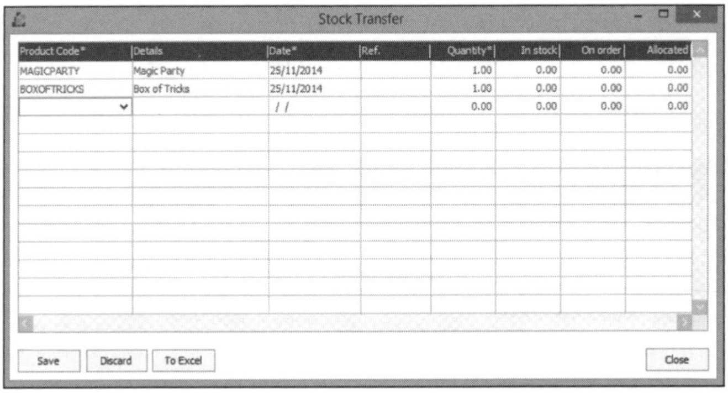

Figure 12-6: Transferring stock to BOMs.

When you carry out a stock transfer, Sage carries out the following postings:

✔ Sage increases the in-stock quantity of the finished product by the quantity entered. This transaction is recorded as a *movement in (MI)* on the product activity file.

✔ Sage reduces the in-stock quantity of each individual component type. The transfer is recorded as a *movement out (MO)*.

> ✔ Sage updates the product activity file with each transfer made.
>
> ✔ Sage updates the cost price of the finished product in the product record.

Processing Stock Returns

You may have stock returned for a variety of reasons – maybe the item doesn't fit, doesn't suit the customer's needs, or is the wrong colour or size. When you receive returned stock, you have to adjust your stock levels by issuing a credit note and updating the system (which in turn updates the stock levels) or by making an *adjustment in* to stock.

The Stock return option isn't available if you selected the product code as a non-stock or service item. I explain this in more detail in Chapter 3.

If the returned items are damaged or faulty, you use a different method to process the stock return to accommodate the ultimate destination of the defective goods:

✔ **Damaged goods returned to you (damages in):** If a customer returns a product that is damaged or doesn't work, you can't just add the faulty item back into your stock and sell it again. Instead, you create a record of the stock return that doesn't increase the in-stock quantity, as I show in Figure 12-7.

✔ **Damaged goods you return to your supplier (damages out):** If you return goods to your supplier for repair or replacement, you don't update the quantity in stock, sales value, or sales quantity figures.

Figure 12-7: Recording a stock return.

✔ **Write off:** You use this option if you need to *write off* the stock, which means determining the stock has no value and you can't sell it. Sage makes an adjustment to the stock levels in the same way that an adjustment out does.

At least once a year, you have to value your stock for accounts purposes. Any written off stock reduces the value of the stock in the accounts. You can obtain a Product Write Off Details report from the Product reports window, in a subsection of Product damage and write off reports. This report helps you identify the value of stock to be written off in the accounts. I suggest you talk to your accountant about processing this type of adjustment in your accounts.

To record a stock return, follow these steps:

1. **From Products and services, select the product you want to record a return for.**

2. **Click the Returns icon in the Products toolbar.**

   The Returns window appears.

3. **Enter the stock return details.**

   You can complete the following boxes:

   • **Code:** If necessary, change the product code by using the drop-down arrow.

   • **Description:** This field automatically appears when the record is selected.

   • **Type:** Click this box to reveal a dropdown arrow and select Damage In, Damage Out, or Write Off.

   • **Reference:** Enter a reference if required.

   • **Date:** Change the date if you don't want to use today's date.

   • **Reason:** Enter a reason for the return.

   • **Quantity:** Note the quantity of stock being returned.

4. **To post the stock return, click Save – otherwise, click Discard.**

If you want, click Memorise to temporarily save the stock return details and then post the items at a later date. To access the memorised information, click the Returns icon and then Recall. Open the saved file to bring up your previously memorised items, which you can then save and post.

Allocating Stock

If you run the Plus or Professional version of Sage, you can manually allocate stock for general use or project use and allocate it to a project by way of a purchase order. Both manual and purchase order stock allocations affect the committed costs of a project. *Committed costs* are costs allocated to a project. Committed costs are not formally charged to a project until the stock allocated to a project is issued – see the later section 'Issuing allocated stock' for more on this.

When you record a stock allocation, you can't allot more than the amount of available stock, called *free stock*, unless you set Sage to allow negative stock. After you assign stock, the stock is no longer free and can't be used for other sales orders.

To allocate stock, follow these steps:

1. **From Products and services, click the Allocations icon.**

   A dropdown menu appears, giving your three options. You can allocate stock, amend allocations, or issue allocations.

2. **Select Allocate stock.**

   The Allocations window appears.

3. **From the Allocations window, enter the stock allocation details.**

   Using the dropdown arrows, enter the product code, the project reference, and the cost code, if required. Figure 12-8 shows allocation information for Jingles – Jeanette decides to allocate 5 balloons to an order, and Sage has calculated that 15 balloons are available.

   Sage automatically shows the amount of free stock, but you need to enter the quantity of stock you want to allocate.

4. **To print a copy of the stock information you've entered, click Print List.**

5. **Click Save to save the allocation, or click Discard if you don't want to save it.**

   Click Close to return to the Products window.

You can view how much stock is allocated by looking at the bottom left corner of the Product Record, as in Figure 12-9. The record shows how much of that item is in stock, how much of the stock is allocated, and how much is free stock.

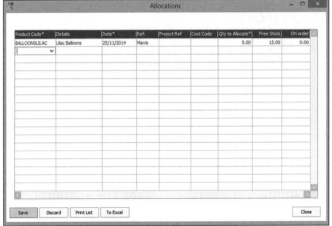

Figure 12-8:
Jeanette decides to allocate some lilac balloons to a customer's order.

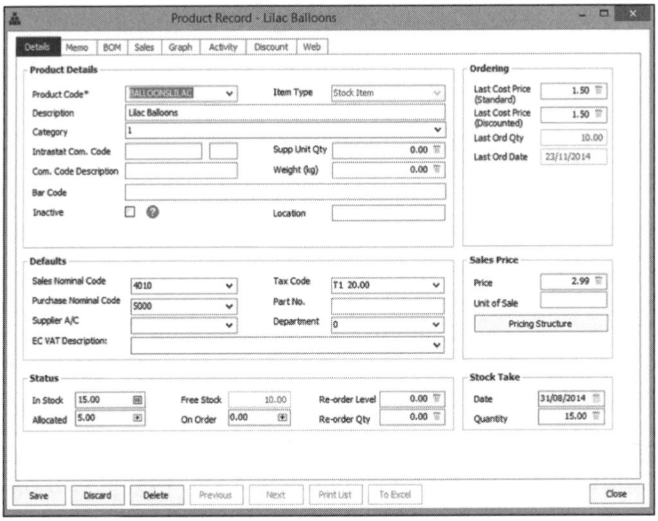

Figure 12-9:
The product record after stock is allocated.

Changing stock allocation

You can amend any previous allocations you made to stock by following these steps:

1. **From Products and services, click the arrow under the Allocations icon.**

2. **From the dropdown list, select Amend Allocations.**

   The Amend Allocations window appears.

3. **Select the product you want to amend or delete using the dropdown arrow.**

   Click OK.

4. **Change the allocated quantity by overtyping.**

   You can only change the quantity. Press 0 (zero) to remove a product allocation. By removing a product allocation, you increase the amount of free stock available for that product and reduce the allocated amount.

   For example, you may want to do this if you receive a big order from a valued customer and you need to ship it quickly. You can decide to take stock that had been previously allocated to another customer and real-locate it to your priority order.

5. **To generate a copy of the stock allocation information, click Print List.**

6. **Click Save to save the details of the stock allocation. If you want to clear the allocation, click Discard.**

If you allocate any of the stock to projects, the costs are committed to the project. You can view this stock on a committed costs report.

Issuing allocated stock

After you have allocated stock, you need to issue the stock. By issuing stock, you update your stock records and stock allocation records. When issuing an allocation associated with a project, the value of the issued stock is applied to the cost of the project. In other words, Sage converts *committed costs* to *actual costs* for the project.

To issue stock, follow these steps:

1. **From Products and services, click the Allocations icon.**

2. **From the dropdown list, select Issue Allocations.**

   The Issue Allocations window opens.

3. **Use the dropdown arrow to select the product you want to issue.**

   The product must be allocated before you can issue it.

4. **Enter the quantity of stock you want to issue and click Save.**

   You can choose to issue less than the whole quantity of stock. Only the stock you choose to issue is allocated and charged to the project – the balance remains as committed stock.

   Alternatively, you can click Issue All, as in Figure 12-10.

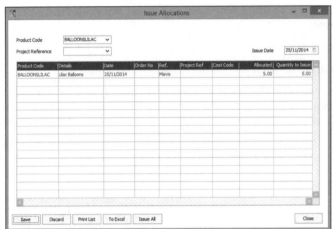

Figure 12-10:
Issuing
allocated
stock.

5. **To print a list of the stock allocation information, click Print List.**

6. **To issue the stock, click Save. To clear the information, click Discard.**

Be aware of the following rules when you issue allocated stock:

- When you issue stock to a project, you must ensure the status of the project allows postings.

- You can't change the details of a stock allocation, such as the project reference or cost codes, during a stock issue. You can only change the stock quantity.

- A stock issue can't exceed the allocation amount, regardless of the negative stock setting.

Chapter 13

Managing Projects

. . . .

In This Chapter

▶ Assigning status and costs to a project

▶ Managing project resources

▶ Recording and analysing project costs

▶ Charging project costs to your customers

▶ Completing a project

. . . .

Sage's Project Costing tool, available to users of Accounts Plus and
Accounts Professional, enables large and small businesses to successfully manage a project.

In Chapter 3, I describe how to set up a project using a blank record. You
can follow that process or access the Project Record wizard by clicking
New Project from the Projects Task pane. After you set up the project, the
information in this chapter comes into play, because here I tell you how to
manage projects.

With Sage, you can track costs and ensure you capture every expenditure
associated with a project. You can then charge the client a fee that produces
a profit for your company. You can evaluate future projects more accurately
and target your business towards more profitable ventures.

Appointing a Project's Status and Costs

Project status helps you track a project's progress. You can set the status
to allow or disallow postings. Sage has five status categories for you to use,
according to where the project is in its lifecycle.

Each status has its own rules as to whether or not you can make postings to
it. Postings that assign costs to a project are usually allowed when a project

is in full swing, but postings are no longer allowed in a project's later stages. You can also decide at which point in the lifecycle to change a status or to delete the project record.

Two statuses don't allow postings:

✔ The project is complete and you don't expect any more costs to come in

✔ The project has been suspended

Every project is specific to an individual business, so only you can determine whether you need to change a project's status. For example, when an active project ends, you give it the status *complete* because you don't want additional postings being made in error to a finished project.

To be absolutely sure that a completed project doesn't incur further costs, you can delete the project record after you change the status to complete. Personally, I think you should consider deleting a project only if you know for certain you no longer require any analysis information for the project.

Assigning status

You assign your project one of five default status categories. A project status changes according to the stage of the project. The default status categories are as follows:

✔ **Active:** This status indicates that a project is open and ongoing. You can make postings to the project, but you can't delete the record.

✔ **Snag:** Although completed, the project remains open so you can still make final postings. You can't delete the record.

An example of a snagged project is a building project that is essentially finished, and you've charged the major costs. You still need to work out the wrinkles to rectify minor defects, however, so you can assign additional costs to the job.

✔ **Completed:** The job is closed and you can't post to the project. You can delete the record if you want to.

✔ **Suspend:** The project has been suspended. You can't post to the project or delete the record. This status usually indicates a problem with the project.

✔ **Initial:** The project is at a pre-acceptance stage. Although you can make postings to the record, you can't delete it. You can use this status for very new projects that are just getting off the ground. You may decide to start recording the costs in case the project gets the official go ahead.

If it doesn't get the go-ahead, no harm is done. But if the project does proceed, you've begun the process of recording costs and can monitor the project effectively.

You can access the Configuration Editor and change the names of the status categories to names that suit your business better, as I explain in the later section 'Changing status and costs'.

Looking at costs – types and codes

You give each project a project reference and use that reference when recording costs to the project by using cost types and cost codes:

- ✔ **Cost type:** This is a label that describes an activity or resource. Labour and materials are examples of cost types. A cost type on its own is meaningless – it must be associated with a cost code. The default cost type is *other*, which is linked to the default cost codes in the next point.

- ✔ **Cost code:** This is a way to further differentiate cost types. For example, you can further divide the cost type *labour* into plumbers, carpenters, bricklayers, and so on. You can create the cost code yourself, according to the needs of your business. You have just eight characters to name your cost codes, but you don't have to use all eight. The default cost codes are labour (LAB1), materials (MAT1), overheads (OHD1), and mixed (MIX1).

A cost type can link to many cost codes, but a cost code can link to only one cost type.

You can set up budgets for a project against each cost code. When you apply costs to a project, the cost code rather than the cost type records the charge. For example, when you enter a purchase invoice, you have a column for the project reference and a column for the cost code. The cost codes are linked to the cost types in the Configuration Editor. You can view cost types and cost codes in the Configuration Editor, as in Figure 13-1.

Changing status and costs

If you use the default status set, the only time you need to change the status of the project is when the project reaches a different stage in its lifecycle. For example, all projects start at the default status of Active, but when a project is complete you no longer want to accept costs against that project so you need to change the status, as I outline in the later section 'Completing Your Project'.

You can change the default project status names so they better describe your business needs. You can make the same name changes to the cost types and cost codes.

You amend the project status, cost code, or cost type by using the Configuration Editor window:

1. **From the Menu bar, click Settings and then click Configuration.**

   A message appears saying that this option can't be run with any other windows open. Click Yes to close all other open windows. The Configuration Editor appears.

2. **Click the Project Costing tab.**

   Figure 13-1 shows the types of field you can change.

3. **Amend the project status, cost type, and cost codes by clicking the Edit button and changing the necessary details.**

   If you want to edit the cost codes, click Edit Code in the cost code section. The Edit Cost Code window appears, and you can change the description or cost type. Then click OK.

4. **Click Apply to use this configuration on your accounts data.**

5. **Click Close.**

   A message appears asking if you want to save the changes. Click Yes and then click Close again to return to the Welcome screen.

You can edit and apply your own project status names using titles that are more meaningful to your business.

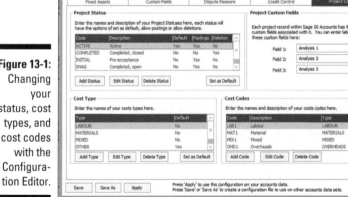

Figure 13-1: Changing your status, cost types, and cost codes with the Configuration Editor.

Managing Project Resources

To undertake work on a project, you need personnel and equipment. Plant, machinery, computer equipment, and people cost money, and you need to apply these costs to your project.

The term *resource* applies to any cost applied to a project. For example, you apply people costs via a timesheet. You can use the timesheet to apply labour costs to a project. Machinery has some sort of hire charge or other cost associated with it, which you can also apply to the project.

When you record a project charge, you select the type of resource used. You can use the resource information to calculate a total cost for the charge, but you can override this as the charge is recorded.

Creating or amending a resource

You can create as many resources as you want, but each resource must have a unique reference. You create or amend a resource as follows:

1. **From the Navigation bar, click Projects and then click the Resources icon.**

   The Resources box opens.

2. **Click Add to add a new resource, or click Edit to edit an existing resource.**

   If you want to add a new resource, enter the details here. You must give each resource a unique reference number, name, unit of measure (such as hour), cost rate, and cost code (use the dropdown arrow).

   When you edit an existing resource, you can change the name, unit of measure, cost rate, and cost code – but not the reference number.

3. **Click OK.**

   Your newly created or amended resource appears in the Resources box.

In Figure 13-2 I have added Jingles' new labour resource, Dave. You can create resources for different people with individual charge rates. For example, you can set up each member of your staff as a resource and charge them to the specific projects they work on.

Add Resource	✕
Reference*	005
Name	Dave - Disco Man
Unit of measure	Hour
Cost Rate	20.00 🗑
Cost Code	LAB1 ⌄
	OK Cancel

Figure 13-2:
Adding a
new labour
resource.

Deleting a resource

You can easily delete a resource if you no longer need it. Follow these steps:

1. **From the Navigation bar, click Projects and then click the Resources icon.**

2. **From the Resources window, highlight the resource you want to delete and click Delete.**

3. **A confirmation message appears.**

   Click Yes to delete or No to return to the Resources window.

4. **Click Close to return to the Projects window.**

Tracking Project Costs

You can record costs or charges against a specific project as soon as you incur them. For example, you can apply timesheets to a specific project as soon as you receive them. The following sections outline the mechanisms for applying project charges, invoices, bank payments, and stock issues to the accounts and projects.

To apply costs to a project, the project must be set up to allow postings. See the earlier section 'Appointing a Project's Status and Costs' section to find out about allowing postings.

Sharing out project charges

A project charge applies a cost to the project but doesn't charge the nominal ledger and therefore doesn't affect the accounts. For example, labour costs go through the accounts by way of wages journals, which directly affect the accounts. But you can't post to Projects directly from a journal – so, at a later stage, you need to allocate the applicable labour costs directly to the project by way of a project charge.

The types of project charge you can make include the following:

- **Labour charges:** You can take these from the rates and hours entered on timesheets.

- **Costs:** You can include costs that don't affect your stock, such as costs involving non-stock items or service items. You can't issue non-stock items to a project, so the only way to post a charge to the project for items of this nature is to process a project charge. You can only charge service items to a project this way. (I discuss non-stock and service items in Chapter 3.)

- **Adjustments or corrections:** You can incorporate amendments to other costs for the project. For example, if you post an invoice to the wrong project, you can do a credit from the project without having to reverse the invoice. You can then put the appropriate charge in the correct project.

Sage shows project charges as transaction type CD (costing debits), but you can also issue a cost credit (CC) if you need to make an adjustment to the project cost.

To record a *project only* cost or credit (the 'only' indicates you're only charging amounts to the project, not affecting your nominal ledger), follow these steps:

1. **From the Navigation bar, click Projects.**

   The Projects window opens. Select the project you want to process a charge for.

2. **Click the Charges icon or the Credits icon if you need to credit the project.**

   The Project Charges or Project Credits window appears.

3. **Enter the details of the charge or credit in the boxes provided, using one line per charge.**

   You must enter a cost code for the cost, otherwise Sage shows an error message when you try to save the cost.

   If you select a resource for the charge or credit, Sage automatically fills in the rate and cost code as the default rate from when you entered it on the resource list. You can overwrite this rate if you require.

When you enter the quantity, Sage automatically calculates the total cost and displays it in the Total Cost column.

4. **Click Save to save your entries, or click Discard to exit without saving.**

5. **Click Close to return to the Projects window.**

Figure 13-3 shows the charge to Jingles for hiring Claris the Clown for the Fun Day project. Claris is set up as a resource and given cost code LAB1. The Fun Day project is allotted the costs of the number of hours that Claris will work.

Figure 13-3:
Applying
a project
charge to a
project for
Jingles –
Claris the
Clown is
a labour
charge to
the Fun
Day project.

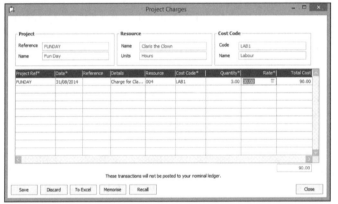

Issuing stock to a project

Sometimes you don't use all of the stock on a project. You can use the Products and services module to allocate stock to a project and put returned or unused products back into stock. These stock postings are shown as adjustments in (AI) or adjustments out (AO) on the Product Activity screen. You can find details about allotting stock in Chapter 12. Remember to select a project reference and ensure the project status allows postings.

When you allocate stock to a project, that stock is set aside for the use of that project. The cost of the stock becomes a *committed cost* to the project, but it only becomes an *actual cost* to the project when the stock is issued.

Sage uses a *first in first out (FIFO)* method of allocating stock, meaning it uses the oldest stock first. If you order stock specifically for a project and get a special price for it, you have to make a price adjustment to assign the correct price to the stock allocated to the project – otherwise, Sage uses the stock price of the oldest stock first, which may be different from the price you paid.

Use the Products and services module to issue the stock, which then shows up in your project reports. (See the section 'Integrating POP with project costing' later in this chapter for more information.)

Figure 13-4 shows the issue of party poppers stock to Jingles' Fun Day project. The stock shows as an adjustment out of stock and against the project.

Stock issues are a cost to the project. Usually, when stock leaves your hands, you invoice a customer, the customer pays the invoice, and money subsequently flows back into your business. When you allocate stock to a project, you don't get paid for it immediately or directly.

You can use the Clear Stock option as part of your month-end or year-end routine. This option involves removing stock transactions from your product activity record, up to and including a specified date. Note that any project active at the point you clear your stock still holds the details of all the transactions showing in its product activity, so you can maintain a complete history for that project.

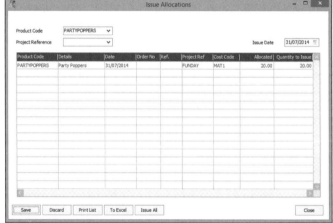

Figure 13-4:
Party popper stock issued to Jingles' Fun Day project.

Counting costs from a supplier invoice

You can post purchase invoices (PI), purchase credit notes (PC), and bank payments (BP) to a project. By doing so, you update your accounts with the cost and also link the cost to your project. (To see how to post a supplier invoice, refer to Chapter 7.) Remember to enter the project reference in the Project Reference column and enter a valid cost code in the Cost Code column.

When you post an invoice to a project, you post a value but not a quantity to the project. The Batch Entry screen for posting invoices doesn't have a quantity column – it just registers an amount. If you need to post quantities of an item to a project, post the invoice without a project reference, and then post a separate project charge to the project.

You can apply costs using bank payments. When you make a bank payment, select a project reference and a cost code. That cost is then applied to the project. (For details on how to process a bank payment, refer to Chapter 8.)

Integrating POP with project costing

As Sage is an integrated system, you can link purchase order processing (POP) and projects. The project is updated at various points of the purchase-order lifecycle:

- ✔ **Creating an order:** At the time of creating an order, give the order a project reference and enter a cost code.

- ✔ **On order:** After you place the goods on order, those costs are *committed* to the project, meaning the value of those goods and services is applied to that project.

- ✔ **Goods received:** After you receive the goods, you can automatically allocate them to stock and then allocate the stock to the project. You can see the stock has been allocated to the project by clicking the product record and looking at the Stock Allocated box in the lower left corner of the record.

- ✔ **Stock issued:** After the stock is issued, the amount of allocated stock reduces. *Actual costs* are applied to the project and committed costs are reduced. The transaction is shown as an AO (adjustment out of stock) transaction type and shows the project reference and cost code associated with that transaction.

  You can look at the Activity tab of the project record to see the transaction.

- ✔ **Invoice:** For stock items, you apply the actual cost to the project at the point the stock is issued. When stock is issued to a project, the costs convert from *committed costs* to *actual costs*. You can update the invoice at a later point to ensure the accounts and supplier ledger have been updated.

You must manually issue the stock to the project by going into the Products and services module. The purchase order only allocates stock to your project and labels it a committed cost. When you formally issue the stock to the project, the committed costs change to actual costs.

When you update your purchase order, in the Batch Supplier Invoice screen the project reference and cost code are blank. Do not re-enter the project reference and cost code, because this posts the actual costs for a second time, thus double-counting. Click Save instead. Sage flashes up a warning message about double-counting. Click Yes to continue and return to the Purchase Order Processing window.

For non-stock items, the actual cost to the project is applied when you generate and update the invoice. When you produce a purchase order for these items, enter the project reference and cost code on the Batch Supplier screen, as this lets you post the actual costs to the project. When you click Save, a warning message appears, stating:

```
If you have already entered a project reference for these
items on the purchase order, they will automatically become
a realised cost when the stock is issued. You may be double-
counting for these items. Are you sure you want to continue?
```

Click Yes. You've created a service invoice, not a stock invoice, so you're not issuing any stock and therefore can't be double-counting.

You can review the value of both committed costs and actual costs by looking at the Analysis tab of the relevant project record.

Analysing Project Costs

Sage has several features that help you track your projects and analyse your costs and revenues. Tracking and analysing gives you the ability to respond to customers' enquiries about the projects.

Looking at the project's activity

When you analyse a project, the first thing you may want to do is look at the Project Activity screen. This screen shows you all the transactions with a specific project reference. You can also filter the transactions by type with the Custom Range button, as in the following steps:

1. **From the Navigation bar, click Projects and then click the Activity icon, or select the specific project and click the Activity icon.**

   The transaction information for the project appears.

If the project you select is a multi-level project, tick the Include Rolled Up Transactions checkbox to show all the transactions for all the projects linked with the one you're viewing.

2. **Filter the transactions by clicking the dropdown arrow next to the Show field to select specific calendar months or by clicking the Custom Range button.**

   Clicking the Custom Range option opens up an Activity Range window, as in Figure 13-5. You can view the project activity by specific transaction types or display all transactions.

Sage remembers the filter you used, so the next time you view the activity Sage applies the same filter until you change it.

Figure 13-5: Filtering the project activity with the Custom Range button.

You can look at the transactions that are recorded against a project. These transactions may include the following:

- ✔ **CD:** Project charge (costing debit)
- ✔ **CC:** Project credit (costing credit)
- ✔ **AO:** Stock adjustment out of stock into the project
- ✔ **AI:** Stock adjustment out of the project back into stock
- ✔ **PI:** Purchase invoice, which you can generate from a purchase order if you have Accounts Professional
- ✔ **PC:** Purchase credit note that may be issued to the project
- ✔ **BP:** Bank payment

✔ **VP:** Credit card payment

✔ **CP:** Cash payment, for example something bought using petty cash

✔ **CR:** Cash receipt

✔ **SI:** Sales invoice issued to charge the customer, as part of the project billing process

✔ **SC:** Credit note issued to the customer in respect of adjustments to the project billing process

Stock allocations aren't displayed as part of the project activity.

You can also check the customer record associated with the project. Access the Projects tab from the customer record to view a list of every project associated with that customer. Figure 13-6 shows the customer record for Any Town Parish Council and the Fun Day project associated with it. The record shows the price quoted for the project and the costs billed to date.

Comparing costs and budget

Comparing the actual costs of a project against a budget gives you an indication of how well the project is being managed. Costs at or below budget suggest a well-managed project. Costs starting to exceed the budget indicate the project isn't going as planned and you need to control costs. You may need to investigate each aspect of the project to see why costs are exceeding budget.

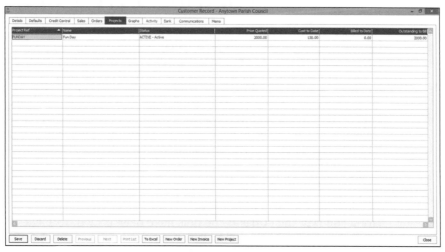

Figure 13-6:
A project associated with a customer, viewed from the Projects tab of the customer's record.

To assign a budget to a project, follow these steps:

1. **From the Navigation bar, click Projects, then select the project you require, and click the Edit icon.**

2. **Click the Budgets tab.**

   The budget information shows all cost codes currently set up in Sage 50 Accounts.

3. **Select the Budget column for each cost type and enter a figure.**

4. **Click Save to save your entries, or click Discard if you want to clear the data and start again.**

5. **Click Close to exit the project record and return to the Projects window.**

To see how the project costs compare with the budget, click the Analysis tab on the project record to view a summary of actual costs, budgeted costs, and committed costs.

You can run many reports to check the progress of your project. You can run reports showing committed costs for each project and cost transactions by cost code, and to check stock issued for a project. You can also run a number of daybook reports to see postings to the project by various transaction types. To print a report, click the Reports icon from the Projects module and select whichever report you require from the array available.

Charging Your Customers for a Project

Ultimately, you need to charge your customers for work carried out on your project. If the project is large, you may want to charge your customers on a continual basis. If the project is a small one-day affair, as in the Jingles Fun Day example, you probably invoice at the end of the project.

Project costing doesn't automatically bill your customers, but the Analysis tab of the project record helps you calculate how much to charge. You can see how much you've billed a customer already or how much you've quoted a customer and therefore what amount is outstanding. Sage provides a variety of project-costing reports that can help you decide how much to charge your customers.

Figure 13-7 shows that Any Town Parish Council was quoted a price of £2,000 for a Fun Day and currently no bills have been issued, so Jingles needs to raise an invoice for the full £2,000.

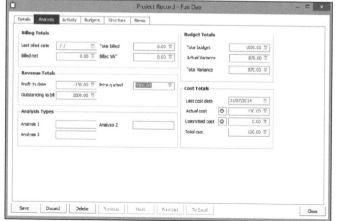

Figure 13-7:
Using the
Project
Analysis
screen to
extract data
for billing
purposes.

After you know how much you need to charge, you can invoice your customer in a number of ways:

- Issue a service invoice, showing details of work carried out.

- Issue a product invoice, using special product code S3 if you have Accounts Professional. This product code lets you issue service charges and product charges on the same invoice.

- Issue a product invoice showing non-stock or service items. You can use this type of invoice if your business is service-based, but you use product records to keep track of your services or to produce price lists.

If you overcharge a customer for a project, you can credit your customer by raising a credit note. (Refer to Chapter 6 for how to raise product and service invoices.)

When you enter the invoice, you must ensure you include the project reference and cost code. When the invoice is posted to the ledger, it updates the project activity information and the Analysis tab.

A number of reports provide you with the information necessary to produce an invoice based on time and materials used. This process isn't automated, so you need to produce your bills manually, as I explain in Chapter 6.

Completing Your Project

After the project has come to an end and you no longer have any invoices or transactions to post to it, you mark the project as complete. Changing the status to *complete* ensures no further postings can be made to the project. You change the status of the project with these steps:

1. **From the Projects window, highlight the project you want to complete.**

2. **Click the Edit icon.**

   This takes you to the Details tab.

3. **On the status line, use the dropdown arrow to select the status** `completed`**.**

4. **Click Save to save your changes, or click Discard to exit without saving.**

If you no longer need to view this project record and have no need for any further analysis of the project, you may delete the project. You can delete a project only if the project status is complete. To delete a project, simply highlight the project you want to delete and click Delete.

Chapter 14

Using Foreign Currencies

*T*his chapter is all about getting your head around the foreign currencies element of Sage. I always found the topic of foreign currencies a bit scary, so in this chapter I go through it step by step and make things as easy as possible for you to understand.

In this chapter I show you how to set up foreign currencies and deal with exchange rates in Sage. I introduce you to the Foreign Trader facility and show you how it fits into the day-to-day working of your business. You can find out how to deal with the extra paperwork when it comes to foreign customers, suppliers, and banks. And I show you how to use the Revaluation wizard to keep your foreign currency bank accounts in line.

Foreign Trader is available for all variants of Sage Accounts from Sage Instant Accounts, but only as an additional module. This chapter applies mainly to businesses that receive multiple foreign invoices and pay suppliers in foreign currencies. If you only have the occasional foreign invoice, converting the foreign currency to pounds sterling and processing the invoice as usual is probably easier than bothering with the Foreign Trader module. (Head to Chapter 7 for the low-down on how to process invoices.)

Setting Up Foreign Currencies

If you deal with foreign currencies, you need to set up those currencies in Sage. To process an invoice in a foreign currency, you have to convert the foreign currency into your base currency, which you select when you run the Active Setup wizard (which I cover in Chapter 1). For this book, I assume your base currency is pounds sterling.

To do the conversion, Sage needs to have exchange rates in place – but these fluctuate constantly. I suggest you agree a rate or set a time to check the current rate with your customers and suppliers. For example, you may agree with your supplier to use the exchange rate issued by HMRC on the first day of each week for a month, or you may set a rate to use for the whole of that month.

The HMRC website at www.hmrc.gov.uk provides useful information on exchange rates. To find the correct exchange rates, enter the words 'exchange rates' in the search box and then click the HMRC exchange rates link that should appear. Select the year you want to find the appropriate rate for, and then choose the month or week. For example, if you have a May 2014 invoice from the USA, you can select May 2014 rates of exchange and find the dollar exchange rate to convert your invoice to pounds sterling.

Entering the exchange rate for a currency

One of the best places to find information on exchange rates is the HMRC website at www.hmrc.gov.uk. You can enter the rates from this website into Sage so that you can use the Sage foreign currencies options. To register the exchange rate, follow these steps:

1. **From the Menu bar, click Settings.**

2. **Select Currencies.**

   The currency you selected when you first set up Sage is displayed as the base currency. (See Chapter 1 for more on setting up Sage.) The Currencies box opens, showing a list of all currencies available in Sage, along with the currency code and symbol (for example, US dollars is USD $). If you want to add a new currency or edit an existing one, do it here.

Converting currencies with F5

The F5 key works as a currency converter if you're in any numeric field. This nifty function comes in handy when you process invoices in pounds sterling and convert the foreign invoice value before you enter invoices into Sage.

Press F5 key and a currency converter box appears. Type in the amount of foreign currency and specify which currency it is (for example, US dollars), and Sage converts it to your base currency.

You need to set up the exchange rate you want to use to convert the currencies in your Currencies table, as I explain in the section 'Entering the exchange rate for a currency'.

3. **Select the currency you want to enter an exchange rate for.**

   The currency you select appears at the bottom of the Currency screen and shows an exchange rate of zero if you haven't already entered an exchange rate.

4. **Enter the exchange rate you want to use.**

   You can enter exchange rates for as many currencies as you require.

5. **Click Close to exit the Currencies screen and save the exchange rate details.**

Amending the Countries table

The Countries table consists of a list of countries and their country codes. Sage indicates members of the European Union (EU) with a tick in the EU column. The Countries table is used for Intrastat reporting. *Intrastat* is a system that collects data about the movement of physical goods between member states of the EU. You may have to amend the Countries table when countries join or leave the EU.

Intrastat has been in operation since January 1993 and replaced the customs declarations. The supply of services is excluded from Intrastat, which is closely linked with the VAT system. Companies that aren't VAT registered have no obligations under the Intrastat system.

To amend your Countries table:

1. **From the Menu bar, click Settings and then Countries.**

   The Countries table appears. The table has three columns showing the country, the country code, and a checkbox indicating with or without a green tick if the country is a member of the EU.

2. **To add a country, click Add.**

   Type the country name in the Add/Edit Country Details box that opens.

   Alternatively, to edit the details for a country, highlight its name and click Edit.

   Figure 14-1 shows how easy adding a country to the Countries table is. Sage automatically generates the country code.

   Tick the EU Member box if you add a country that's part of the EU. You can change EU status by clicking the EU Member box to add or remove the tick.

Foreign currency checklist

Use this checklist to get through the maze of working with Sage 50 Accounts and foreign currency.

✔ Activate the Foreign Trader Setup wizard.

✔ Enter exchange rates for all currencies you use.

✔ Set up new customer accounts for customers that use foreign currencies.

✔ If you have customers who may pay you in more than one currency, use a separate customer account for each currency.

✔ Set up new foreign currency supplier accounts – with separate accounts for each currency.

✔ Set up bank accounts for each foreign currency.

---

   3. **Click OK to save the changes, or click Cancel to exit without saving.**

   Sage returns to the Countries table.

   4. **Click Close to exit the Countries table.**

Figure 14-1:
Adding a country to the Countries table is almost as easy as filling in the blanks.

Tailoring the Foreign Trader Tool

Turning on Foreign Trader is a choice, but if you trade using foreign currencies, you have to activate Foreign Trader.

The Foreign Trader facility is the crux of the foreign currencies part of Sage. When activated, this facility can process customers and suppliers based in a foreign currency, let you use foreign currency bank accounts, and process invoices, credit notes, bank payments, and receipts in different currencies.

After you activate the Foreign Trader option, you can't switch it off! Activating the Foreign Trader option causes numerous changes to the mechanics of Sage – if you encounter anything odd, press F1, type `foreign trade` into the Help box, and read the Help sheet called 'How Foreign Trader affects Sage 50 Accounts'.

You set up the Foreign Trader option using the Foreign Trader Setup wizard as follows:

1. **From the Menu bar, click Tools, Activations, and then Enable Foreign Trader.**

   A warning message may say you can't run this wizard with other windows open, so click Yes to close all other windows.

Figure 14-2: Welcome to the Foreign Trader Setup wizard.

2. **The Foreign Trader Set Up window opens, as in Figure 14-2.**

   Work through the following screens of the wizard, clicking Next after you finish each screen:

   • **Welcome:** This screen explains that you can process customer, supplier, and bank transactions in foreign currencies. Sage offers a link where you can access a complete guide to Foreign Trader.

   • **Setup:** This screen explains that you need to use a nominal code to handle exchange rate variances and to choose how you want to update exchange rates. The default nominal code is 7906 and the default update method is 'Always prompt to save exchange rate changes'. You can use the dropdown arrows to change either of these.

- **Finish:** In the Finish screen, Sage recommends you click Settings and then Currencies to check your currency codes and the exchange rates you want to use.

  If you need to make any changes, click Back. If you don't want to proceed, click Cancel. Otherwise, click Finish to activate your Foreign Trader option.

When you run the Foreign Trader option, the Currency Exchange Rate box appears in the Invoice defaults on the General tab. You can use the dropdown arrow to choose a different exchange rate change method from the default setting.

Keeping Trade Status in Mind when Setting Up Accounts

Getting your customer, supplier, and bank records ready for foreign trade is as simple as making sure you give them a touch of the exotic when you set them up. In Chapter 3 I explain the basic set-up procedures for Sage, so check there for help.

When you set up customer and supplier records for foreign trade, keep the following points in mind for individual records:

- ✔ Click the correct country when you enter the customer or supplier's address.

- ✔ Select the correct currency on the Defaults tab. (If you don't select the currency, the currency rate box won't appear when you issue an invoice for that foreign customer.)

- ✔ Adjust the tax code accordingly. If you supply goods to a VAT-registered customer in another EU member state and the goods are moved from the UK to that EU country, your supply may be zero-rated. (See HMRC Notice 725, The Single Market, for more information on this.) Some supplies of services to overseas customers are zero-rated, but many are standard-rated – seek advice from your local tax office.

You need a separate bank account for every currency you deal with. For example, if you trade in pounds sterling, US dollars, euros, and Japanese yen, you need four bank accounts. Sage shows you the balance in the original currency and also what it converts to in the base currency. Use these accounts just as you do any other bank account.

After you enter a transaction, you can't delete it or change its currency.

To convert a bank account to foreign currency usage, change the currency by using the dropdown arrow of the Currency box on the Account Details tab within the bank account. Figure 14-3 shows an example of an American bank account set-up: Notice the Account Details tab shows a field for both the US dollar balance and the pounds sterling base currency.

Figure 14-3:
Setting up a
foreign bank
account.

Processing the Paperwork

In this section, I show you how to raise sales invoices and purchase invoices using foreign currencies and how to apply receipts and payments using foreign currency bank accounts.

Raising invoices, credit notes, and orders

You can raise invoices, credit notes, and orders in the usual way. (I explain raising invoices and credit notes in Chapter 6 and raising orders in Chapter 10.) When you open a foreign customer record, a Rate box appears under the Address box on the Details screen of both the Invoice and Sales Order screens, and the currency symbol changes from pounds sterling to the currency you have chosen for that customer.

You can change the currency rate in the Rate box by overtyping the current rate shown.

Exchange rates fluctuate all the time, often in the time between processing one foreign invoice and the next. You can apply a new exchange rate as you enter your sales invoice, credit note, or order. As soon as you attempt to change the exchange rate (assuming you've accepted the defaults for the exchange-rate method), Sage asks if you want to update your currency record with your new exchange rate. Click Yes or No depending on your requirements.

Choosing VAT codes

You must make sure Sage shows the VAT correctly. For example, exporting goods to a customer outside the EU is normally zero-rated. (Read HMRC Notice 703, Export of Goods from the UK, for more on this.) When you process a sales invoice, credit note, or order to a zero-rated country, make sure Sage calculates the VAT using the T0 tax code.

You may need to press F3 and edit the information on your invoice to ensure you've selected the correct VAT code. Click OK to apply these changes. Figure 14-4 shows an invoice for goods sold to a business in the USA.

For VAT-registered customers outside the UK but within the EU, use the tax code T4 (Sales to Customers in the EU) and make that you include the customer's VAT registration number on the customer record.

Figure 14-4:
Changing
the VAT
code is easy
and often
necessary
when
dealing
with foreign
trade.

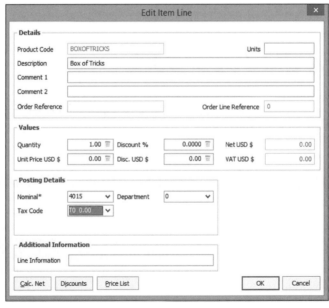

Other useful VAT codes include the following:

- ✔ T7 for zero-rated purchases from suppliers within the EU
- ✔ T8 for standard-rated purchases from suppliers in the EU.

For EU VAT codes for purchases, Sage allocates a notional rate linked to the UK VAT system. For example, T8 is linked to the UK standard VAT rate of 20 per cent.

Figure 14-5 shows an invoice to American Events for a box of tricks, which retails at £50 in the UK. Sage converts this amount to $78.45 in US dollars.

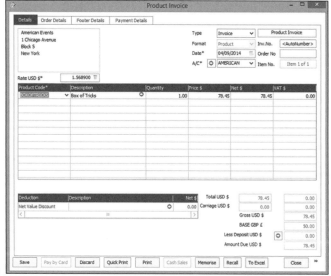

Figure 14-5: A Jingles sales invoice raised to an American customer.

Converting currencies and viewing invoices

Although you create the invoice in a foreign currency, after saving the invoice shows on the Invoice list in pounds sterling. The invoice in Figure 14-5 shows a value of £50 on Jingles' Invoice list, even though the invoice itself is in US dollars.

After you update the invoice to the nominal ledger and the customer ledger, the balance on the Customer screen shows in pounds sterling, just like all the other balances outstanding. If you double-click the customer record and look at the Details tab, the balance in sterling still shows. On the Activity tab, you see the foreign currency, as in Figure 14-6. The right side of the screen shows the customer balance in US dollars and the year-to-date (YTD) turnover is shown in pounds sterling. The invoice details are in US dollars, and the balance outstanding is aged in dollars at the bottom of the screen.

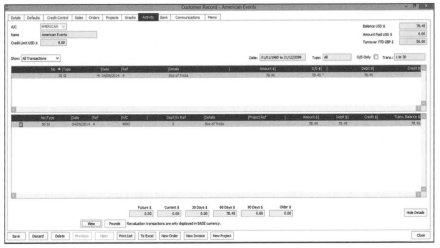

Figure 14-6:
Customer activity for an American customer's account.

Entering batch invoices and credit notes

You can use the batch-entry method of inputting invoices for customers and suppliers in the currency that appears on their record. For example, if you have a German supplier, you can enter the invoice in euros as it appears on the German invoice.

Figure 14-7 shows an invoice from Tiki Toys in Japanese yen for some robot toys. The Batch Entry has an additional Currency box showing Japanese yen, the exchange rate used for processing the invoice, and the T0 tax code used for zero-rated supplies.

After you enter the batch invoice and are happy with the details, you can save the invoice. You can now view the transaction in the supplier's Activity screen. The transaction is shown in yen and the balance on the account is in yen, but the turnover YTD is in pounds sterling. The balance outstanding is aged into current, 30 days, 60 days, 90 days, and older than 90 days.

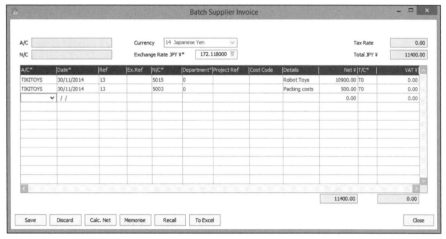

Figure 14-7:
A batch of
invoices
from a
foreign
supplier.

Banking on Foreign Currencies

Banking tasks with foreign currencies are no different from the same tasks in sterling, although you have additional boxes on some of the screens that highlight the exchange rate, and you see references to the foreign currency.

Coping with customer receipts and supplier payments

When you deal with businesses and customers in foreign countries, you expect to receive and send invoices and payments in different currencies. For example, if you send customer invoices to America, you send the invoice in US dollars and you expect to be paid in US dollars.

Make sure you process the transaction in the same currency from the customer or supplier account through to the bank account.

Sometimes you may receive money in a foreign currency that doesn't relate to any invoices you issued, or you may need to make foreign currency payments where you have no invoice associated with the payment. To accommodate these invoice-less transactions, follow the procedure I explain in Chapter 8 for bank payments or bank receipts – but note that the Bank Account screen shows the currency and the exchange rate you entered in the Currency table. You can change this rate if required. Depending on the defaults you chose, you may be able to update your currency record here.

The Net and Tax columns show the currency code associated with the bank account. For example, if you have a US dollar account, you see the $ sign at the top of the Net and Tax columns.

Depositing foreign currencies

You process receipts in a foreign currency in the bank account that you set up to deal with that type of money – Japanese yen in the yen bank account, euros in the euros account, and so on. When Jingles receives payment from American Events for the sum of $78.45, Jeanette deposits the money in the US dollar account.

To process a receipt in foreign currency, follows these steps:

1. **From the Navigation bar, click Bank accounts and highlight the foreign bank account you're processing a receipt for.**

   Click Customer Receipt.

2. **Select the customer account.**

   Outstanding invoices appear in the main part of the screen.

3. **Enter the date of the receipt.**

   Sage automatically defaults to the current day's date, so change the date if you need to.

4. **Enter a reference.**

   Putting a paying in slip or BACS reference is a good idea.

5. **Check you're happy with the exchange rate given (taken from your Currency table) and change it as needed.**

   If you change the currency rate, Sage asks if you would like to update your Currencies List.

   If you used the HMRC website to obtain your previous exchange rate, check the rate is still valid; if not, amend the rate.

6. **Enter the amount received against the invoice, or click Pay In Full in the Receipt box.**

7. **Click Save to process the data, or click Discard to exit without saving.**

8. **Click Close to exit the Customer Receipt screen.**

   You return you to the Bank screen.

Paying a foreign supplier

Businesses generally like to receive payments in the same currency as the invoice. Consider what happens when Jingles pays Tiki Toys for the robot toys. The total amount outstanding on the account is 11,400 yen – you can see the invoice in Figure 14-7. Jeanette processes this transaction through the Japanese bank account in the usual way – check out Chapter 7 for a reminder on how to process supplier payments.

Carrying out a bank transfer

In this section, I describe how to make transfers from your base currency to a foreign currency and from one foreign currency to another.

Use the exchange rate shown in the table at www.hmrc.gov.uk and follow these steps:

1. **From the Navigation bar, click Bank accounts, and then click the Bank Transfer icon.**

2. **Use the dropdown arrows to select the account you want to transfer from and the account you want to transfer to.**

   The Reference and Description fields have details entered already, but you can change these to something more meaningful to you.

3. **Use the dropdown arrow to select a department, if required.**

4. **Enter the date of the transaction.**

5. **Enter the amount you want to transfer from account to account.**

6. **Enter the exchange rate you want to use if you're transferring from your base currency to a foreign currency account.**

   The Bank Transfer screen for foreign to foreign bank accounts, shown in Figure 14-8, appears slightly more complicated than the screen for transferring from a UK account to a foreign account because Sage needs to calculate the exchange rate conversion between two foreign accounts.

   If you want to transfer funds between foreign currency accounts, you must enter the currency amount you're transferring from – Sage automatically calculates the value of currency to be received in the other foreign account, which shows in the Receipt Value field. Sage uses the exchange rates shown in the Currency table for the two currencies involved.

7. **Click Save or click Discard to exit without saving.**

   Figure 14-8 shows a 30 November transfer of $200 in US dollars from the Bank of America into Jingles' Japanese bank account. Sage calculates the value to be received in yen for the Bank of Japan and deposits the proper sum – in this case, 21,445.05 yen – in the Japanese bank account. Jingles can use the money in this account to pay its Japanese suppliers and receive payments from Japanese customers.

Figure 14-8:
A bank
transfer
between
two foreign
accounts.

When you perform bank transfers between foreign accounts and you enter a payment value for a transfer from a particular account, Sage uses the exchange rate information held within the Currency table to calculate the receipt value in the other account. If you decide to change any part of the information in this transaction, Sage may need to recalculate the figures. Sage makes these changes according to the order in which you change the data.

For more on how Sage deals with a number of different scenarios regarding changes of information on the Bank Transfer screen, type `foreign bank transfers` into Sage Help.

Expecting changing exchange rates

Exchange rates vary from week to week and even from day to day. The exchange rate is likely to change in the time between you receiving and paying an invoice.

When you post invoices and make payments to your ledgers, you do so in the relevant foreign currency. For example, a $100 invoice is likely to prompt a $100 payment in US dollars. That payment clears the balance on the account to zero – but the payment doesn't take into account any exchange rate differences that occurred between posting the invoice and posting the payment.

Sage secretly works in the background to make adjustments for exchange rate fluctuations. To accommodate exchange rate differences, Sage cleverly creates a dummy invoice with the reference Reval (short for Revaluation). Sage works out the differences on the two parts of the invoice and posts the necessary adjustment using the 7906 exchange rate variance nominal code. If the exchange rate works in your favour so you pay less, Sage posts a purchase credit note to account for the fluctuation.

You can view these adjustments by looking at the nominal activity of account 7906. (Chapter 20 covers how to access a Nominal Activity report.) In addition, opening the foreign supplier record and clicking the Activity tab reveals a button at the bottom of the screen that says Pounds. Click this to see the transactions in pounds sterling instead of the foreign currency.

Figure 14-9 shows the Nominal Activity screen for Exchange rate variances. You can see the result of a movement in exchange rate for the Tiki Toys transaction. Between the time Jingles ordered robot toys from the supplier and the time Jingles paid the invoice, the exchange rate changed – instead of £74.38, the 11,400 yen was worth £66.23, so the robot toys cost £8.15 less than expected. Sage automatically posted the necessary adjustments into nominal account 7906, which you can see on the Nominal Activity screen in Figure 14-9.

Figure 14-9:
Accommo-
dating
exchange
rate
fluctuations.

Exchange rate revaluations go on all the time as you process your foreign currency transactions. For more information on this subject, type `exchange rate fluctuations` into Sage Help.

Doing Revaluations with the Wizard

The Revaluation wizard is useful for keeping your monthly foreign currency bank accounts straight. Sage does a lot of automatic adjustments in the background, but from a housekeeping point of view you need to ensure you update and review all your foreign currency bank accounts on a regular basis. Doing so at the end of each month ensures your financial reports are correct.

For example, a bank account with a balance of $1583.20 at an exchange rate of 1.5832 contains $1,000. But at the month-end, if the exchange rate falls to 1.4723, the account contains $1,075.32. You need to take account of these fluctuations by running the Revaluation wizard.

To run the Revaluation wizard, follow these steps:

1. **From the Menu bar, click Modules ⇨ Wizards ⇨ Foreign Bank Revaluation.**

   Click Yes to the confirmation message that appears. The Revaluation wizard opens with the Welcome screen, as in Figure 14-10.

2. **Highlight the account you want to revalue and then click Next.**

3. **Enter the date you want to revalue.**

Figure 14-10: Running the Foreign Bank Revaluation wizard.

The last day of a month is a good choice. Enter the exchange rate for the foreign currency on the date of revaluation. Click Next to continue.

4. **Check the details of the revaluation are correct and then click Post.**

   The wizard posts a journal, using your revaluation control account nominal code, to revalue your foreign currency bank accounts.

You can check your journals have been posted by clicking on the Transactions link from the Navigation bar. You can also check revaluations from the Revaluations tab of the bank record, where you see the date of the revaluation and the exchange rate used. You can make changes to these revaluations.

If you need to correct the exchange rate you used or reverse the revaluation because you made an error, follow these steps:

1. **From the Navigation bar, click Bank accounts, select the bank account you want to make the adjustment for, click the New/Edit icon, and select Edit from the dropdown list.**

   The bank record opens.

2. **Click the Revaluations tab.**

3. **Click Show Balances.**

   The information updates to show the foreign balance and the prior base currency balance. The revalued base balance also shows.

   Note that the Edit and Reverse buttons are activated and available to use. The Reverse button comes in handy if you mess up a transaction and want to reverse it. If you click the Reverse button, Sage automatically reverses the revaluation and creates and posts the appropriate journals to the necessary accounts.

4. **Select the revaluation you want to adjust and click Edit.**

5. **Change the exchange rate in the Edit Revaluation box.**

6. **Click OK to complete the adjustment, or click Cancel to take you back to the Bank Record Revaluation tab.**

Part IV

Running Monthly, Quarterly and Annual Routines

In this part . . .

✔ Discover how to reconcile your bank accounts.

✔ Understand the procedures you need to carry out when you prepare monthly accounts and year-end reports.

✔ If you're a VAT-registered business, ensure you meet the key quarterly deadline of the VAT return.

Chapter 15

Reconciling Your Bank Accounts

*I*f you like to know to the penny what's in your bank account, you're reading the right chapter. Reconciling your bank accounts normally forms part of your monthly accounting routine. Running through the bank reconciliation process gives you a thorough review of your bank statements and provides a good opportunity to investigate any unusual or incorrect transactions. As a result, you're fully aware of the financial transactions flowing in and out of your bank accounts.

Recognising Reasons to Reconcile

Performing a bank reconciliation requires you to check you've matched all the bank transactions in Sage against the entries on your bank statements. Ultimately, you should be able to tick off every item on your bank statement against a corresponding entry in Sage.

Most businesses have at least one current account, a deposit account, a business credit card, and a petty cash tin. Each separate account needs statements of one sort or another. Sage assumes you have all of these accounts and provides defaults for each account, which you can rename or add to as required. (Refer to Chapter 3 for the low-down on amending accounts.) Additionally, Sage includes a building society account and credit card receipts account as default, as I show in Figure 15-1.

Figure 15-1:
Sage
assumes
your busi-
ness has
various bank
accounts.

After you reconcile your accounts, you can be sure that the data and any reports run from your information are accurate

You need to reconcile all your bank accounts to ensure the accuracy of your accounting records. Reconciling all your bank accounts particularly important if you're VAT registered, because reconciling helps you pick up all transactions associated with VAT. Credit card transactions in particular can attract a lot of VAT. If you don't reconcile your credit card statements, you may miss VAT-liable transactions and render your accounts and your VAT return incorrect.

When you set up your bank records, Sage lets you determine whether you want each bank account to be a reconciling account. If you don't want to reconcile an account, click the bank record and put a tick in the `No Bank Reconciliation` box on the account details tab. Use this feature with caution – most bank accounts need to be reconciled to ensure accuracy of information.

Doing your bank reconciliations on a regular basis guarantees the accuracy of your information and lets you run meaningful reports to help you manage your business and make sensible decisions.

Getting Ready to Reconcile

The aim of a reconciliation is to match transactions in Sage with your bank statement. The process is easier if you've entered as many transactions as possible before you look at the bank statement. Before you start a reconciliation, make sure you've accomplished the following tasks:

> ✔ **Enter all the payments from your cheque stubs for the period you want to reconcile.** Refer to Chapter 7 for a reminder on how to process supplier payments and Chapter 8 for all other payment types.
>
> ✔ **Enter the receipts from your paying-in book for the period you want to reconcile.** Refer to Chapter 5 for help with processing customer receipts and Chapter 8 for recording other bank receipts.

Make sure you enter the cheque numbers and payslip numbers in the Reference field so you can easily identify those items on your statement.

If your bank statements contain any transactions that aren't yet in Sage, input those transactions before the reconciliation. Items in this last-minute batch may include:

> ✔ Bank interest (paid and received)
>
> ✔ Bank charges
>
> ✔ Direct debits – to pay suppliers, for example
>
> ✔ Direct credits and BACS from customers
>
> ✔ Transfers between accounts

Tick off the items on your bank statement as you enter them in Sage. That way, you can see if you missed anything that needs to be entered.

Doing the Reconciliation

You need your bank statements in front of you as you work through the reconciliation process. Tick off each item as you enter it into Sage, and then put a line through the tick or use a highlighter pen to indicate you've reconciled that item. Make your mark visible so you can easily spot anything that you haven't reconciled. In Figure 15-2 I show an example of a bank statement with marks for items entered and reconciled. The payments are all entered into Sage and reconciled; the receipts have been entered but aren't reconciled yet.

To begin the reconciliation process, follow these steps:

1. **From the Navigation bar, click Bank accounts.**

   Make sure the cursor highlights the bank account you want to reconcile. Sage defaults to account 1200, which is the Bank Current account, so move the cursor if necessary.

BISI BANK LTD
Statement Period ended 30.04.14

Account No: 51235467   Sortcode: 21.45.85

		Payments	Receipts	Balance
01.04.14	Account Opened			£0
01.04.14	100001		£2000 ✓	£2000
01.04.14	Cheque No 1	£100 ✗		£1900
15.04.14	Cheque No 2	£29.38 ✗		£1870.62
15.04.14	100002		£200 ✓	£2070.62
15.04.14	DD Denby DC	£120 ✗		£1950.62
30.04.14	balance carried forward			£1950.62

Figure 15-2: A bank statement showing items that are and aren't reconciled.

2. **Click the Reconcile icon to bring up a Statement Summary, as I show in Figure 15-3.**

3. **Enter the Statement Summary information.**

   Your statement summary contains the following fields for you to fill in:

   • **Statement Reference:** Sage gives you a default reference, with the first four digits being the bank account nominal code and the remaining reference being today's date. You can overwrite this reference with a more meaningful name. Giving your statement a reference lets Sage archive the reconciliation as a PDF document so you can pull up a copy of the bank reconciliation at any time.

Statement Summary

Bank : 1200   Bank Current Account

Statement Reference : 1200 2014-12-19 01

Ending Balance : 2152.87   Statement Date 30/04/2014

Interest Earned :
Amount : 0.00   Date : 19/12/2014   NC :   TC : T2 0.00

Account Charges :
Amount : 0.00   Date : 19/12/2014   NC :   TC : T2 0.00

OK   Cancel

Figure 15-3: Statement Summary for bank reconciliation.

   • **Ending Balance:** Enter the final balance shown on the bank statement for the period you're reconciling. Most people reconcile to the end of the month, but I find it easier to reconcile one statement page at a time, as you have fewer transactions to reconcile – which means fewer transactions to check back through in the event of an error. To reconcile by page, use the balance at the bottom of the statement page and reconcile each item on that single page.

- **Statement Date:** Sage automatically defaults to today's date, so change this to the date of the bank statement you want to reconcile.

- **Interest Earned:** If you've earned any interest on the bank statement, enter it here. Alternatively, you can enter any interest as an adjustment in Step 6.

- **Account Charges:** Enter any bank charges on this screen, or enter an adjustment on the Bank Reconciliation screen in Step 4.

4. **Click OK to bring up the Bank Reconciliation screen, as in Figure 15-4.**

   If you click OK without changing any of the information on the statement summary, you can still change the statement balance and date on the actual Reconciliation screen.

Figure 15-4:
The Bank Reconciliation screen.

The Bank Reconciliation screen is split into two parts. The top part shows all the transactions currently entered in Sage that need to be matched against the bank statement (up to and including the statement end date, shown at the top of the screen). Items move to the bottom part of the screen after you match them against the bank statement. The bottom part of the screen shows account charges and interest earned if you entered these on the statement summary, and shows the last reconciled balance. If you're doing a reconciliation for the first time, the last reconciled balance is zero – otherwise, you see the balance from the previous reconciliation.

Sage only brings up transactions posted to the system up to the statement end date that you enter on the Summary screen. In Figure 15-4, the end date is 30 April 2014, so only items dated on or before that date appear. If you don't specify a date on the Summary screen, Sage brings up all transactions posted to the system date, which is today's date.

You can change the statement end balance and the date in the Bank Reconciliation screen by overtyping the date and end balance at the top of the screen.

5. Match items on Sage against the bank statement.

Match each item on your bank statement against the same item in the top part of the Bank Reconciliation screen. To match an item, double-click the item in the top box, or highlight it and click the Match Transaction button to the right of the screen. As soon as you match an item, it moves to the bottom part of the screen and the values of the Matched Balance and the Difference boxes at the bottom right of the screen change accordingly.

As you double-click each item in Sage, make a corresponding mark on the bank statement. If you originally ticked items on the statement, now put a cross through the same tick or highlight the item so you can identify anything not reconciled at the end.

If you move a transaction to the bottom section in error, double-click the transaction or highlight the transaction and click Unmatch Transaction to move it back to the unmatched items at the top.

The three boxes at the bottom right corner of the screen keep track of the balance between the transactions you match and what your statement says. If you get everything to agree, the Difference box contains a zero.

6. Click the Adjust button (above Difference at the bottom right of the screen) to make any adjustments.

You may find you missed inputting an entry that's on the bank statement. Figure 15-5 shows what you can adjust.

7. Save the reconciliation.

Ideally, you work through the bank reconciliation until you've matched all the items from the bank statement. If you need to stop halfway through, however, you can save the work you've done so far by clicking the Save button, near the bottom left of the screen, and then clicking OK.

To continue reconciling, click the Reconcile icon. A pop-up screen asks whether you want to use or discard the previously saved statement. Click the Use Saved button, and Sage takes you back to the point where you left off.

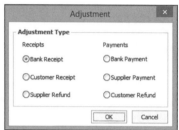

Figure 15-5:
Adding an adjustment directly to your bank reconciliation.

Clicking Discard Saved wipes out your previous work, and you have to start your reconciliation again.

8. **Reconcile your bank transactions.**

When all your transactions match and the Difference box reads zero, click the Reconcile button at the bottom left of your screen. Sage saves your reconciled statement in a history file (using the reference you gave your reconciliation at the start of the reconciliation process), so you can review it later if you need to.

To access your archived reconciliations, click the Reconcile button and then click OK from the Statement Summary screen. This opens up the Reconciliation screen, where you can click the View History button at the bottom of the screen. A list of PDF files appears, displaying your historical bank reconciliations, as I show in Figure 15-6. Double-click the file you want to view to open the relevant PDF file.

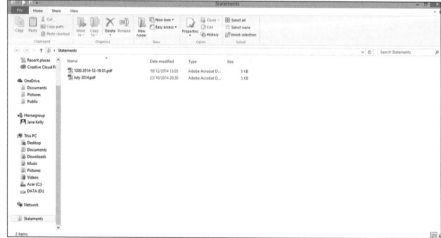

Figure 15-6:
Viewing the historical bank reconciliations.

Troubleshooting when Your Account Doesn't Reconcile

In an ideal world your accounts always reconcile, especially if you follow my recommendations in this chapter. But if your accounts don't reconcile, try the suggestions in this section:

- ✔ **Check you've ticked off every item on your bank statement.** You may have missed something, which is easy to do when you have lots of transactions on one page or lots of pages in a statement.

- ✔ **Make sure all the items left in the top part of the screen haven't cleared your bank account.** On a bank statement several pages long, you can easily overlook a transaction, especially if you're going through the statement page by page.

- ✔ **Check off each item again to make sure you've haven't entered the same entry twice.** If you've entered something twice, double-click the offending item in the matched section of the Bank Reconciliation screen to unmatch it. Then find the transaction number of that item and delete it.

When the Difference box reads zero, save or reconcile the account.

If you reconcile a transaction by mistake, go to File Maintenance, click Corrections, and find the transaction. Then Click Edit Item, uncheck the Bank Reconciled box, and save your changes. Click Yes to confirm the changes. The next time you open the bank reconciliation, that transaction appears.

Rounding Up Stragglers

You may find that even though the Difference box is zero, you still have some unmatched items in the top part of the screen. This situation is perfectly normal – it just means you've entered cheques or receipts that haven't cleared the bank account and don't show on the current bank statement.

For example, if you're preparing accounts to the end of March, you must enter all cheques up to and including 31 March. However, the 31 March bank statement may not include cheques you wrote on 31 March, 30 March or even 29 March because they haven't cleared your bank yet.

Cheques that show on Sage but aren't yet on your bank statement are known as *unpresented cheques*. You may also have an *outstanding lodgement* or two – a deposit paid in towards the end of the month that doesn't appear on your bank statement because it hasn't cleared the banking system.

Figure 15-7:
The accoun-
tant's
year-end
bank recon-
ciliation for
Jingles.

Bank Reconciliation as at 30.04.2014	
	£
Balance per Bank Statement	1950.62
Less unpresented cheques	0.00
Add back outstanding lodgements	55.00
Balance per Cash book	2005.62

Listing unpresented cheques and outstanding lodgements

At the year-end, your accountant has to perform a traditional bank reconciliation and needs to know your outstanding cheques and lodgements are. In
Figure 15-7 I show an example year-end reconciliation using some of Jingles'
figures.

You can print a list of unpresented cheques and outstanding lodgements
at the end of any month. To do this, click the Report icon within the Bank
module (click on the small chevron to the right of Recurring Items to see the
rest of the icons), scroll down the report headings on the left of the screen,
and at the bottom click Unreconciled Transactions. Click Bank Report –
Unreconciled. If you click the Preview icon, you see this report lists all the
unreconciled items for the period selected.

Remembering recurring entries

The Recurring Entries feature helps speed up your data-entry process, particularly where the same types of entry occur every month. If you set up recurring entries, you no longer have to laboriously enter them manually each
month. I explain how to do this in Chapter 8.

Entering recurring entries only works when the value is the same each month.

Recurring entries can be used for the following:

- ✔ **Regular supplier payment on account:** If you pay off a large supplier
  balance in instalments, you can set up a regular payment on account to
  the supplier using recurring entries.

- ✔ **Customer payment on account:** You may have a customer who pays
  you a regular instalment each month or week.

✔ **Bank receipts and payments:** You may have payments that go out of your account on a regular basis, such as car or equipment loans.

✔ **Bank transfers:** You may want to transfer a regular sum of money into a deposit account to put aside money for bills, such as VAT or PAYE.

✔ **Nominal journals (debits and credits):** If you're confident with your double-entry bookkeeping, you may have regular journals for the same value that need to be done each month.

Chapter 16

Running Your Monthly and Yearly Routines

*T*he nominal ledger lists all the nominal codes that your company uses. These nominal codes, when grouped together, form the record of your company's assets, liabilities, income, and expenditure. The codes are grouped together in categories identified in your chart of accounts, which I talk about in Chapter 2.

Sage uses the accounting principle of *accrual accounting*. Accrual accounting is all about recording sales and purchases when they occur, not when cash changes hands – you match revenue with expenditure. For example, if you prepare your accounts for the month of June, you need to make sure that you enter all the sales invoices for June, even if your customers haven't paid them yet. You also check that all the purchase invoices relating to June are posted, so you get an accurate reporting position.

In this chapter, I show you how to run wizards and create journals by using the nominal codes to run the monthly and yearly routines. You need these routines to produce timely and accurate reports for management decision making.

 Checklists are vitally important to the smooth running of month-end and year-end processes. You can design your own checklists or use the wizards to guide you through the processes – but either way, you need a routine.

If you don't have Accounts Plus or Accounts Professional, you can't perform some of the steps I outline in this chapter. Instead of benefiting from the wizards, you have to manually process your accruals, prepayments, and depreciation by using a nominal journal. If you're not happy dealing with journals, I suggest you leave these tasks for your accountant.

Adding Up Accruals

An *accrual* is an amount you know you owe for a product or service you've received but for which you haven't yet received the invoice. An accrual occurs for items that you pay in arrears, such as telephone bills. To maintain an accurate set of accounts, you post an accrual into your nominal ledger by using the appropriate journals. These journals increase the costs to the business and create an accrual for the value of the outstanding invoice. The accrual is treated as a liability within the accounts because the business owes money. As soon as you receive the bill, you can reverse the accrual.

Charging a monthly amount for a service that you normally pay in arrears has a smoothing effect on company profits. For example, if you have a £3,000 telephone bill that you pay quarterly, the bill is accrued in the accounts for the three months before you receive the bill and you put a charge of £1,000 in your accounts each month. If you don't do this, the first two months of the quarter show artificially high profits and the third month shows artificially low profits when the full cost of the telephone bill hits the profit and loss account in one go. The cumulative effect over the three months is the same, but the monthly effect can make the difference between a profit and a loss for your company. Reviewing your accruals and prepayments (which I talk about in the next section) is important for monthly reporting purposes.

If you're confident with your double-entry bookkeeping, you can post a debit to the cost account and a credit to the accruals account. Sage likes to make things easy for you and provides a wizard for setting up adjustments for any invoices you're likely to pay in arrears.

To access the wizard and set up the accruals, follow these steps:

1. **From the Navigation bar, click Nominal Codes.**

   Click the Accruals icon. The Accruals window opens up.

2. **Click the Wizard button to open the Accruals wizard.**

3. **Select the code you want to set up an accrual for.**

   Enter a transaction description, for example `Telephone accrual for June—Sept 2014`. Click Next.

4. **Enter the total amount of the accrual, followed by the number of months the accrual should run for.**

   In the three-month telephone bill example, you enter £3,000 in the Total Amount box, followed by 3 in the No. of Months box.

5. **Click Create to continue.**

   The Accruals window opens, displaying the information for the accrual that you're setting up. If you're happy with the information shown, click Save; if not, close the window. A confirmation message appears saying that the accruals will be posted to the ledgers when you run the month-end option.

If you're happy with the accrual process and don't need step-by-step guidance from your friendly wizard, you can set up a nominal ledger accrual manually as follows:

1. **From the Navigation bar, click the Accruals icon.**

2. **Manually fill in the fields in the Accruals window.**

   Enter the following information:

   - **Nominal Code:** Using the dropdown arrow, select the nominal code affected by the accrual. In the telephone bill example, the code is 7550.

   - **Details:** Enter details of the accrual. These details show up in the nominal activity reports.

   - **Department:** Enter the department, if required.

   - **Accrual Nominal Code:** This field is set to the default accrual nominal code 2109. Don't change this code, because it's a control account. If you're not using the Sage default codes and chose a customised set of nominal codes during Active Setup (which I talk about in Chapter 1), your accrual account may have a different code.

   - **Value:** Enter the total value of the accrual. In the telephone bill example, the amount is £3,000.

   - **Months:** Put in the number of months to spread the accrual over, from between 1 and 12 months.

   - **Monthly Amount:** Sage automatically calculates this field after you enter the total amount and the number of months. It shows the monthly amount that's debited when you run the month-end post accruals option.

3. **When you're happy with the information entered for your accruals, click Save.**

   A confirmation message states that these details will be posted to Sage when you run the month-end option. The accrual now appears on the Accruals list.

If you use the basic Sage Accounts program, you have to complete a nominal journal for your accruals. For the telephone costs example, the double-entry is a debit to the cost code (telephone 7550) and a credit to default accrual code 2109.

Counting Out Prepayments

A *prepayment* is payment in advance for services you haven't completely received. For example, if your business buys a year-long radio advertising campaign for £12,000, which is invoiced in March, you enter the invoice in March for the full value of the advertising campaign – but most of the invoice relates to a future period of time, so you create a prepayment for the 11 months of advertisements to come.

Registering a prepayment has the effect of decreasing the cost code in the expenses and increasing the prepayments account in the debtors ledger because you've paid in advance for services that haven't been supplied in their entirety (effectively, the supplier owes you).

You can set up prepayments in much the same way as accruals. If you want to use the wizard method, follow these steps:

1. **From the Navigation bar, click the Prepayments icon.**

   The Prepayments window opens.

2. **Click Wizard.**

   The Nominal Ledger Prepayments wizard opens.

3. **Select the nominal code you want to set up the prepayment.**

   In the advertising example, you set up an advertising prepayment for, using the nominal code 6201.

In the nominal record, you can sort the nominal code list into alphabetical or numerical order by clicking the Name or Nominal Code fields. But the system doesn't let you sort differently in the Prepayments screen.

4. Enter the description of the prepayment, and a department if relevant.

Click Next to continue. For example, the advertisement description may read Radio Advertising Prepayment April 2014 - February 2015. (The prepayment is only for 11 months because the initial payment paid the bill for March.)

5. Enter the total amount, followed by the number of months for the prepayment.

Click Create to continue.

6. Review the summary of the prepayment.

Click Save if you're happy with the details, or close to exit without saving.

7. Click Save.

A confirmation message states the payments will be posted only when you run the month-end option. Click OK to return to the Nominal Ledger window.

Alternatively, follow Step 1 above and then manually enter the details directly on to the screen (see the example in the section 'Adding Up Accruals' earlier in this chapter). This manual method is quicker than using the wizard, as you don't click through so many screens.

If you use basic Sage Accounts, your nominal journal double-entry is a debit to prepayments and a credit to the cost code.

Depreciating Fixed Assets

A *fixed asset* is an item likely to be held in your business for more than 12 months. Fixed assets are usually large and expensive items with a long useful life, such as machinery, land, buildings, and cars.

Because fixed assets last so long, you can't charge the profit and loss account with the full asset value. Instead, you *depreciate* the asset, assigning a proportion of the asset to the profit and loss account and offsetting that amount against any profits you make.

Depreciation or *writing down your assets* is an accounting method used to gradually reduce the value of a fixed asset in the accounts. Depreciation applies a charge through the profit and loss account and reduces the value of the asset in the balance sheet.

If you have many different asset types, figuring out individual depreciation amounts can be quite time-consuming. Fortunately, Sage has the useful Fixed Asset Register that lets you enter the details of each asset and the method of depreciation you intend to use. Each time you run your month-end option, Sage calculates the depreciation due for each asset and automatically posts this to the appropriate accounts. Head to Chapter 3 for more on assets.

Writing down your assets

Sage provides two accepted methods of calculating depreciation and a write-off facility. If you use the Fixed Asset Register, Sage calculates the depreciation for you.

If you don't have Accounts Plus or Accounts Professional, you have to depreciate your assets manually by posting a nominal journal each month, as fixed asset records aren't available in the basic Sage Accounts program.

You can choose your method of depreciation, but after you choose it you must use the same method consistently every year. This method becomes part of your accounting policy and is referred to in the Notes to the Accounts section of your year-end accounts prepared by your accountant.

Your accountant can help you decide which of the methods I explain in the next sections is best for you.

Ruling on the straight line method

In *straight line depreciation*, the value of the asset is depreciated evenly over the period of its useful life. For example, an asset that depreciates over a four-year period has a quarter (25 per cent) of the value depreciated each year. The same amount of depreciation is charged each month. For example, an asset that cost £24,000 and is due to be depreciated over a four-year period is depreciated by £6,000 each year, which equates to £500 per month.

Counting down the reducing balance method

In *reducing balance depreciation*, the value of the asset is depreciated by a fixed percentage but the calculation is based on the net book value (NBV) each year, so the NBV reduces each year. The *net book value* is the cost price of the fixed asset less the accumulated depreciation to date. For example, at the end of year 1, a £12,000 asset with a four-year lifespan depreciates by £3,000 (at 25 per cent), leaving the NBV as £9,000 – as in Table 16-1.

Table 16-1	Depreciation on a £12,000 Asset over Four Years	
Year	*Net Book Value*	*Depreciation Amount*
1	£9,000	£3,000
2	£6,750	£2,250
3	£5,062.50	£1,687.50
4	£3,796.88	£1,265.63

Using the reducing balance method means the asset never fully depreciates. The amount of depreciation just gets smaller and smaller each year. You're actually likely to write off the asset because it's obsolete before the NBV is anywhere near zero.

Going for the one-time write-off

If you use the *write-off* method, you make a single posting to write off the remaining value of the asset in one go. You may choose to write off an asset if you disposed of it and need to remove the value from the books. Alternatively, if the asset is so old that it's no longer worth the value shown in the books, it's a candidate for write-off.

Posting assets and depreciation

You post the actual capital cost of an asset when you make the invoice or bank payment and you've coded the item to fixed assets. You make the depreciation postings when you run month-end routines or if you've chosen to manually post your journals each month-end. You can only make the postings once in a calendar month. If you use the month-end option and forget to run the depreciation, you need to set the program date back to the month that you forgot to run and post the depreciation.

If you post your depreciation journals manually, the double-entry way to complete your journals is to debit the depreciation account in the profit and loss account and credit accumulated depreciation in the balance sheet account.

To ensure you post the correct amount of depreciation, check your fixed asset records are up to date and you correctly set up the asset and the required depreciation.

Entering Journals

If you use the basic Sage Accounts program, pay special attention to this section, as it explains what journals actually do. You need to understand the principles of double-entry bookkeeping to make journal entries competently.

A *journal* is where you transfer values between nominal accounts. You can use journals to correct mistakes if you post incorrectly. You also use journals to do your accruals and prepayments in basic Sage Accounts or if you don't want to use the wizards in Accounts Plus or Accounts Professional.

You use debits and credits to move values between nominal accounts. The journal must balance, so you need equal values of debits to equal values of credits before Sage can post the journal.

Only use journals if you're confident with double-entry bookkeeping. Otherwise, stick to the wizards because they perform the double-entry for you.

You may need to update several journals on a monthly basis, including depreciation journals if you don't use the Fixed Asset Register, wages journals, and any other journals that you may need to correct *mispostings* – items posted to the wrong account.

To complete a journal, follow these steps:

1. **From the Navigation bar, click Nominal Codes and then click the Journal entry icon at the top of the screen.**

   The Journal Entry screen opens.

2. **Enter the necessary information in the Nominal Ledger Journal sheet.**

   You need to supply the following information:

   - **Reference:** For example, your reference may be November 2014 depreciation if you're manually posting depreciation and not using the Fixed Asset Register.

   - **Posting Date:** The system uses the current day's date, so specify the date on which you want to post the journal.

   - **Nominal Code:** Use the dropdown arrow to select the first nominal code for your journal. For example, if you post a journal for depreciation, you may show a debit entry for depreciation (N/C 8000) for the sum of £200. The detail reads Plant and Machinery Depreciation. The corresponding credit entry uses plant and machinery accumulated depreciation (N/C 0021) for the sum of £200, as in Figure 16-1.

- **Name:** The nominal code name automatically comes up on the screen.

- **Ex.Ref:** This column lets you provide any extra detail.

- **Department:** Choose a department, if you need one.

- **Details:** Enter details of the journal to appear on the nominal activity report.

- **Tax Code:** The system defaults to T9, but you can change the code using the dropdown arrows.

- **Debit or Credit:** Fill in the appropriate column according to whether it's a debit or a credit.

When you finish, the Balance box shows zero and the totals of the debits and credits are the same.

3. Click Save if you're happy with the journal.

The journal is posted to the nominal codes shown.

Before you save the journal, you can reverse it at a future point in time. This option is particularly useful if you post an accrual or prepayment type of journal. Tick the Reverse Journals box and then enter the date you want the journal to reverse on. These boxes only show up on your nominal journal if you tick the Enable Reversing Journals box on the Parameters tab of Company Preferences, which you access by clicking Settings on the Menu bar.

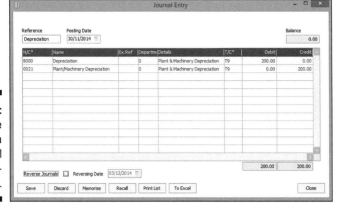

Figure 16-1:
An example
of posting a
journal
for depre-
ciation.

Rattling skeleton journals

If you do the same journals on a regular basis, you can take advantage of the option to create a *skeleton journal*, which you can reuse. After you save a skeleton journal, you can recall the journal and see all the details that you saved.

You can only save values in your skeleton journals if you tick the Copy Skeleton Journal Values box in Settings ⇨ Company Preferences ⇨ Parameters.

Creating a skeleton journal

To create a skeleton journal, enter the journal details as described above but click Memorise instead of saving the journal. The Memorise box opens, and Sage prompts you for a filename and a description of the journals. Type these and then click Save, which saves the journal for reuse another time.

Recalling a journal

When you want to reuse your skeleton journal, from the Navigation bar, click Nominal codes, and then click the Journal entry icon to bring up the Journal Entry window. Click the Recall button to see a list of the memorised journals. Highlight the journal you want and click Load. The journal comes up on the screen, as if you'd just entered it. If you want to make changes to the journal, you can overtype the details. Click Save to post the journal, or click Close to exit followed by No to discard the journal and return to the Nominal codes window.

Reversing journals

Sometimes you may want to cancel a journal. Making a mistake when you're trying to reverse a journal manually is very easy, especially if you get the double-entry accounting wrong. Sage can help you with the reversing journal option.

The main reason you may want to reverse a journal is because you got the double-entry bookkeeping wrong – maybe you got your debits mixed up with your credits. As long as you can identify both the debit and the credit that need to be corrected and these have individual transaction numbers, you can reverse them. You may not need to reverse the whole thing.

Before you undertake the nominal journal reversal, take a backup in case things go wrong and you need to restore your data.

To reverse a transaction, follow these steps:

1. **From the Navigation bar, click Nominal Codes and then click the Journal reversal icon.**

   Sage prompts you to take a backup and print a copy of the Nominal Ledger Daybook report.

2. **Click Print Now to obtain a printout or to Preview the Nominal Ledger Daybook report.**

   Click Run to produce the reports you need. You can select the date ranges and nominal codes from the usual criteria box.

3. **Click Backup.**

   The usual Backup screen appears. Click OK. After the backup is complete, you return to the Journal Reversals screen. Click OK.

4. **Enter the transaction range your journal appears in.**

   You can find this information on the Nominal Ledger Daybook report that you printed.

5. **Enter the date of the original journal and then click OK.**

   The Journal Reversal window opens, showing the journal transactions that you want to reverse.

   If the journal you're trying to reverse doesn't come up, check you used the correct transaction number. Make sure the journal you want to reverse balances, otherwise Sage won't accept the reversal.

6. **Highlight the items for reversal and click Reverse, followed by Save.**

   The journal you reversed shows on the audit trail with the reference `REVERSE`, and the details state `Reversal of transaction XX`.

After you reverse an offending journal, don't forget to post the correct one.

Carrying Out Your Month-End Routine

Running the month-end process in Sage lets you automatically run the accruals, prepayment, and depreciation journals that I describe in other sections in this chapter. When you run the month-end process, you also get the opportunity to clear your customer and supplier month-to-date turnover figures, remove fully paid and reconciled transactions, clear the audit trail, and remove stock transactions.

The month-end process gives you the opportunity to review your accounts and prepare for the next accounting period. After you post all your journals and run all monthly routines, you can start running reports (which I cover in Chapter 18).

Ticking off your checklist

Following a checklist is probably the easiest way to run the month-end in a controlled manner. Before you run your month-end process, use the following to ensure you remember everything:

- ✔ Change your program date to the month-end (Settings ➪ Change Program Date).
- ✔ Enter all transactions for the current period.
- ✔ Process bank recurring entries for the month.
- ✔ Reconcile all bank accounts (including credit cards).
- ✔ Post all journals (including skeleton).
- ✔ Post revaluation journals if you use foreign currency. (Refer to Chapter 14 for more on dealing with foreign currencies.)
- ✔ Set up prepayments, accruals, fixed assets, and depreciation.
- ✔ Post opening and closing stock journals (use Modules ➪ Wizards ➪ Opening Closing Stock Wizard).
- ✔ Take a backup and label it, for example `June 2014 month-end`.

As you run your month-end processes, be sure to cover the following points:

- ✔ Remove stock transactions, if required.
- ✔ Clear audit trail, if required.
- ✔ Take another backup entitled `After month-end` together with the date.

As you work through the month-end processes, tick off each item in the checklist so you can see which tasks remain.

Running the month-end

The month-end procedure lets you clear down the month-to-date turnover figures on all your customer and supplier records. In clearing the month-to-date turnover figures, Sage zeroes down the sale or purchase values in the Month to Date field, which helps for reporting purposes. If you have Accounts Plus or Accounts Professional, you can process your accruals, prepayments, and depreciation as well.

If you have foreign currency set up, you have the option to run the Foreign Bank Revaluation, which ensures exchange rate fluctuations are taken into account at the month end.

You can post transactions beyond the month-end date, and Sage designates them to the appropriate month. Even after you post the month-end, you can still post transactions to any previous accounting period: Sage just slots them into the appropriate month. If you don't want this to happen, you can enter a lock date when you run the month-end – this means that if you tick the Lock Date box and enter a specific date, you won't be able to post a transaction with a date before the lock date. This helps control the accuracy of the reporting – for example, if you request reports with a prior period date, then the numbers in those reports should remain the same and not be adjusted by late invoices being posted to prior periods.

To run the month-end, follow these steps:

1. **Click Tools➪Period End➪Month End from the Menu bar to bring up the Month End window.**

   Click Yes prior to the Month End window opening, as in Figure 16-2.

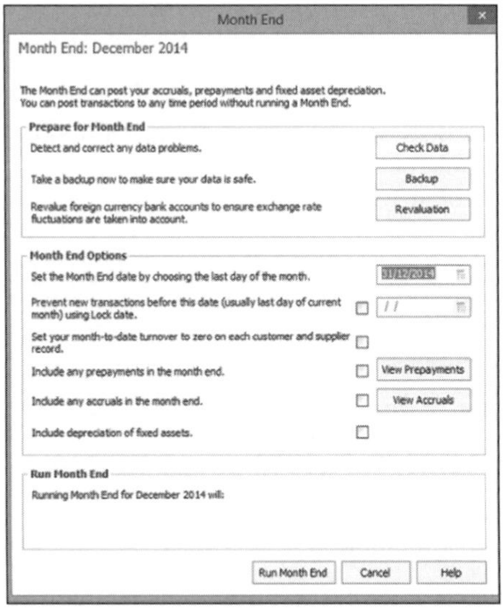

Figure 16-2:
Running the month-end procedure.

2. **Sage suggests you check your data, take a backup, and run your foreign bank revaluation wizard if you have enabled the foreign trader option.**

3. **After you're happy that your data is suitably updated and checked, review the Month End options section and tick the appropriate boxes.**

   You can select the month-end date, run the accruals, prepayments, and depreciation journals, and tick the Clear Turnover Figures box to set your month-to-date turnover figures for your customers and suppliers to zero. You can also set a lock date, which ensures you can't post information with a prior date to the date that you tell Sage to lock from.

4. **Click the Run Month End button to begin the month-end process.**

   A confirmation message says that the process has been completed.

Clearing stock transactions

Clearing stock transactions is a way to reduce the number of transactions on your product activity ledger. You clear the transactions up to a date you specify. You may decide to do this if your system is slowing down as a result of the vast number of records it has to process. A year-end is often a good time to clear stock transactions. You don't have to clear the stock transactions, however, and many people prefer not to, as they like to be able to view a complete history of transactions.

You must print off your Product Valuation and Product Activity reports before you clear your stock transactions.

When you run the Clear Stock option, it removes all individual product transactions from each product record, leaving Adjustment In (AI) and Movements In (MI) – records of stock movements – which are brought forward as opening balances.

To clear your stock, follow these steps:

1. **Take a backup of your data.**

2. **From the Menu bar, click Tools⇨Period End⇨Clear Stock.**

3. **The Data Management box opens and gives you two options:**

   • **Clear transactions on all stock records:** This clears all transactions up to the date specified.

   • **Clear transactions on selected records:** This lets you select specific product records and clear the transactions for those products only.

4. **After you select one of the options, Sage asks for a date to clear trans-actions up to.**

   Enter the date you want and then click Clear Stock to continue or Close to exit. The Sage backup window appears and suggests you run a backup. Once the backup has completed, the clear stock process begins and a confirmation message tells you the process has been completed. Click OK to close the Clear Stock box, and then click Close to exit the Data Management box to return to the Getting Started screen.

Deleting stock

After you clear stock transactions, you can delete any stock records that you no longer want. Sage scans your product list and checks for any records that meet the following criteria:

- ✔ There are no transactions in the stock activity (you can ensure this is the case by clearing stock as I explain in the previous section).
- ✔ The stock record is not part of a component for another stock item.
- ✔ The product has zero items on order or allocated (which indicates it's part of an active stock item).

If these criteria are met, Sage lets you delete the stock records.

To delete stock, work through the following steps:

1. **From the Menu bar, click Tools, Period End, and then Delete Stock.**

2. **If you have other windows open, say Yes to the warning message that asks you to close all other windows before you run the process.**

3. **The Data Management – Delete Stock window opens.**

   Click the Start Scan button for Sage to check for product lists to see if any products meet the criteria listed above.

4. **The Backup window opens.**

   Sage asks you to back up your data before you select the stock records you want to delete. Click OK.

5. **Sage provides you with a product list highlighting all the products that meet the deletion criteria.**

   Select the records you want to delete. To select all of the records in the list, click the Swap button.

6. **After you select the products to delete, click OK.**

   A warning message asks you if you want to permanently delete the selected records. If you aren't sure, click No; otherwise click Yes. A message confirms the number of records that you've deleted. Click OK.

7. **Close the Data Management window.**

   You can check the Products and services main window to check the products have disappeared from the product list.

Clearing the audit trail

Clearing your audit trail removes fully paid and fully reconciled transactions from the audit trail up to a date that you choose. You're left with fewer transactions on the screen, which makes your life easier and speeds up the process of running reports and backing up your data. The process of clearing your audit trail is usually done at year-end. Several criteria must be met before a transaction can be cleared – for example, transactions must be from a prior financial year, transactions must be fully paid and allocated, and all VAT and bank entries must be reconciled.

Taking backups before you run the process of clearing your audit trail is absolutely essential. Clearing your audit trail is irreversible. Make sure you print your audit trail, daybook reports, sales, purchase, and nominal activity reports, and any VAT return reports before you run the Clear Audit Trail option.

You can look at the deleted transactions by clicking Transactions from the Navigation bar, followed by the Reports icon. The Transaction Reports window opens. Selecting Cleared Audit Trail Reports shows you a variety of reports on the right side of the screen – if you scroll down the list, you can see that the last report shows Removed Audit Transactions.

During the process of removing transactions, Sage posts journal entries to the nominal codes the transactions were linked to. This posting ensures the balances on the nominal accounts stay the same as before the Clear Audit Trail process was run. The journals are displayed with the detail opening balance and appear at the end of the audit trail when the Clear Audit Trail process is complete.

To run the Clear Audit Trail, follow these steps:

1. **From the Menu bar, click Tools ⇨ Period End ⇨ Clear Audit Trail.**

   The Data Management – Clear Audit Trail window opens. Enter the date you want to clear transactions up to and including. Then click Clear Audit Trail.

2. The backup window opens.

You may want to amend the name of the backup file to make it clear that it refers to prior Clear Audit Trail data.

If transactions are removed, you can view the deleted transactions by clicking I would like to review details of removed transactions and then OK. Click OK again and then close the Data Management window.

Managing Cash Flow

You probably wonder sometimes if you have enough money in the bank to pay your suppliers, staff salaries, and imminent bills. Keeping an eye on your cash flow is the only way to know how much spare cash you have.

Sage's cash-flow facility helps you plan your payments and work out what monies are due in, so you can calculate whether or not you have the cash to carry out your day-to-day banking transactions.

You need to be in the Bank accounts module to run the cash-flow forecast. Then follow these steps:

1. **From the Navigation bar, click Bank accounts, and then click the select the Cash flow icon.**

   The Cash Flow Forecast screen opens, with two boxes at the top of the screen. The box on the left is a summary of the bank balance and notes any regular receipts or payments (recurring entries). The left-hand box also shows any forecasted receipts and payments and provides a projected bank balance up to the period specified. The box on the right shows bank accounts; the default shows the main bank account only, but you can include more accounts if you want to. The bottom section of the screen shows a list of all outstanding receipts and payments in date order.

2. **In the main body of the screen, remove the tick in the Include? column to remove the corresponding transaction from the cash flow.**

   The forecast bank balance adjusts accordingly. Figure 16-3 shows the Cash Flow screen with the Include? column.

   To make a manual entry to see what effect a transaction may have on the cash flow, place the cursor on the first vacant line on the main body of the cash flow and enter the details of the manual entry. The forecast bank balance adjusts for the new transaction.

Figure 16-3:
Posting
a manual
entry on to
your cash
flow.

3. **Print the cash flow by clicking Print, or send the cash flow to Microsoft Excel by clicking To Excel.**

Excel opens and you can view the cash-flow details on a spreadsheet. The spreadsheet allows you a lot more flexibility to play around with the figures.

The layout of the Sage cash flow exported to the spreadsheet may not suit you. Many people like to see a much more detailed or daily cash-flow analysis. You can design your own spreadsheet layout. Alternatively, most banks can provide you with examples of cash-flow statements – go and have a word with your friendly business banker.

Additional features on the cash-flow tool include a Manage Payments button at the bottom of the screen, which opens up a window showing a list of supplier accounts with a summary of their current payment position. You can see which supplier accounts are overdue. You can click the Suggest Payments icon to help you allocate amounts of monies to suppliers, and then make payments to suppliers by clicking the Make Payment button.

Clicking the Chase Debt button opens a window showing a list of customers and the amount of monies overdue on each. You then have access to the usual customer icons and can send statements or run reports using the icons at the top of the screen.

You can find more details about the Manage Payments and Chase Debt options by pressing the F1 key and typing manage payments or chase debt into the Help field.

Clicking the Graph button shows you a graphical analysis of your receipts and payments.

Doing a Year-End Routine

The year-end procedure is principally a financial accounting process. You must run your month-end for the last month of your accounting year, which takes care of the usual journal routines.

The year-end procedure clears down the profit and loss accounts to zero and transfers any current-year profit or loss to the retained profit account. You carry forward the balances on the balance sheet to the new year and transfer any future-dated transactions into the relevant months for each nominal record.

You transfer the actual values for the current year to the prior year, so you can make comparisons in the new financial year.

You must take a backup before you run this process. Sage actually recommends taking two backups, so you still have a copy if one backup is lost or damaged. You also need to check you've run all the reports that you require for your accounts and you've adjusted your system date to the same as your year-end date by clicking Settings⊅Change Program Date. Check your chart of accounts doesn't contain any errors, although you should notice these sorts of mistakes when you run your profit and loss and balance sheets for the year.

To run your year-end procedure, follow these steps:

1. **From the Menu bar, click Tools⊅Period End⊅Year End.**

   The Year End window appears, which is essentially a checklist of things to do before and during the year-end process. In the Prepare for Year End section, you can check your data and chart of accounts before you run your backups. You can also archive your data and choose the location of the archive.

2. **In the Year End Options section, choose whether to base next year's nominal or stock budgets on current year actual or budget data by ticking the Budget Options box.**

   The Budget options window opens. You can increase your budget by a percentage increase if you want to. You must also check the Year End Postings Date and the Lock Date that Sage suggests.

3. **In the Run Year End section, Sage summarises the options that you've chosen.**

   If you're happy with the details, click Run Year End. A message asks you to confirm that you want to run the year-end process. Click Yes if you are, or click No to cancel.

4. **If you click Yes, a message says that processing the Year End will apply to any existing layout of accounts.**

   Click Yes to continue.

5. **The Year End Report window asks which method of output you need.**

   You can choose Printer, Preview, or File. I usually choose Printer. Click OK. The Print Year-end Report window opens and you can select your printer and the number of copies. Click OK.

6. **A confirmation message says your year-end has now completed and gives you the dates of your new financial year.**

   I suggest you take another backup and label it `After the year-end`.

Chapter 17

Running Your VAT Return

*V*alue-added tax, or VAT, can induce a state of panic when a tax inspection suddenly looms. You can avoid this hysteria by keeping proper accounting records with a system such as Sage and running your VAT returns in a systematic, methodical manner.

Running a VAT return takes mere seconds as a result of the integrated nature of the Sage software.

In this chapter, I take you through the two different VAT schemes that you can operate with Sage, and show you how to switch VAT schemes if you need to. I also cover fuel scale charges and Intrastat reports.

The VAT return involves working through three stages and ticking tasks off as you go along. You can process your whole VAT return from the VAT Return window in Sage, where you can check, reconcile, and perform the journal transfers all in one area.

Understanding some VAT Basics

You need to worry about VAT only if your business is VAT registered. After you register, you can reclaim VAT on certain purchases, but you also have to charge and pay VAT on your sales.

Your company can voluntarily register for VAT – and doing so is usually worth the extra hassle if you can reclaim VAT on a significant proportion of your purchases. VAT registration is mandatory if you exceed certain VAT thresholds – at the time of writing, you must register for VAT if your annual sales reach £81,000 or above.

A basic knowledge of what you can and can't claim VAT on pays off. You can find many books on this subject, and the VAT office also provides plenty of publications for specific industries. A quick look on the HMRC website at www.hmrc.gov.uk gives you a list of the various publications. You can find the main VAT rules and procedures in HMRC Notice 700/1.

Knowing your outputs from your inputs

VAT inputs and outputs have nothing to do with the Hokey Cokey. I wish they were that enjoyable.

Output VAT is just a fancy name for the VAT element of your sales. *Input VAT* is the opposite – it represents the VAT element of your purchases.

A VAT return compares the totals of your VAT inputs and outputs, and subtracts one from the other. If the outputs exceed the inputs, you owe HMRC. If the inputs exceed the outputs, HMRC owes you a refund.

Cracking the codes

When you enter invoices, credit notes, or orders for your customers and suppliers, you need to know which tax code to use. Sage automatically provides you with the following list of UK tax codes, or T codes:

- ✔ **T0:** Zero-rated – VAT is not payable on zero-rated supplies, such as books, children's clothes, and some items of food.

- ✔ **T1:** Standard rate – currently 20 per cent.

- ✔ **T2:** Exempt from VAT – for example, postage stamps.

- ✔ **T4:** Sales to customers in the European Union (EU).

- ✔ **T5:** Lower-rate VAT – usually 5 per cent. This applies to the purchase of energy-saving materials and reclaiming VAT on DIY building work.

- ✔ **T7:** Zero-rated purchases from suppliers in the EU.

➔ **T8:** Standard-rated purchases from suppliers in the EU.

➔ **T9:** Transactions not involving VAT – for example, wages.

For unexplained reasons, Sage doesn't use T3 or T6.

Comparing Sage's VAT accounting methods

Sage supports three types of VAT schemes: the standard VAT accounting scheme, VAT cash accounting, and the flat rate VAT scheme. HMRC provides some helpful information about the VAT schemes available on its website, so go to www.hmrc.gov.uk if you want to find out more.

Set up your accounting method before you enter any transactions onto Sage. The Active Setup wizard I talk about in Chapter 1 includes the VAT accounting method as one of its steps. If you're not sure which method you chose, click Settings ⇨ Company Preferences and then click the VAT tab. In the VAT Details box, you'll find the VAT scheme that you selected. Use the dropdown arrow to view the other VAT schemes available for you to use, as in Figure 17-1.

Setting the standard scheme

In the standard VAT scheme, Sage calculates the amount of VAT based on when you issue an invoice. As you raise each invoice, you're liable to pay the VAT on it when your next VAT return is due. You can reclaim the VAT on invoices sent to you from your suppliers, regardless of whether or not you've paid them.

Considering cash accounting

VAT cash accounting calculates the VAT based on when your customer pays an invoice and when you pay your supplier. You benefit if your customers are slow to pay, as you don't need to pay the VAT until they pay you.

VAT cash accounting in the Republic of Ireland is slightly different from VAT cash accounting. In the Republic of Ireland, the scheme is also known as the _monies received_ scheme – you calculate your VAT on the money you actually receive from customers and on the invoices or credits you receive from your suppliers. Sage 50 Accounts can operate both schemes.

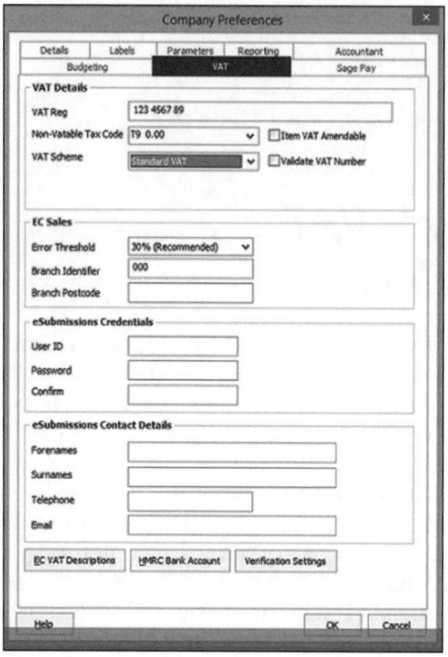

Figure 17-1:
Checking your VAT scheme.

Figuring out the flat rate VAT scheme

The flat rate VAT scheme lets you pay VAT as a fixed percentage of your VAT-inclusive turnover. You don't claim VAT back on any purchases, making it a very simple system to operate. The actual percentage you use depends on what type of business you run.

You can only join the flat rate scheme if you estimate your VAT taxable turnover (excluding VAT) in the next year to be £150,000 or less. You can then stay on the scheme until your business income is more than £230,000.

Sage lets you set up both invoice and cash-based flat VAT rate schemes.

Managing Your VAT

Running a VAT return in Sage is remarkably easy, but you do have to check your VAT return before you send it in.

To access the VAT ledger, from the Navigation bar, click VAT and then the VAT Return icon. The VAT Return window opens, where you find three tabs:

- ✔ Prepare the VAT Return
- ✔ Reconcile the VAT Return
- ✔ Complete the VAT Return.

Also included within the VAT ledger are icons to help you calculate your fuel-scale charges, print EC sales lists, and produce a reverse charge Sales list. You can also access a Prepare for Audit checklist and a selection of tax analysis reports. The Show Me How icon is like a VAT help centre to help you process your VAT return from start to finish.

When you work out your VAT, appreciating what items carry VAT and what you can reclaim VAT on helps. If you're unsure, contact your accountant or HMRC for help.

Preparing your VAT return

Before you start figuring out your VAT return, make sure your books are up to date for the period. Enter all your sales invoices, purchase invoices, receipts, and payments, and reconcile all your bank accounts and credit card accounts to ensure you've accounted for all elements of VAT.

The first step of running your VAT return is to calculate the amount owing or owed by following these steps:

1. **From the Navigation bar, click VAT.**

   The VAT window opens.

2. **Click the VAT Return icon.**

   The VAT form opens. The screen is split into two parts: The right side of the screen looks like the manual VAT return form that you may have received from HMRC before. The left side of the screen is the data entry part.

3. **Click Backup.**

   Sage advises you to run a backup before you run the VAT Return.

4. **Under Date Range, enter the period the VAT return relates to.**

   In my Jingles example, I use 1 April 2014 to 30 June 2014.

5. Under VAT Verification, click the Settings button.

Here you can view the eight checks Sage carries out to ensure your VAT return is as accurate as possible, as I show in Figure 17-2.

6. Click Calculate VAT Return.

Sage tells you how many transactions it found for this VAT return, and how many transactions are dated before the specified period but haven't been reconciled. You can choose whether you want to include these. If you choose not to include them, they remain as unreconciled items in the audit trail and appear again when you do your next VAT return.

7. Click OK.

The VAT return fills with figures, and you can see how much Sage thinks you owe HMRC or vice versa. Sage also jumps to the Reconcile VAT Return tab – note the boxes on the left side of the screen have changed.

Figure 17-3 shows a VAT return for Jingles. Sage calculates that Jingles is owed £44.13.

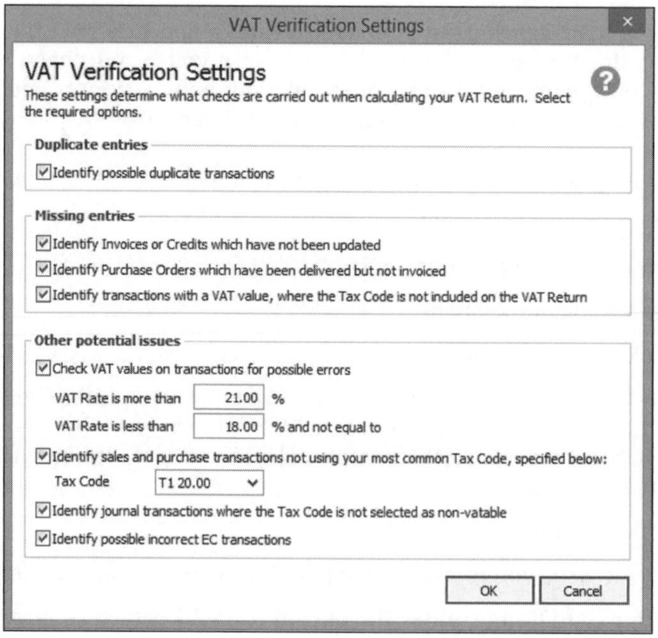

Figure 17-2: Checking your VAT verification settings.

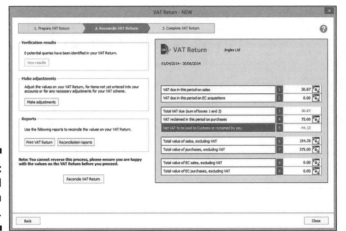

Figure 17-3:
A standard
VAT return
for Jingles.

Reconciling your VAT return

After you calculate your VAT, you can reconcile your VAT Return. On the Reconciling your Vat Return tab, you have the following options:

- ✔ **Check your verification results:** This box shows how many queries have been identified with your VAT return. The Jingles return shows zero queries. Click the View Results button if you have any queries that Sage has targeted.

- ✔ **Make adjustments:** Clicking this button opens the VAT Manual Adjustments screen opens, as in Figure 17-4.

- ✔ **Reports:** This section lets you print your VAT return and run reconciliation reports. When you click Print VAT Return, the VAT Return Report box opens, as in Figure 17-5. The VAT Return box is already ticked, but you can also run the detailed or summary VAT report – I like to always run the detailed VAT report. You can choose to preview, print, email, or file – I always print a copy for my VAT return folder.

- ✔ **Check the reconciliation reports:** After you print your VAT return, you need to check the results by using Sage's reconciliation reports. Click Reconciliation Reports to open the Reconciliation Reports window. Double click the Reconciliation Reports option on the left side of the screen. Two further options appear: Standard VAT and Transaction Analysis. If you double click the Standard VAT, a further series of options appear. If you click once on the Bank option, a series of reports appear on the right side of the screen. Here you can print a copy of all the bank reports that contribute towards checking the detail of your VAT report. Work through each of the report options (you see most of them in Figure 17-6) to find all the reports necessary to check your figures.

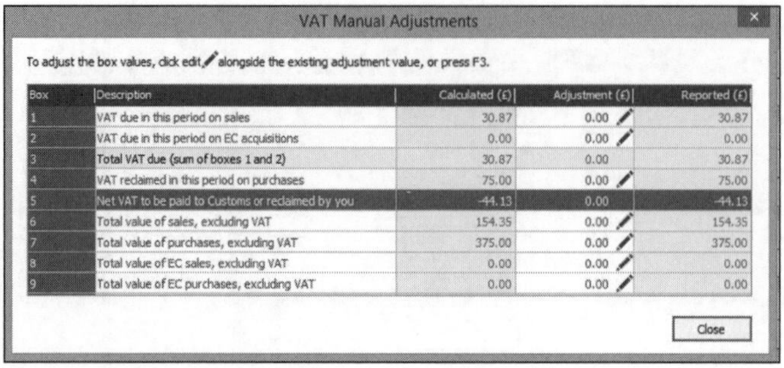

Figure 17-4:
Making
VAT manual
adjustments.

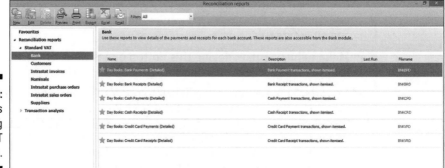

Figure 17-5:
Running
your VAT
reports.

Figure 17-6:
VAT reports
for checking
your VAT
return.

After you print out your reconciliation reports and are happy with your VAT return, click Reconcile Your VAT Return to continue. Sage asks if you want to Flag Transactions as Reconciled. Click Yes if you're certain you want to complete your VAT return, otherwise click No.

Checking Your VAT Return Using Reconciliation Reports

You have to run some reconciliation reports to check the figures in your VAT return. The information supplied by Sage is only as good as the person who enters it, so you need to check your VAT return against the nominal ledger. The checks are different depending on which VAT scheme you operate. In this section I look at each scheme in turn and examine which reconciliation reports you need to check to ensure the accuracy of your VAT return.

Checking under the standard scheme

Your sales tax and purchase tax control accounts must agree with box 1 and box 4 respectively on the VAT return. To make sure that the accounts agree, print the nominal activity report for the sales tax control account and the purchase tax control account and compare the totals with the relevant boxes on the VAT return. Ensure the dates for the nominal activity report are the same as for the VAT return. The nominal activity report identifies all elements of VAT on sales and purchases. If necessary, you can check each entry line by line and compare them with the information in the VAT return detailed report.

The detailed VAT report provides a breakdown of all the transactions behind each number on the VAT return. If you use the VAT standard accounting scheme, the detailed VAT report shows every sales invoice and credit note and every purchase invoice and credit note.

Sage groups the transactions on the report according to the box they belong in on the VAT return. For example, you see each individual transaction contained within VAT box 1.

Getting a hard copy of the nominal activity report

As I mentioned in the preceding section, a copy of the nominal activity report is required so that you can check the totals of your Sales Tax control account and your Purchase Tax control account compared to the detail shown on your VAT return.

Follow these steps to print the nominal activity report:

1. **From within the VAT return process, click Reconciliation Reports.**

   The reconciliation report window opens, initially showing that you have no favourite reports added.

2. **Double click Reconciliation Reports in the list, and then double click Standard VAT.**

3. **Choose Nominals with a single click.**

   Some report options appear on the right side of the screen.

4. **Choose the Nominal Activity Report and click on the Preview icon.**

   The Criteria Value box opens, as in Figure 17-7. Enter the nominal codes for the sales tax control account and the purchase tax control account – 2200 and 2201, respectively.

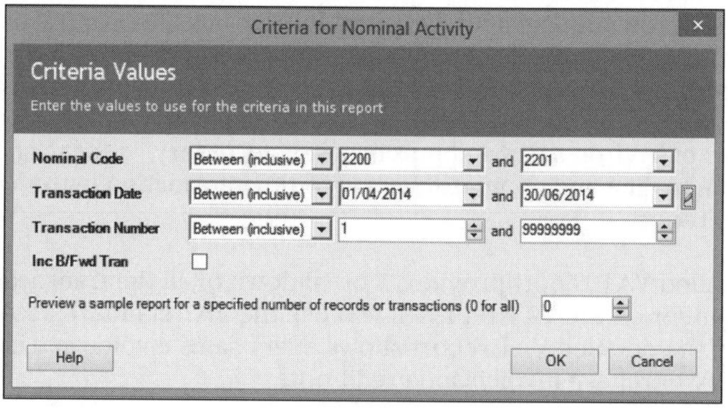

Figure 17-7:
The Criteria
Value box
for running
the nominal
activity for
VAT.

5. **Enter the transaction dates.**

   Make sure the dates are for the same period as the VAT Return, and then click OK.

6. **View the report and ensure the figures for the sales tax control account and purchase tax control account are the same as the figures on the VAT return in boxes 1 and 4.**

   If the figures are not the same, check through the following reasons:

   • Make sure you select the same dates for the Nominal Activity report and the VAT return. That way, you select data for the same period and it should agree, unless you've said Yes to any unreconciled items from a previous quarter.

- Check if the VAT control accounts include any totals for tax codes that aren't included in your VAT return. For example, T9 by default isn't included in your VAT return.

- Check your clear-down journals have been correctly posted from the previous quarter. (The clear-down journals are done automatically by Sage if you select the option when processing your VAT return. I talk about these journals in the 'Clearing Down Your VAT' section later in this chapter.)

- See if any journals were posted to the VAT control ledgers. You don't normally need to post journals to the control accounts.

- Check the audit trail. You can check which items have already been reconciled by looking for R (for reconciled) in the V (VAT) column. Items with an N in the column haven't been reconciled and need checking as part of the current VAT return.

- If you still can't find the discrepancy, print the Customer daybook reports and the Supplier daybook reports and manually tick off each item against the tax control accounts. You can find these reports by clicking the Reconciliation Reports button on the VAT Return and then selecting Standard VAT Return followed by either Customers or Suppliers. This last-resort check can be time-consuming, but it does usually work.

- If you still have a discrepancy, print the daybooks for your bank, cash, credit receipts, and payments, and check these reports.

Checking with cash accounting

If you operate the VAT cash accounting system and work from a cash-based instead of an invoice-based system, you need to print the following reports:

✔ Nominal Ledger daybook reports

✔ Customer Receipts and all other daybook reports

✔ Supplier Payments and all other daybook reports.

You can find all of these reports using the Reconciliation Reports button within the VAT Return module. Make sure you select the same dates for your reports and your VAT return. Check the reports against your VAT return for all bank and cash accounts within your business.

Completing your VAT return

After you calculate, check, and reconcile your VAT return, Sage jumps into action and begins the process of completing all the tasks involving your VAT.

When Sage is finished, the VAT return appears with a big stamp marked RECONCILED on it, as in Figure 17-8.

The final screen of the VAT return process is the Complete Vat Return tab, where you can also print a copy of the VAT return. You can click Verification Results to see the verification results summary, as in Figure 17-9. This outlines possible duplication entries, missing entries, uncommon tax codes, incorrect EC transactions, and other issues. You can also review any adjustments that you made.

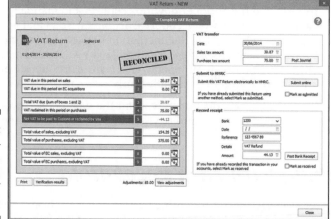

Figure 17-8: Success – you have reconciled your VAT return!

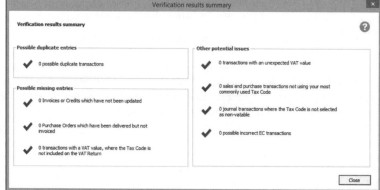

Figure 17-9: Viewing the verification results summary.

To check if the transactions have definitely been reconciled, try to calculate the VAT return again for the same period. A message appears stating you've selected a date range that's already been reported on. Click Yes to continue. Sage confirms that no transactions were found for that period – evidence that the transactions have been reconciled. You can also check that the individual transactions have been reconciled by viewing the Audit Trail screen and looking for an R in the VAT column.

To finalise the VAT return process, Sage gives you some further options on the right side of the Complete Vat Return screen:

- ✔ **Post the VAT transfer:** If you click Post Journal, Sage automatically does the double-entry bookkeeping for you. A big green tick appears when this is complete. (See the later section 'Clearing Down Your VAT' for more details.)

- ✔ **Submit to HMRC:** You can directly submit your VAT return from this screen if you have your Government Gateway details to hand. You don't have to submit your VAT return straight away, however, if you're within your deadline period.

- ✔ **Record receipt/payment:** You can submit your payment or receipt, depending on whether you owe VAT or HMRC owes you. You can post the bank payment or receipt directly from this screen, or tick the box to tell Sage if you've already completed the transaction directly through the Bank module.

After you reconcile your VAT return, a copy of the return is archived in Sage. The reconciled and archived VAT return appears on the VAT ledger window and has a return number as a method of identification. The listing shows the period and the amount of the return. The Paid column shows N if the return hasn't been submitted to HMRC.

You can view a saved return by highlighting the return in the VAT ledger and clicking View. You can delete a VAT return from Sage by highlighting the return and clicking Delete, but I suggest you keep your VAT returns on Sage. I recommend you also keep a hard copy of all your VAT returns and put them somewhere safe – you must keep copies for possible VAT inspection for at least six years.

Submitting Your VAT Return

You can submit your VAT return directly from Sage, as I describe in the section above, or you can print off all the reports and submit your VAT return via the HMRC website. I describe both methods in this section.

In this section I assume you've calculated and reconciled your VAT return but haven't sent it yet.

Posting your return online via Sage

Nearly all VAT-registered businesses have to submit their VAT return online. You also have to pay electronically – this works in your favour as you get an extra week to pay your VAT liability.

You must have a Government Gateway account to make e-VAT payments. Go to www.hmrc.gov.uk for details on how to obtain an account.

You must enable e-VAT submissions on your VAT preference settings. To do so, click Settings ➪ Company Preferences ➪ VAT tab and tick the e-VAT Submissions box.

To send your online VAT return, follow these steps:

1. **From the VAT screen, double click the VAT return you want to send.**

   The VAT Return window opens. The return's status must be pending or partial.

2. **Click the Submit Online button.**

   If this is the first time you've sent an online VAT return, Sage asks you to enter your e-submission credentials. Click Yes to open the e-submission details window, as in Figure 17-10.

<table>
<tr><td colspan="2" align="center">e-Submission Details</td></tr>
<tr><td colspan="2">VAT Details</td></tr>
<tr><td>VAT Reg</td><td>123-4567 89</td></tr>
<tr><td colspan="2">eSubmissions Credentials</td></tr>
<tr><td>User ID</td><td></td></tr>
<tr><td>Password</td><td></td></tr>
<tr><td>Confirm</td><td></td></tr>
<tr><td colspan="2">eSubmissions Contact Details</td></tr>
<tr><td>Forenames</td><td></td></tr>
<tr><td>Surnames</td><td></td></tr>
<tr><td>Telephone</td><td></td></tr>
<tr><td>Email</td><td></td></tr>
<tr><td colspan="2">EC Sales List</td></tr>
<tr><td>Error Threshold</td><td>30% (Recommended)</td></tr>
<tr><td>Branch Identifier</td><td>000</td></tr>
<tr><td>Branch Postcode</td><td></td></tr>
<tr><td>Help</td><td align="right">OK Cancel</td></tr>
</table>

Figure 17-10: Submitting your credentials.

Submitting your VAT return manually via HMRC

To submit your VAT return manually, you need to print out all the reports and then enter them into the HMRC system. Ensure you have a printed copy of the final VAT return and follow these steps:

1. **Access the HMRC website at `www.hmrc.gov.uk` and click the Online services button.**

   Using the login details you were given when you registered to use the Online services, access the VAT Return service.

2. **Submit the figures from the VAT report in Sage into the relevant boxes on the HMRC website.**

   Follow the online instructions to submit your VAT return, and print out a copy of the confirmation that the VAT return has been submitted. File this with your hard copy of the VAT return.

   If the value in box 5 is negative, you have a VAT reclaim and HMRC owes you money. If the figure in box 5 is positive, you owe HMRC.

Posting your refund or payment in Sage

If you haven't posted your payment or receipt, you need to process a VAT payment or a VAT refund. To post a VAT refund, post a Bank receipt to the VAT Liability account (2202), coded to T9. To make a VAT payment, post a bank payment via the Bank module, using the nominal code 2202.

As soon as you save the bank payment, the Paid column changes from N (no) to Y (yes) on the VAT ledger list of returns.

Clearing Down Your VAT

Clearing is transferring the values from your sales tax and purchase tax control accounts to your VAT Liability account. The balance created in your VAT Liability account should agree with the amount due to or from HMRC.

After you make the VAT payment or refund and post it to the VAT Liability account, the balance on the Liability account becomes zero.

Sage has a VAT transfer wizard to help you. You find the wizard on the final page of the VAT Return screen: Click Post Journal in the VAT Transfer section and the job is done.

Changing VAT schemes

You can change from VAT cash accounting to standard or flat rate accounting, and vice versa, but you have to prepare carefully for the change.

You can't change to the VAT cash accounting scheme in Sage unless you create a new company if you have the Foreign Trader option enabled in Sage 50 Accounts 2013 and below. Doing so is possible in Sage 50 Accounts 2014 onwards.

Going from standard to VAT cash accounting or the UK flat rate

You need to switch methods at a month-end or quarter-end, after reconciling the VAT on standard accounting.

Always take a backup of your data, just in case anything goes wrong and you need to restore. Label the backup disk something like 'Prior to VAT scheme change'.

After you take a backup, follow these steps to begin the switch from standard to VAT cash accounting or the UK flat rate:

1. **From the Navigation bar, click VAT and then the VAT Return icon.**

2. **Calculate and reconcile the VAT return for your final standard VAT return.**

3. **Post the journal for the VAT Transfer on the last page of the VAT Return wizard.**

4. **Double-check the reconciliation flags have been set by running the VAT return again for the same period and checking that it finds no transactions.**

After you're happy that you've reconciled all your VAT transactions, you're ready to transfer to the VAT cash accounting system by following these steps:

1. **From the Menu bar, click Settings and then Company Preferences.**

   Click the VAT tab and then select the new VAT scheme you want to change to. If you have transactions that haven't been VAT reconciled, Sage shows a warning message. You can't change your VAT scheme until you calculate and reconcile all the items for your final VAT standard accounting return.

   If no unreconciled items exist and Sage can change the VAT scheme, Sage asks you to check your recurring entries before you process them.

2. **Click OK.**

   The Sage desktop appears.

3. **Change the VAT codes so you don't reconcile the VAT that you reconciled under the old VAT standard scheme a second time under the VAT cash accounting scheme.**

   In the next section I show you how to change the VAT codes.

Changing VAT codes

To make sure the VAT reconciled under the old standard scheme isn't reconciled again under the new scheme, you change the VAT codes so you don't include the old codes in the VAT return, as I show in Figure 17-11.

Figure 17-11: Changing VAT codes when you change your VAT accounting scheme is vital.

To change the VAT codes:

1. **From the Menu bar, click Settings and then Configuration, and then select the Tax Codes tab.**

   A list of all tax codes appears.

2. **Select the tax code you want to change, and then click Edit.**

   The Edit Tax Code window appears.

3. **Amend your current tax codes so they don't appear on your VAT return.**

   Clear the green tick from the Include In VAT Return box.

4. **Click OK.**

   You return to the list of tax codes.

5. **Repeat Steps 1–4 for each tax code from T0 to T8 and remove them from the tax return.**

6. **Edit tax codes T10–T18 and select the Include In VAT Return box.**

   Use these tax codes when entering transactions from now on. Sage uses these new codes to calculate your VAT return.

Table 17-1 shows what your new UK tax codes should look like.

Table 17-1		Altered VAT Codes
New Code	**Tax Rate (%)**	**Category**
T10	0	Zero-rated transactions
T11	20	Standard-rated transactions
T12	0	Exempt transactions
T14	0	Sales to VAT-registered customers in the EU
T15	5	Lower rate
T17	0	Zero-rated purchases from suppliers in EU (link to T10)
T18	0	Standard-rated purchases from suppliers in EU (link to T11)
T19	0	Non-VATable tax code

Preparing to process with the new VAT cash accounting scheme

Here's a checklist of tasks to do before you start processing with your new VAT cash accounting scheme:

✔ Change all the default tax codes in your customer records, supplier records, and product records.

✔ Amend tax on unposted invoices.

✔ Amend tax codes on incomplete sales and purchase orders.

✔ Amend tax codes on all memorised batches and skeleton journals that you've saved.

To see which codes to use for the Republic of Ireland, press F1 for the Help screen, click Index, and type switching. The Help screen for switching to VAT cash accounting appears, and you can follow the links for more information about the Republic of Ireland.

Making the switch from VAT cash to standard accounting

Make sure you run the changes after the month-end or quarter-end for VAT purposes, after reconciling the VAT on the VAT cash accounting scheme and before entering any transactions under the standard VAT scheme. Always take a backup before you make any changes. Label the backup something like 'Backup before changing to standard VAT accounting'.

Any future dated sales invoices or credit notes must be deleted before the VAT changeover and re-entered in the new standard scheme, otherwise VAT won't be accounted for correctly.

Get ready to switch from VAT cash to standard accounting by taking the following steps:

1. **Reconcile all unreconciled VAT transactions.**

2. **Post the VAT Transfer journal from the last page of the VAT return wizard.**

3. **Check the reconciliation flags have been set properly by running a VAT return again for the same period and making sure it doesn't find any transactions.**

After you reconcile transactions included in your last VAT cash accounting return, follow these steps to switch systems:

1. **From the Menu bar, click Settings and then Company Preferences.**

   Click the VAT tab.

2. **Clear the tick from the VAT Cash Accounting box and click OK.**

   A warning message states that if you have any transactions that haven't been VAT reconciled, you won't be able to change VAT schemes.

   From the VAT dropdown box, select Standard VAT.

Reconciling the sales tax and purchase tax control accounts

When you change from VAT cash accounting to the standard VAT scheme, you need to be sure that the items of VAT currently sitting in the sales tax control account and the purchase tax control account are valid. Essentially, you are changing from a system where you have to account for VAT on a cash basis, that is, when cash has either been paid or received from customers or to suppliers. Your new system will account for VAT as soon as invoices are raised for customers or received by suppliers. Whether or not the invoices have been paid is irrelevant.

You may find invoices raised under the cash accounting scheme but that have not been paid. The VAT will not have been accounted for on these outstanding invoices. You need to ensure that they are included under the standard VAT scheme, so that the VAT can be accounted for. To correctly account for the VAT, you need to make an adjustment in boxes 1, 4, 6 and 7 to include the correct VAT figures.

Another situation that might occur, is where you've made a payment on account within your cash accounting scheme (which will trigger a VAT payment) and then, when the invoice is actually posted onto the system in the standard VAT scheme, Sage calculates VAT again. Hence, you are double counting. To correctly account for the VAT, you must make an adjustment to boxes 1, 4, 6 and 7 of the VAT return to include the invoice value that has been allocated to the payment on account.

Sage has created four different reports that you can run at the point of switchover, but prior to entering transactions under the newly changed standard VAT scheme. To download these reports, go to www.sage.co.uk/accountsupdates and choose Reporting Updates. You will need to download and install the Sage 50 Accounts additional report backup. (For further information about these reports and where to run them from, take a look at article 28447 on the Sage website.)

One of the easiest ways to ensure that you do everything correctly is to use the Sage help menu. In the search field, enter the words 'VAT Scheme' then choose Vat Settings from the list that appears. Scroll down the screen that appears until you get to the VAT scheme section. At the bottom of this section, there is a hyperlink – 'Switching your VAT scheme'. Click on this link and follow the screen instructions to confirm which scheme you are switching from, and you'll be given step-by-step details and a checklist of how to perform the switch.

As this can be a tricky process, you might not feel confident in doing this yourself. If so, you are wise to talk to your accountant before attempting to change your VAT scheme.

Posting Scale Charges

Fuel-scale charges occur when you use a company vehicle for private use. According to HMRC, if an employee buys fuel for business use and that vehicle is also used privately, the business must account for output tax on the private use by using scale charges.

If you use scale charges, you can claim back all the VAT charged on road fuel without splitting your mileage between private and business use. The calculations are based on the CO_2 emissions of the vehicle and the engine size.

Scale charges apply only to cars, not to commercial vehicles. Also, if you use the UK flat rate VAT scheme, scale charges don't apply.

Sage makes claiming back VAT much easier with a wizard that guides you through the process:

1. **From the Menu bar, click Modules, click Wizards, and then select Scale Charges.**

   Before you continue with the wizard, you need to calculate the scale charge for each vehicle. HMRC publication Notice 700/64 from www.hmrc.gov.uk helps you do this.

2. **The Scale charge window opens.**

   Sage confirms the use of nominal code 7350 as the default nominal code for scale charges.

Enter the date you want to post the scale charges for and any reference or details that you wish to include. Enter the gross scale charge and click Next. Sage calculates the posting.

3. **Review and check the posting, and then click Post.**

Reporting Intrastat

Intrastat is concerned with collecting statistics surrounding the physical movement of goods between countries in the EU. It's closely linked with the VAT system. If you're not VAT registered, you don't have any obligations under the Intrastat system.

If you exceed the *assimilation threshold* in the amount of goods you supply to customers in the EU, law requires your company to submit certain details about your trade to HMRC. You can find details about Intrastat in HMRC Notice 60 – 'Intrastat General Guide'.

You have to complete Supplementary Declarations (SD) forms, which Sage can help you prepare. You then transfer the information from Sage on to the official SD forms.

For information about Intrastat reporting and how Sage can help, press F1 and type `Intrastat` into the Sage Help function.

You need to submit a European Community (EC) Sales list if you're VAT registered and supply products to customers in EU member states. The information on the lists is used by the UK and other member states to ensure the appropriate amount of VAT has been calculated.

Some of the information shown on the sales list comes from details contained within Company Preferences in Sage, but you must enter the appropriate quarter-end and click Calculate. Sage extracts all the relevant data and shows it on the EC Sales list. You can see the country code, the customer's VAT registration number, the total value of supplies, an indicator field, and a submitted field.

The indicator field shows a zero for the supply of a product or service from one business to another. For a *triangulation*, meaning a transaction involving three parties – for example, products ordered from a French company and sold by a UK company to a Spanish company – a 2 is displayed. To save time and costs, the French company sends the goods directly to the Spanish company. The number 2 indicates the goods never entered the UK.

You can use the arrows on the Values boxes to see what transactions make up the values on the EC Sales list. When you're happy with the list, click Save and Sage adds your EC Sales list to the VAT Ledger list, showing a status of pending.

For more information about the EC Sales list, visit `www.hmrc.gov.uk` and enter `VAT 101 - EC Sales lists` into the search box to reveal lots of information about completing the forms.

The Rev Charge icon on the VAT ledger refers to the Reverse Charge Sales list, which some businesses have to submit to HMRC. HMRC Business Brief 24/07 relates to businesses that trade in mobile phones and computer chips. For more information on the reverse-charge legislation, visit `www.hmrc.gov.uk`.

Part V
Using Reports

In this part . . .

✔ Make the most of the many reports that you can produce in Sage and create your own reports in Microsoft Excel.

✔ Check your Chart of Accounts layout to ensure that your Profit and Loss account and Balance Sheet are accurate.

✔ Follow the audit trail and review the different transaction types.

✔ Use e-banking and the Accountant Link, to see how it can save your business time and money.

✔ Let the Document Manager help you organise your paperwork.

✔ App happy? Use Sage 50 on your mobile.

Chapter 18

Running Monthly Reports

*R*unning reports is an opportunity to see how well your business is progressing. Reports show you if your business is meeting your targets, if you're bringing in as much revenue as you projected, and how actual costs compare with your budgeted or forecasted expenditures. Good reports are easy to understand and use headings that are meaningful to your business.

In this chapter I talk about the reports you can produce at the end of each monthly accounting procedure. I assume you've already run the month-end procedure and processed all the necessary journals, as I explain in Chapter 16.

Making the Most of Standard Reports

Whenever possible, I suggest you use the standard reports provided by Sage, as they're simple to run and provide most of the information you need.

Each section on the Navigation bar (apart from Quotations) contains its own reports. The Report icon is usually the last icon on the right hand side. For example, if you go to Customer and then Reports, you can bring up the aged debtors and customer activity reports; if you go to Bank and then Reports, you see copies of unpresented cheques. Clicking Nominal codes on the Navigation bar and then selecting the appropriate icon brings up the profit and loss report or the balance sheet report – the key financial reports that tell you how the business is doing.

Whenever you select a report, you have five choices of what to do with the data:

- ✔ **Preview**: This lets you preview the layout of the report on the screen and check that it provides you with the information you require. You can then print, export, or email from this screen.

- ✔ **Print:** This lets you print a hard copy of the report without previewing.

- ✔ **Export:** You can save the file in various different formats, such as PDF or CSV.

- ✔ **Export to Excel:** You can send the contents of the report into an Excel document and save and amend as necessary.

- ✔ **Email:** Depending on how your email system is configured, you can send the report as an attachment or you can link to your email software and send the report directly.

Checking the Chart of Accounts

Before you run your financial reports, you must check your chart of accounts (COA) for errors because errors in the COA can affect the accuracy of your reports. (Refer to Chapter 2 for more information on the COA.) If you try to run a balance sheet without checking your COA, Sage is likely to show you a message telling you your COA has and your reports may be inaccurate.

To check the COA for errors, click the Chart of Accounts icon from the Nominal codes module, highlight the COA you want to check, click Edit, and then click the Check box. Sage lets you know if no errors exist. If there are errors, Sage lets you print or preview them.

Figuring Out the Financial Reports

The trial balance, profit and loss, and balance sheet reports give you a view of your business. You generally run each report at the end of your account- ing period, which is probably monthly, quarterly, or annually. I cover these reports in the following sections.

Trying for an initial trial balance

The trial balance report forms the basis of your profit and loss and balance sheet reports. The trial balance report lists all debit and credit balances in nominal code order for the period you specify. The report only shows nominal codes that have a balance, so any codes with a zero balance don't make the list. As I show in the Jingles example in Figure 18-1, the debits and credits are in separate columns with totals at the bottom of each. Double-entry bookkeeping principles mean the two columns balance.

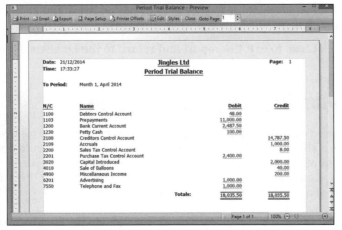

Figure 18-1:
Jingles' trial
balance for
the period
ended April
2014.

Jingles is quite a new company – it doesn't have many transactions yet and it doesn't use many nominal codes. As the Jingles business increases, the number of codes will likely increase and the trial balance report will get longer.

The trial balance report shows at a glance the extent of your assets and liabilities. You can use the report as an investigative tool. For example, if something seems out of whack, you can run more detailed reports to see where the numbers came from. You can drill down further into each of the numbers in the report: If you want to look at the detail behind any of the figures, clicking on the number takes you to the nominal activity for that nominal code and you can see exactly which transactions make up the number.

To run a trial balance report, follow these steps:

1. **From the Navigation bar, click Nominal codes.**

   The Nominal codes window opens.

   Alternatively, from the Menu bar, click Modules and then Nominal codes.

2. **Click the Trial balance icon.**

3. **In the Print Output box, select Preview and then click Run.**

4. **In the Criteria box, use the dropdown arrow to select the period you want to view.**

   In the example in Figure 18-1, I use April 2014.

5. **Click OK.**

   The trial balance report appears.

6. **Click Print, Email, or Export to send the report to the destination of your choice.**

7. **Click Close to exit the report and return to the Financials window.**

Accounting for profit and loss

Owners and directors of businesses really like the profit and loss report because it shows whether they're making any money. The profit and loss report shows the total revenue (sales) your company has made in the specified period and then deducts direct costs and overheads for the same period to arrive at a profit or loss for the period.

The layout of the profit and loss report is a standard format, but you can use the COA function to rename headings and group together your nominal codes so the report appears with terminology suited to your business. (Check out Chapter 2 to see how to edit your COA.)

To run your profit and loss report, follow these steps:

1. **From the Navigation bar, click Nominal codes and then click the Profit and Loss icon.**

2. **Select the print output want and then click Run.**

   You can print, preview, send to file, or email. I suggest you preview first so you can see if you're happy with the report criteria you chose.

3. **In the Criteria box, select the period you want to run the report for by filling in the From and To dates.**

4. **Use the dropdown arrow to select the COA layout you want (which I explain in Chapter 2), and then click OK.**

   The profit and loss report appears. The report has two columns, one showing the current period and the other showing the year to date (YTD).

   If you select a full year for your From and To dates, both columns show the same figures. If you choose a single month (for example, April), the Period column differentiates the current period (April) from the YTD figures. The numbers for the first month of the year and the YTD numbers are the same.

5. **Choose to Print, Email, or Export the report.**

In Figure 18-2, I selected the period from April 2014 to 30 April 2014. This represents the first month of trading, and goes some way to explaining why the business made a loss: low sales and large advertising costs. You'll also notice that the Period and Year to Date columns contain the same data. As the year progresses, these figures cease to be the same and you'll see some useful data appearing.

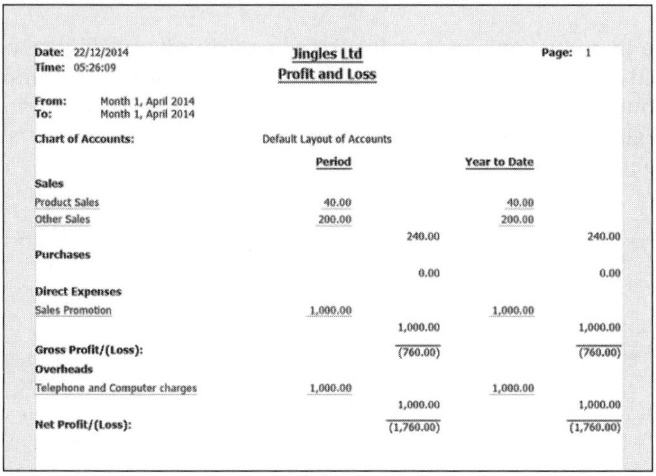
Date: 22/12/2014
Time: 05:26:09

Jingles Ltd
Profit and Loss

Page: 1

From: Month 1, April 2014
To: Month 1, April 2014

Chart of Accounts: Default Layout of Accounts

	Period		Year to Date	
Sales				
Product Sales	40.00		40.00	
Other Sales	200.00		200.00	
		240.00		240.00
Purchases				
		0.00		0.00
Direct Expenses				
Sales Promotion	1,000.00		1,000.00	
		1,000.00		1,000.00
Gross Profit/(Loss):		(760.00)		(760.00)
Overheads				
Telephone and Computer charges	1,000.00		1,000.00	
		1,000.00		1,000.00
Net Profit/(Loss):		(1,760.00)		(1,760.00)

Figure 18-2: A profit and loss report for Jingles.

Comparing profits and losses

Sometimes you need additional analysis from your reporting. With the comparative profit and loss report, you can compare your current month values against budget and prior year data. You can also include percentage variations. The report shows current period values and YTD values.

Work through the following steps to run the comparative profit and loss report:

1. **From the Navigation bar, click Nominal codes and then click the Comparative Profit and Loss icon.**
2. **Select the print output you want and then click Run.**
3. **In the Criteria box, select the period you want to run the report for by filling in the From and To dates.**
4. **Use the dropdown arrows to select the appropriate COA.**

Click the dropdown arrow to determine whether you should show, not show, show as a variance, or show as a variance with a percentage. You can choose any or all of the variables – but if you choose them all, the report becomes quite difficult to read.

5. **Click OK and the report generates in a preview format.**

   Adjust any variables if necessary, or choose to print, export, or email the document.

In Figure 18-3 you can see that Jeanette has printed out Jingles' comparative profit and loss report for April 2014. She has chosen to compare against budget but not prior year periods. Choosing not to show the prior year period figures means the report is much easier to read, as Sage shows fewer columns.

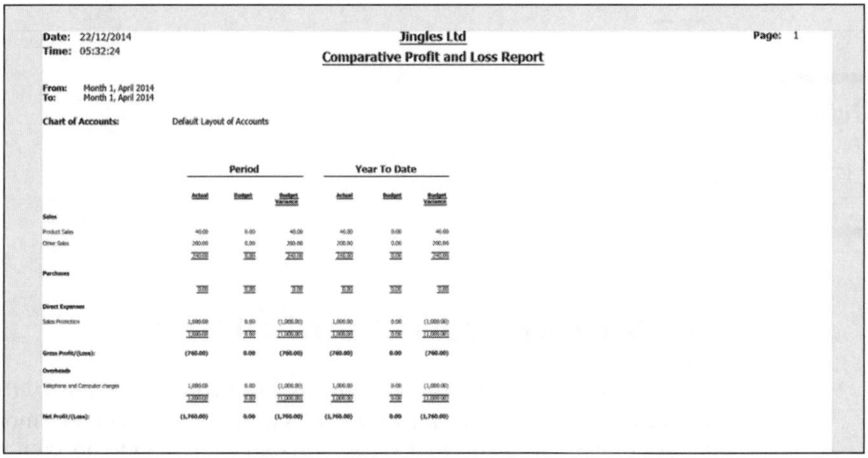

Date: 22/12/2014
Time: 05:32:24

Jingles Ltd
Comparative Profit and Loss Report

Page: 1

From: Month 1, April 2014
To: Month 1, April 2014

Chart of Accounts: Default Layout of Accounts

	Period			Year To Date		
	Actual	Budget	Budget Variance	Actual	Budget	Budget Variance
Sales						
Product Sales	40.00	0.00	40.00	40.00	0.00	40.00
Other Sales	200.00	0.00	200.00	200.00	0.00	200.00
	[illegible]	[illegible]	[illegible]	[illegible]	[illegible]	[illegible]
Purchases						
	[illegible]	[illegible]	[illegible]	[illegible]	[illegible]	[illegible]
Direct Expenses						
Sales Promotion	1,000.00	0.00	(1,000.00)	1,000.00	0.00	(1,000.00)
	[illegible]	[illegible]	[illegible]	[illegible]	[illegible]	[illegible]
Gross Profit/(Loss):	(760.00)	0.00	(760.00)	(760.00)	0.00	(760.00)
Overheads						
Telephone and Computer charges	1,000.00	0.00	(1,000.00)	1,000.00	0.00	(1,000.00)
	[illegible]	[illegible]	[illegible]	[illegible]	[illegible]	[illegible]
Net Profit/(Loss):	(1,760.00)	0.00	(1,760.00)	(1,760.00)	0.00	(1,760.00)

Figure 18-3: The comparative profit and loss report for April 2014 for Jingles.

Weighing the balance sheet

The balance sheet is a really useful tool for establishing your company's financial position. The balance sheet provides a snapshot of the business at a particular point in time. The balance sheet shows your assets, liabilities, and sources of funds that helped finance the business. From the balance sheet, you can see how much money people owe to the business and how much money the business owes.

The balance sheet forms part of the management accounts of the business and is traditionally issued at the month-end, quarter-end, and year-end. Some people prefer to issue just one set of accounts at the year-end, but others prefer to use monthly accounts.

Follow these steps to run a balance sheet for your business:

1. **From the Navigation bar, click Nominal codes and then click the Balance Sheet icon.**

   Alternatively, click Modules and then Nominal codes from the Menu bar.

2. **In the Print Output box, select Preview and then click Run.**

3. **In the Criteria box, use the dropdown arrow to select the period From and To that you want to view.**

   If you have more than one COA layout, select the one you want to preview. Refer to Chapter 2 for details on setting up additional COAs.

   The Jingles example in Figure 18-4 uses the period 1 April 2014 to 31 March 2015 to demonstrate the balance sheet layout. Because the full year has been selected, both columns show the same data.

4. **Click OK to open the Balance Sheet.**

   The balance sheet shows a Period column and a Year to Date column.

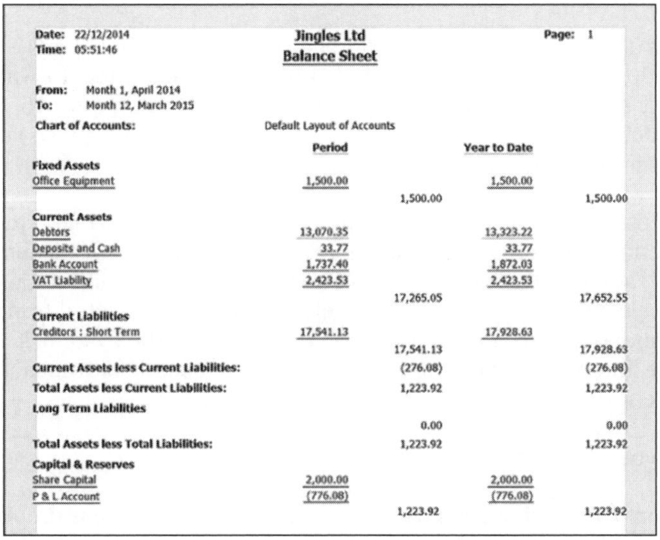

Date: 22/12/2014 Jingles Ltd Page: 1
Time: 05:51:46 Balance Sheet

From: Month 1, April 2014
To: Month 12, March 2015
Chart of Accounts: Default Layout of Accounts

	Period		Year to Date	
Fixed Assets				
Office Equipment	1,500.00		1,500.00	
		1,500.00		1,500.00
Current Assets				
Debtors	13,070.35		13,323.22	
Deposits and Cash	33.77		33.77	
Bank Account	1,737.40		1,872.03	
VAT Liability	2,423.53		2,423.53	
		17,265.05		17,652.55
Current Liabilities				
Creditors : Short Term	17,541.13		17,928.63	
		17,541.13		17,928.63
Current Assets less Current Liabilities:		(276.08)		(276.08)
Total Assets less Current Liabilities:		1,223.92		1,223.92
Long Term Liabilities				
		0.00		0.00
Total Assets less Total Liabilities:		1,223.92		1,223.92
Capital & Reserves				
Share Capital	2,000.00		2,000.00	
P & L Account	(776.08)		(776.08)	
		1,223.92		1,223.92

Figure 18-4: The Jingles balance sheet for 31 March 2015.

Make sure you understand the component parts of the balance sheet. Try to match the debtors figure in the balance sheet with the aged debtors report, and try to find out what transactions Sage includes in the accruals and prepayments. You can check all your figures by looking at your COA and determining which nominal codes represent each section of the balance sheet. You can review any of the numbers by clicking directly on the number in the balance sheet. Sage provides details of the transactions behind those numbers in the nominal activity report.

Viewing the Audit Trail

Your *audit trail* is a list of all the transactions that have ever occurred in your Sage account, including transactions that you delete. If you make a complete mess of something, you can never quite escape it – Sage displays the mess for all to see, including your accountant and the auditors, who may use it at year-end.

Sage lists the transactions in the audit trail chronologically. Each transaction has a unique transaction number. You can use the unique transaction number alongside a search tool to find a particular transaction, which is useful if you need to correct a specific transaction.

You can clear your audit trail periodically to remove the details of the transactions, but Sage keeps the balances and carries them forward so the accounts remain accurate – I explain this properly in Chapter 16. Sage has the capacity to hold 2 billion transactions in your audit trail, so you probably don't ever need to clear it out if you don't want to.

You access the audit trail by clicking the Audit trail report icon in the Transactions module. The Audit reports are available in brief, summary, detailed, and deleted transactions. The brief, summary, and detailed reports show the transactions in varying levels of detail. The deleted transactions report shows all the transactions you deleted from the system. The report lists one line per transaction, so if you have thousands of transactions the whole report is extremely long.

To run your audit trail, follow these steps:

1. **From the Navigation bar, click Transactions and then the Audit trail report icon.**

   The Audit Trail Report window opens.

2. **Enter your choice of audit report – brief, summary, detailed, or deleted transactions.**

   Choose the method of output and click Run.

3. **In the Criteria box, choose the criteria required for this report.**

   Sage recommends you run the report on a monthly basis, so enter the current month dates.

4. **Click OK to generate the report.**

   If you choose to preview the report, you can now print, export, or email it from this screen.

5. **Click Close to exit the report and return to the Financials screen.**

   Printing off your audit trail at the end of each period is a good idea as it provides a hard copy of all your business transactions. Many people print their audit trail at the year-end to provide a copy for the auditors, but you can print more regularly if you want. The longer the reporting period, the longer the print-off.

In Figure 18-5 I show an extract from a brief audit trail report for Jingles.

Figure 18-5:
An extract from Jingles' brief audit trail report.

Date:	22/12/2014			Jingles Ltd				Page:	1
Time:	05:57:28			Audit Trail (Brief)					

Date From:	01/01/1980		Customer From:	
Date To:	31/12/2019		Customer To:	ZZZZZZZZ

Transaction From:	1		Supplier From:	
Transaction To:	99,999,99		Supplier To:	ZZZZZZZZ

Exclude Deleted Tran: No

No	Items	Type	A/C	Date	Ref	Details	Net	Tax	Gross
1	1	SI	ANYTOW	31/03/2014	O/Bal	Opening Balance	200.00	0.00	200.00
2	1	SI	ANYTOW	31/03/2014	O/Bal	Deleted SI	200.00	0.00	200.00
3	1	PI	PAPER	31/03/2014	O/Bal	Opening Balance	387.50	0.00	387.50
4	1	SI	PETE	21/04/2014	1	20 Happy Birthday	40.00	8.00	48.00
5	3	SI	VILLAGE	25/05/2014	2	Snowman cards	49.25	9.85	59.10
8	2	SI	JOHNSON	25/06/2014	3	Wine gift bags	31.00	6.20	37.20
10	2	SI	DAVIS	25/06/2014	4	Party poppers	52.10	10.42	62.52
12	1	SI	BALLOON	13/08/2014	5	Wedding helium	45.00	9.00	54.00
13	1	SC	DAVIS	25/06/2014	1	Party poppers	18.00	3.60	21.60
14	1	SC	BALLOON	14/08/2014	2CR	Wedding helium	45.00	9.00	54.00
15	1	SI	BALLOON	10/03/2014	Op	Opening Balance	52.87	0.00	52.87
16	1	SR	BALLOON	23/04/2014		Sales Receipt	52.87	0.00	52.87
17	1	PI	PAPER	01/05/2014	1	5467 500 Sheets of	286.00	57.20	343.20
18	1	PI	DERBY	13/05/2014	2	Assorted cards	117.00	23.40	140.40
19	1	PI	BRILLIAN	23/07/2014	3	Assorted balloons	102.00	20.40	122.40
20	1	PI	DAGENHA	01/08/2014	4	Party Poppers &	55.00	11.00	66.00
21	1	PI	DIGGORIE	02/09/2014	5	Snowman cards	25.00	5.00	30.00

Forgetting the Periods and Going Transactional

Instead of generating reports based on information from a specific period, Sage can produce profit and loss, balance sheet, and trial balance reports based on transactions instead of time periods. These transactional reports look very similar to period-based reports, but Sage calculates them in a different way. For example, you have to run period-based reports for a complete month, but with a transactional report you can be more precise in selecting your data.

Transactional reports are handy if you want to look at a specific area or time period in your business. For example, if you ran a promotion over a six-week period and want to view the effects on sales of that promotion, you can run a transactional profit and loss report for that specific six-week period.

You can create transactional-based reports for any date range, taking figures from the audit trail, which I talk about in the section 'Viewing the Audit Trail'.

To prepare transactional reports, you need to group the transactions obtained from the audit trail into brought-forward figures, current-period figures, and YTD figures to help structure the reports. I explain these groupings in more detail in the following sections.

Going by date

You can run transactional reports by selecting a specific date range. The dates you use allow Sage to correctly categorise the transactions into three categories:

- ✔ **Brought Forward figures:** These numbers include the current year's activities and also the balance brought forward from the previous year.

- ✔ **Current Period figures:** These numbers come from the From and To dates you select in the Criteria box for the period you want to report on. (See the section 'Running the reports' below for more on this.)

- ✔ **Year-to-Date figures:** This category encompasses the period from the start of the financial year to the end of the period you select. For example, if you select 1 June 2014 to 15 July 2014, the YTD figures show from 1 January 2014 to 15 July 2014 (assuming you have a December year-end). The YTD figures are standard comparative data that Sage uses to compare with the current-period figures.

You need to complete the Criteria box in the report with the specific dates you want to report on. For example, if you choose 1 June to 15 July, that range is your current period – Sage generates the report using those precise dates.

Being number-friendly

You can run transactional reports by selecting a transaction number range rather than a date range. To use transaction numbers, make sure you know what the first transaction number is for the current year. Knowing this number helps Sage determine whether the transaction is prior year or not, which is necessary for balance sheet information. You also need to specify the range of transaction numbers for the specific period you want to report on.

Running the reports

You can run transactional profit and loss, balance sheet, and trial balance reports. To run any of these reports, follow these steps:

1. **From the Navigation bar, click Nominal codes and then the Reports icon.**

   The report browser opens.

2. **Highlight Profit and Loss, Balance Sheet, or Trial Balance on the left side of the Report Browser screen.**

   Sage gives you several report options on the right side of the screen.

3. **Scroll down to the bottom of the screen and over the Transactional Report option. Using the floating icons, select Preview, Print, Export, Export to Excel, or Email.**

   Clicking an icon once loads the Criteria Values screen, as in Figure 18-6. Double-clicking opens the Criteria Values box, where you can preview the report.

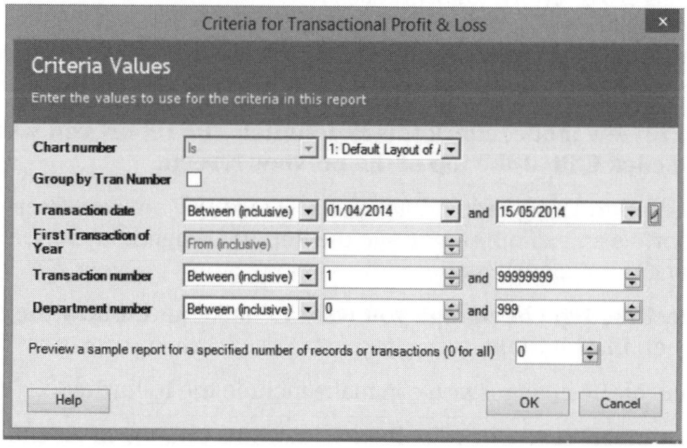

Figure 18-6: Selecting the criteria for a six-week period.

4. **When you're happy with the numbers, click OK.**

   Your report is generated.

This method of reporting lets you track your business progress for any accounting period, even for a single day or week. The report gives you much more flexibility over the information that you produce and can aid your business decisions.

If you run the Clear Audit Trail option up to a given period, you can't run transactional reports for that period.

Designing Reports to Suit Yourself

You may want to personalise one of the many standard reports Sage offers. You can change the existing layouts to suit your needs using Report Designer. Designing reports is a huge topic, and Sage used to produce an entire reference book dealing only with report writing. In this section I scratch the surface by showing you how to take an existing report and tweak it slightly.

The easiest place to start is to find a report that almost but not quite matches your needs. Take this report, save it under a different filename, and then reconfigure it with information that suits your business needs.

Pressing the F1 key in Report Designer opens the very useful Report Designer help module.

To reconfigure a report, follow these steps:

1. **Find the report you want to amend by choosing the Report icon from whichever module you require, and preview the report.**

2. **In Preview mode, check this is definitely the report you want to adapt, and click Edit at the top of the preview screen.**

   The Report Designer module opens. Figure 18-7 shows a Project activity report as an example – you see the Report Designer layout before any changes have been made.

3. **Select the type of change you want to make and follow the online screen instructions.**

   Some of the changes you can make include the following:

   - **Insert text:** Click Toolbox ➪ Text Box. Use the mouse to drag and insert a text box in the appropriate part of the screen.

   - **Insert new variables:** Click View ➪ Variables to open a list of variables on the left side of the screen. You can then drag and drop suitable variables into the main body of the report.

Jeanette decides she wants to change the Jingles report name – she selects 'Set the report name or description' and follows the onscreen prompts to change the name and then clicks OK.

4. **After you make the necessary changes, click File on the Menu bar and then click Save As from the dropdown list. Choose an appropriate file format to save the document as.**

The Save As screen opens. On the left are folders containing saved reports. Sage saves the report you're tweaking in the My Project Reports folder and names it `copy of XX`.

In Figure 18-8, Jeanette has renamed the Jingles file `JK copy of Pjact`.

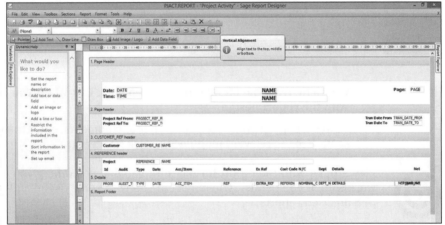

Figure 18-7:
Viewing the project activity report through Report Designer.

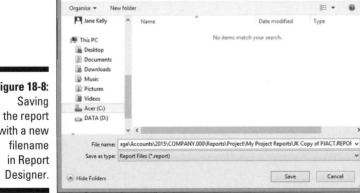

Figure 18-8:
Saving the report with a new filename in Report Designer.

5. Click Save.

You return to the Report Designer screen. Figure 18-9 shows the altered Jingles report with a new heading.

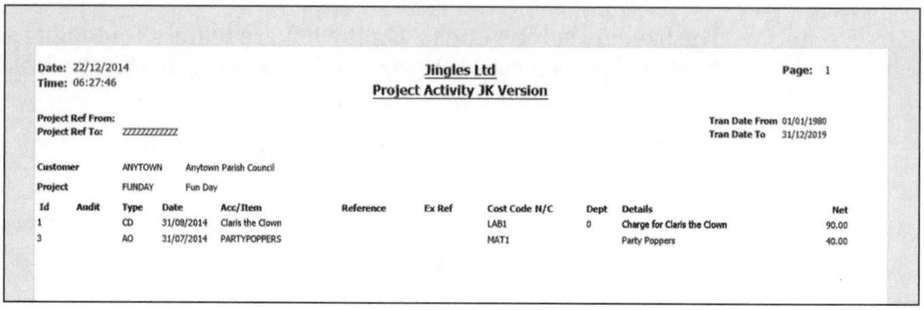

Figure 18-9:
The Jingles
report
viewed
through
Report
Designer,
showing
a new
heading.

Date: 22/12/2014				Jingles Ltd					Page: 1	
Time: 06:27:46				Project Activity JK Version						
Project Ref From:								Tran Date From	01/01/1980	
Project Ref To:	ZZZZZZZZZZ							Tran Date To	31/12/2019	
Customer	ANYTOWN	Anytown Parish Council								
Project	FUNDAY	Fun Day								
Id	Audit	Type	Date	Acc/Item	Reference	Ex Ref	Cost Code N/C	Dept	Details	Net
1		CD	31/08/2014	Claris the Clown			LAB1	0	Charge for Claris the Clown	90.00
3		AO	31/07/2014	PARTYPOPPERS			MAT1		Party Poppers	40.00

6. Click File from the Menu bar and then click Exit when you're happy with the report design.

To see a copy of your report and your amendments, enter the report section of the relevant module and click My Reports.

Play around with the report format until you find something you can work with. If you persist, you may come up with some useful and personalised reports.

Chapter 19

Tackling the Complicated Stuff

. . . .

In This Chapter

▶ Sending data out

▶ Bringing data in

▶ Using the Accountant Link

▶ Banking electronically

▶ Managing paperwork with Document Manager

. . . .

*W*hen you're confident that you've got to grips with the day-to-day mechanics of the Sage system, you can tackle some of the more advanced options that Sage offers.

The extras I explain in this chapter include the ability to extract data from Sage, make changes within a spreadsheet to that data, and then import those changes back into Sage. You can also discover how to relay information to your accountant with minimum disruption to your data and your day-to-day workings.

I also look at the impact of using e-banking to speed up the processing of banking transactions and how the Document Manager can help you organise your paperwork.

Exporting Data

You can send data from Sage to Microsoft Excel, Word, or Outlook. I cover all three in this section.

Sending spreadsheet stuff

You can send all sorts of information from Sage to Microsoft Excel so you can mess about with the data in a spreadsheet without affecting the data in Sage. For example, you may want to edit the data, design specific reports, or create what-if scenarios to suit the purposes of your business.

The list of information you can send from Sage to Excel is too long to provide here. To find out whether you can extract what you want from your Sage data, press the F1 key and type `fileexport` into the Help field to get a list of the reports you can extract from each module.

The easiest way to send information to Excel is to use the Send to Excel icon available in every module: Click the relevant module from the Navigation bar and then click the Send to Excel icon. Sage immediately copies and pastes the contents of the main window into an Excel document, which you can amend as you wish.

Alternatively, click File from the main toolbar, then Microsoft Integration, and then Contents to Microsoft Excel.

You can export to Excel any of the standard reports that you print. Simply choose the Export to Excel floating icon when you want to print the report.

Transferring Outlook contacts

You can send customer and supplier contact information from Sage to Microsoft Outlook. This option is an excellent time-saving device, as it means you don't have to type the information in twice.

The option creates a contact record within Outlook for customers and suppliers who have a name entered on their customer or supplier record.

If you have two accounts with the same name, Sage creates two contact records in case the two contacts are two different people – for example, you may have two John Smiths.

You can make changes in Sage and then send those changes to Outlook with the amended contact details.

To export account information to Outlook, follow these steps:

1. From the Sage Menu bar, click File ➪ Microsoft Integration ➪ Microsoft Outlook Import/Export Wizard.

2. **Select Export Contacts To Outlook.**

    You can choose the other destinations if you prefer.

3. **Follow wizard's instructions, clicking Next to continue on to each screen.**

When you've completed the transfer of information, a confirmation message appears, stating that the transfer has been successful. If a different message comes up, follow the advice on the screen. It may be that the folder you're trying to send information to doesn't allow access – Sage then suggests alternatives.

You can copy the following information from your customer and supplier records to Outlook:

- ✔ Contact name and addresses
- ✔ Telephone and fax numbers
- ✔ Websites and email addresses.

Exporting to Word

You can send data to Microsoft Word from Sage. You can send information to a new or existing document or as a mail-merge. For example, you can send a list of customer records to Word and mail-merge the contact details with a standard letter from Word.

Exporting to Word can be helpful, for example, if you run a sales promotion and want to contact all your customers to make them aware of the promotion. You can produce a leaflet or letter within Word and send the customer contacts from Sage across to Word so that the names and addresses merge into your Word document. You save time as you don't have to type in the individual names and addresses for all your customers.

To merge customer contact details with a Word document, follow these steps:

1. **From Sage, select the items you want to export data from and click File from the Menu bar.**

2. **Click Microsoft Integration ⇨ Contents to Microsoft Word and the option that suits you.**

    Your choices are:

    - **New Document:** You can create a new Word document to hold the information extracted from Sage.

- **Open Document:** You can open an existing Word document, for example a promotion letter. You can insert merge boxes so you can personalise the promotion document with the customer details.

- **Run Mail Merge:** You can use the selected data extracted from Sage in a mail-merged document.

Importing Data

The Data Import Wizard lets you enhance the existing file import options. You can import from a CSV file or from a Microsoft Excel spreadsheet (.xls or .xlsx file).

To structure your files correctly ready for importing, take a look at the File Import Templates that are installed with your Sage software. Press F1 to bring up the Help facility if you want to find out more about the templates.

To use the Data Import Wizard, follow these steps:

1. **From the Menu bar, click File and then Import.**

   Follow the screen prompts that open the File Import Wizard.

2. **Click Next to work through the wizard.**

   You can access Help at any time while using the wizard and move forward and backward through each screen. Take a backup of your data before proceeding with the Data Import Wizard as the procedure isn't reversible.

3. **From the menu of the Data Type window, select what type of data you wish to import.**

4. **Click Next to open the Data Source window.**

   Specify whether the data to import is from a CSV file or an Excel worksheet.

5. **Use the Browse button to choose the file you want to import.**

   If the first line of your CSV file or Excel spreadsheet file contains headings, check the box to say it contains headings. If your Excel spreadsheet contains multiple worksheets, select the one you want to import. Then select the worksheet from the dropdown list provided.

6. **Click Next to open the Field Mappings window**.

   If the field in your imported spreadsheet or CSV files contains the headings appropriate to the supplied template, a mapping template appears, similar to that in Figure 19-1. The imported field name is matched to the corresponding Sage field. In most cases, no remapping is required.

Where you have no header row in your imported file, no data is shown in the left side of the Field Mappings window, but you still have the Sage headings.

Where you see an asterisk in the `Required?` column, you must make a selection in the `Imported Field` column to match with an entry in the Sage field. For example, if your Account Reference is Column A of your spreadsheet, then use the dropdown list to select A to map with the corresponding Sage field.

When you've completed your mapping, click Save Map.

7. **Select a filename and location, and save your Data Import Map file. Click Save.**

   Your map is saved in your Company .000 Import Maps folder. You can reload maps by using the Load Map function in the Field Mappings window of the Data Import wizard. If you make a mistake while mapping your fields, click Clear Map and start again.

Figure 19-1:
Extracts
from exam-
ple CSV
file struc-
tures for
importing
customer
and supplier
records.

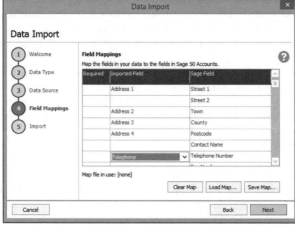

8. **Click Next when your field mapping is complete.**

   The Import window appears. You see a summary of the options you chose in the previous Import wizard windows. If you're happy with the summary, begin importing the data by clicking the Import button. You can modify any of your selections by using the Back button before you click Import.

9. **When the data has finished importing, the Import Results Window appears.**

The top part of the screen shows the fields you've imported. The bottom part of the screen shows the records that haven't imported.

Check your data files after completing the import by clicking File ⇨ Maintenance ⇨ Check Data options.

If you leave a blank line between a heading and the actual information, the data won't import correctly. Delete the line with no information and the import should then work.

Linking to Your Accountant

If your accountant has access to Sage 50 Client Manager, you can use the Accountant Link to save untold amounts of time for both you and your accountant – and reduce your accountant's bill.

You probably employ an accountant to help you with quarterly VAT returns, year-end accounts, and tax computations. Before the Accountant Link existed, at some point after your year-end your accountant took your data files to work on – leaving you unable to use Sage, sometimes for months.

With the Accountant Link, you and your accountant can exchange data in a speedy and accurate fashion. Essentially, you send data to your accountant, who then processes adjustments while you continue to work on your data. Your accountant sends back the adjustments to you to apply to your data. The Accountant Link keeps a log of any changes you make to your data in the intervening period.

The Accountant Link is a wizard that guides you and your accountant through the different stages of the process. To access the wizard, from the Menu bar click Modules ⇨ Wizards ⇨ Accountant Link. The wizard is split into two parts: One part exports data to your accountant, records material changes, and imports your accountant's adjustments; the other part lets your accountant import your data, record adjustments, export the adjustments to a file, and send the back to you, ready for you to apply the changes.

Ensure your accountant's information is up to date by clicking Settings, Company Preferences, and then Accountant from the Menu bar.

The Accountant Link is not available if you have activated Sage Drive. To read more about Sage Drive, head to Chapter 21.

Sending accounts to your accountant

If you select the wizard's Export option, Sage guides you through the process of exporting your file in a secure password-protected file to your accountant via email.

From the moment you export the data, Sage begins to record changes you make. You can print a list of material changes to show to your accountant before you import the records back into your system. The changes that Sage considers important are wide-ranging but include deleting customer records, restoring data, and creating a nominal account.

When you export your data, Sage generates an export file with an .sae extension. You have two options: Navigate to the filename that Sage has given, or email the file. You select one of the options and then click Exit.

If you click Navigate to File, Sage takes you to the folder where you saved the data.

If you click Email File, Sage creates an email and attaches a copy of the export file.

Material changes

After you export your data, Sage begins to record any changes that you make to the dataset. Any amendment to the data is considered a *material change*. You'll know when the system is recording changes, because the word *recording* appears in red at the bottom of the screen.

You can view any of these material changes by clicking on View and then Material Changes from the Menu bar. The Accountant Link – Material Changes window opens. From here, you can view the adjustments that you've made to the data and print the changes if necessary. You can also add comments to the Material Changes file before you click send and then email the file to your accountants.

If you think you need to restart the export process, you can stop recording material changes by clicking the Cancel button. Sage flags up a confirmation message asking if you're absolutely sure that you want to cancel the material changes, as any changes made will be lost. Click Yes or No as appropriate. If you click Yes, the material changes stops recording, and the recording message at the bottom of the screen disappears.

Getting back adjustments and narratives

Your accountant makes the adjustments and sends the file back to you for you to apply the adjustments and bring the accounts up to date. The adjustments fall into two categories:

- ✔ **Adjustments:** You can apply these to the accounts automatically from the Comments and Adjustments window. Examples include journals, journal reversals, bank payments, and receipts.
- ✔ **Comments:** These are instructions that your accountant sends for changes, which you need to make to your records. You must change the data manually according to your accountant's instructions.

The last section of the wizard helps you import the adjustments your accountant has made to your data.

To import the file from your accountant (which will have an .saa extension), from the Menu bar click Modules ➪ Wizards ➪ Accountant Link ➪ Import. Locate the file and enter your password, and then click Import. You can choose to view the comments and adjustments now or later.

You then click the Adjustments tab, click Begin, and then click OK. The adjustments are processed in the order that they appear.

Allow plenty of uninterrupted time to complete the import process.

You can find further details about the Accountant Link by using the Help system within Sage. Press F1 and type in `accountant link` to get more information.

Trying e-Banking

Using e-banking can give you a seamless interface between your bank account and Sage. You can pay your suppliers directly from your bank account, check your online bank statements against your Sage statements, and import transactions from your bank so you can reconcile your Sage transactions.

Before you start using this wonderful product, contact your bank and ask for the necessary software. After you set up your banking software, you can then enable the e-banking options within Sage.

The e-banking features available are limited by your bank and your account type. Some banking products let you download statements, which helps with the bank reconciliation, but these products may not have the electronic payments option for your suppliers.

The benefits of making electronic payments include:

- ✔ **Good control of cash flow:** You know exactly when a payment clears your account – no waiting for cheques to arrive and no delays while cheques are cashed.

- ✔ **Lower costs:** Online banking transactions are cheaper than clearing cheques and cash.

- ✔ **Secure:** You don't need to keep cash on the premises if you pay all your debts electronically.

- ✔ **Speed:** You no longer have to write out cheques. Instead, you click and type your way through invoice payments.

Getting your statements online brings benefits too:

- ✔ **Better cash flow:** You can easily see what funds are available at any time.

- ✔ **Efficiency:** You can keep your accounts up to date by seeing current interest payments, direct debits, and bank charges.

- ✔ **Environmentally sound:** No paper statements means saving trees and sparing the planet the chemicals used to make paper, ink, and stamps.

- ✔ **Saving time:** You don't have to wait for statements to arrive by post and can reconcile straight away.

Configuring your e-banking

To make sure Sage can interpret the file format required by your e-banking system, you need to configure your e-banking facility. Follow these steps:

1. From the Navigation bar, click Bank accounts.

Choose the account you want to configure.

2. **Click the New/Edit icon and select Edit from the dropdown menu.**

   The bank record opens. Select the Bank Details tab and enter the sort code and account details for your bank account. Figure 19-2 shows the Details tab.

   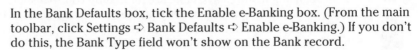

   In the Bank Defaults box, tick the Enable e-Banking box. (From the main toolbar, click Settings ➪ Bank Defaults ➪ Enable e-Banking.) If you don't do this, the Bank Type field won't show on the Bank record.

3. **Select the bank type you want to use.**

   To begin with, Sage doesn't show any bank type options. You need to press F1 and follow the help menu for e-banking. Sage suggests you access the Sage website to download your e-banking components. By following the instructions in Sage, you reach mysage.co.uk, where you can choose the correct bank download component. The option then appears on your bank type dropdown option, as in Figure 19-2.

4. **Click the Configure button.**

   The Sage e-Banking Configuration screen appears for your selected bank type.

5. **Enter the information requested and click OK to save the changes you've made.**

   Click Save in the Bank Details window to close the bank record and save the changes to the record.

You can now access the e-banking options from the Bank Accounts window.

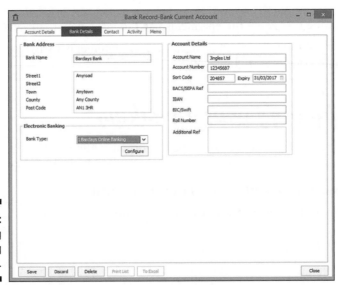

Figure 19-2: Configuring e-banking with Sage.

Opting for e-payments

If your banking software is compatible with Sage 50 Accounts, you can use the e-payments option to pay suppliers directly from your bank account using electronic payments, as in Figure 19-3. You need to know the supplier's sort code, account number, BACS reference, and account name. You also need to make sure the supplier's record is set to allow online payments – to do this, tick the Online Payments box on the Bank tab of the supplier record.

You complete the supplier payment as normal (except the word BACS automatically appears in the Cheque No field) and click Save to process the payment.

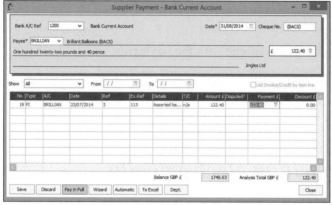

Figure 19-3:
Supplier
payments
using
e-Banking.

After you complete the supplier payment information, you can make the e-payment by following these steps:

1. **From the Navigation bar, click Bank accounts and select the bank account you want to make an e-payment from.**

   Click the Payments icon, and from the dropdown menu select E-Payments at the bottom of the list. The Send Payments window appears, showing details of all the outstanding supplier payments that you've set up to use online banking, as in Figure 19-4. You can restrict the number of transactions that appear by selecting a date range.

2. **Select the transactions you want to send to your bank and click Send.**

   The transfer of information from Sage to your bank account begins. A confirmation message appears, showing the number and value of payments.

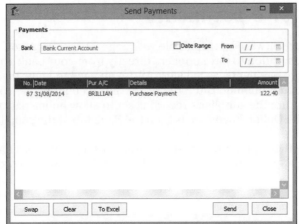

Figure 19-4:
Sending an
E-Payment.

3. Click OK to continue with the payments.

To keep a record of the payment, click Print.

If any problems occur with your e-payment, Sage prompts you to view an error log explaining why the transfer hasn't been successful.

Reconciling electronically

Electronic reconciliation lets you connect to your banking software and see electronic copies of your bank statements so you can reconcile your accounts in Sage.

Make sure you've configured e-banking and set up your bank records to allow online reconciliation.

You need to be able to import files from your banking software. Your banking software saves this data into a file on your computer. You use this file to reconcile your electronic bank statement to Sage.

If you accidentally reconcile a transaction, you can reverse the reconciliation process by using the Amend Bank Transactions option. From the Reconciliation screen, click Tools and then use the dropdown menu to select Amend Bank Transactions. Select the transaction you want to amend and click Unreconcile.

Going automatic

To import your banking transactions, follow these steps:

1. **From the Navigation bar, click Bank accounts, select the bank account you want to reconcile, click the Reconcile icon, and then select e-Reconcile.**

   The Amend Bank Statement window appears.

2. **Enter the statement end date and end balance and then click OK.**

   The Reconciliation From screen appears.

3. **Open the File menu and choose Import Bank Transactions, browse to the required file, and then click Open.**

   The Open window for your selected bank appears. The left side of the window shows the files on your computer and the right side shows the bank statement files.

4. **Open the folder where your bank data is saved in the panel on the left.**

   The bank files for the selected bank account are now visible on the right panel.

5. **Select the bank file you want to import from the right panel and click Open.**

   The Reconciliation From window appears, showing your imported transactions. The imported transactions from your bank appear in the top part of the screen and the Sage account transactions in the bottom part of the screen.

6. **Select a method to match transactions.**

   Choose one of the three automatic matching buttons:

   - **Full Match:** Use this button to match items with the same reference and amount.

   - **Match Amount:** Click this button to match transactions of the same amount.

   - **Match Reference:** Use this option to match transactions that share the same reference as shown on the bank statement, such as 'British Gas DD'.

   If no transactions can be matched, a message appears and you can't reconcile your bank transactions with the automatic function. Click OK to go back to the Reconciliation screen.

   If Sage finds more than one matching transaction, the Duplicate Transaction window appears. Select the transaction you want to match by using the Confirm button. If you don't want to confirm the matching transactions but want to carry on with the automatic matching process, click Next. To close the window and not match any transactions, click Cancel.

Matching transactions then appear, highlighted in green. The Matched With column shows the number of transactions that have been matched.

7. **Click Confirm to verify the matched transactions and remove them from the list.**

    You can view your confirmed transactions by clicking View and then Confirmed.

8. **When you're happy with your confirmed transactions, click Reconcile.**

    Sage marks the matched transactions as reconciled and they no longer appear on the Bank list or the Sage list.

Reconciling manually

Sage recommends you use both the automatic and manual reconciling options. Use the automatic option first, to match the majority of the items, and then finish off the reconciliation with the manual reconciling option. To do a manual e-reconciliation, follow these steps:

1. **From the Navigation bar, click Bank accounts, click the Reconcile icon, and then select e-Reconcile.**

    The Amend Bank Statements window appears.

2. **Enter the statement end date and end balance details and then click OK.**

    The Reconciliation screen appears.

3. **Match transactions from the bank list or the Sage list by clicking Match Manual.**

    If the Automatically Confirmed Match Manual box is checked (the default setting), the Match Manual button confirms the transactions. If you haven't ticked this box, the transactions are highlighted in green and you must click Confirm before you reconcile those transactions. You can view the confirmed transactions by clicking View and then Confirmed.

4. **To finish the reconciliation, click Reconcile. If you aren't happy with the reconciliation, you can exit without reconciling by clicking Discard.**

5. **Click Yes to the confirmation message that appears, or click No to return to the Reconciliation screen.**

    The matched and reconciled transactions no longer appear on the Sage or Bank transactions.

Working with Document Manager

Sage's Document Manager helps you organise your paperwork. Document Manager lets you match contact information and documents with customers, suppliers, and bank records within Sage. You can then link electronic and paper documents to the associated records on Sage.

You can use the Memo tab located on your Sage customer, supplier, and bank records to attach electronic files such as Word documents and statements produced in Sage. You can make a filing system reference to note the location of an actual physical document for this record. You can also type free text into the blank section at the bottom of the Memo tab.

Adding attachments and filing system references

A useful feature is the ability to attach a file or even a photograph to a record, using the memo tab. For example, you could attach a photograph to a project record to provide visual evidence of the project concerned.

To attach a memo to a specific record, use Document Manager and follow these steps:

1. **Open the relevant record and then click the Memo tab.**

2. **Click Add Attachment.**

   Choose the type of attachment to add and click OK.

   The Add New Attachment box appears and asks which type of attachment you want to add. Your attachment choices are Electronic (for any electronic file) and Filing System Reference (for a reference to a file location).

3. **Browse your computer to find the electronic file you want to attach.**

   If you want to add a file system reference, enter the location where your paper document is held, such as the filing cabinet. Type in the name that you want to appear on the Attachment pane for this filing system reference – choose a meaningful name, such as Invoice File Location. Click OK.

4. **If you select an electronic file, double-click the filename and it appears in the Attachment pane of your record.**

   The attachment now shows in that supplier record.

Deleting attachments

If you no longer need an attachment linked to a record, you can delete it. Click the Memo tab of the relevant record and highlight the attachment that you want to delete. Click Delete Attachment and a confirmation message appears. Click Yes to continue. The attachment disappears.

Chapter 20

Running Key Reports

. . . .

In This Chapter

▶ Looking at your customer and supplier activity

▶ Working out who owes you money and who you owe money to

▶ Running simple management reports

▶ Searching for your top customers

. . . .

Sage produces so many reports that just thinking about them can make your head spin. In this chapter, I pick out the reports I find most useful on a day-to-day basis. I show you how to run each report and use examples to demonstrate how to use them. I provide lots of lovely pictures so you can see what Sage should look like.

Sage contains lots of other useful reports as well as the ones I talk about in this chapter. I suggest you have a good root through and pick the ones that suit you.

Checking Activity through the Nominal Codes

The nominal activity report identifies transactions posted to specific nominal codes. The report includes transaction types such as purchase invoices, sales invoices, bank payments and receipts, and journals. I use this report on a daily basis. I often just view the activity on screen, but sometimes I print out the information for further analysis.

This report is useful if you see a figure in the accounts that you want further information on, or if you want to know how you've spent on an item for a specific time period. For example, Jeanette notices that Jingles has allocated £286 to Party Gifts (N/C 5015) in May 2014 and wants to know the breakdown data for this expense item. Jeanette decides to run a nominal activity report for the nominal code 5015 to give her more details, as in Figure 20-1.

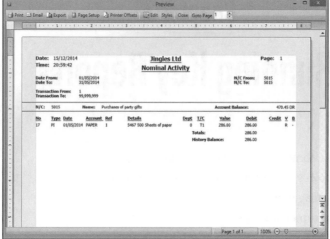

Figure 20-1:
An example
of a nominal
activity
report,
showing
party gift
expenses
for Jingles.

Jeanette spots an invoice for £286 posted to the 5015 nominal code. Scanning through the details column, she sees that she has given the invoice a reference of number 1, and the supplier invoice number is 5467. Jeanette can check the invoice in the file to confirm that she knows what the items are and is happy with the result of her investigation.

To investigate your own nominal codes, follow these steps:

1. **From the Navigation bar, click Nominal codes and then click the Reports icon.**

   The Nominal code reports window appears.

2. **Click on Nominal activity from the list on the left side of the screen.**

   A variety of report options appear on the right side of the screen. Highlight the activity report you require and then click the floating preview icon that appears. This brings up the Criteria Values box, as in Figure 20-2.

3. **Select the nominal code you want to generate a report for and the date range you want to look at.**

   If you can't remember the code, use the dropdown arrow to identify the nominal codes. You can run the report by using a range of transaction numbers, if you know them.

   If you don't put a code in the boxes, Sage uses the default codes 0010–9999. All nominal activities for all nominal codes then print. If you have lots of nominal codes, you'll probably run out of paper before the report finishes printing.

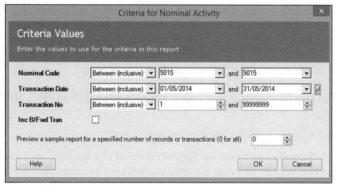

Figure 20-2:
Select the
parameters
for your
report from
the Criteria
Values box.

Criteria Values

Enter the values to use for the criteria in this report

Nominal Code	Between (inclusive)	5015	and	5015
Transaction Date	Between (inclusive)	01/05/2014	and	31/05/2014
Transaction No	Between (inclusive)	1	and	99999999
Inc B/Fwd Tran	☐			

Preview a sample report for a specified number of records or transactions (0 for all)   0

Help   OK   Cancel

4. Click OK.

The report preview appears on screen, unless you've requested to print directly.

5. Choose to print, email, or export the report or just view it on screen.

If you select print preview, you can scan the report on screen to make sure it's presented the information as expected.

If you want to print the report, click the Print icon at the top of the Preview screen. This takes you to the Print Options box, where you can click OK to continue printing or Cancel to return to the report.

In Chapter 19 you can find out how to export data from Sage into Excel.

6. Close the report by clicking the white cross in the red box at the top right corner of the screen.

Alternatively, click Close at the top of the Preview screen.

7. Click the white cross in the red box to exit the Nominal code reports screen.

You return to the Nominal codes window.

Looking into Supplier Activity

How often do you receive supplier statements that don't agree with the figures you think you owe? Performing a quick reconciliation helps you make sure suppliers don't charge you for things you haven't bought.

You can print a supplier's activity screen to show you the transactions you entered in the supplier's account within a specific period and compare that with your supplier's statement. You can then see whether you have any invoices missing.

You can also use a supplier activity report if you want to see how much you spend with a specific supplier or see the volume of transactions for a given period of time.

To run a supplier activity report, follow these steps:

1. **From the Navigation bar, click Suppliers, and then click the Reports icon.**

   The Supplier reports window opens.

2. **Click Supplier activity on the left side of the screen, and then highlight the report of your choice, shown on the right side of the screen.**

   I recommend looking at the Supplier Activity (Detailed) report. After you highlight the report, click the Preview Icon to open the Criteria Values window, as in Figure 20-3. Double-clicking on the report you wish to view also opens the Criteria Values box.

3. **From the dropdown arrow in the Supplier Reference field, select the supplier and the transaction dates you want to view.**

   In Figure 20-3, Dagenham Party Suppliers is my chosen supplier and 1 April 2014 to 31 August 2014 are the specified dates.

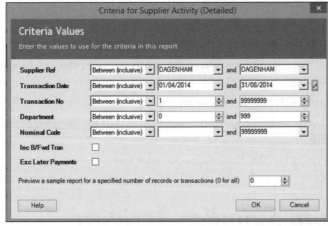

Figure 20-3: Choosing the criteria for your supplier activity (detailed) report.

4. **Click OK to display the report in preview format.**

   After you preview the report, you can choose to print, export or email from the toolbar on the report.

   Figure 20-4 shows the Supplier Activity (Detailed) report for Dagenham Party Suppliers.

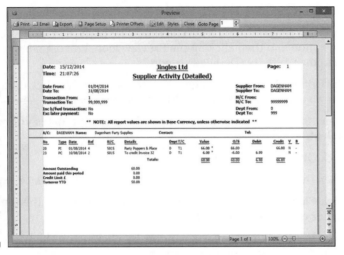

5. **Print the report if you want to.**

   To exit, click Close or click the white cross in the red box at the top right of the Preview window.

6. **Click the white cross in the red box to close the Supplier reports screen.**

   You return to the Supplier window.

Tracking Customer Activity

You may be keen to look into the activity of one of your customers for a variety of reasons. You may want to see how much business has tailed off with a particular customer, or you may want to see what goods another customer usually orders you so you can work out what other products to recommend to them. The customer activity report shows you the transactions with a customer for a specified period of time. You can view all transactions, including invoices, credit notes, payments, and payments on account.

To bring up a customer activity report, follow these steps:

1. **From the Navigation bar, click Customers and then click the Reports icon.**

   The Customer reports window opens.

2. **Click on Customer activity on the left side of the screen.**

   Choose a report option from the right side of the screen by highlighting the option and then clicking the Preview icon. I recommend using the Customer Activity (Detailed) report.

   The Criteria Values box opens. You can also double-click on the report you wish to view to open the Criteria Values box.

3. **Select the customer and the range of transaction dates you want to look at.**

4. **Click OK to run the report.**

   When the report's done, choose whether to print, email, or export.

5. **Click Close, or click the white cross in the red box at the top right corner of the Preview screen.**

6. **Close the Customer reports window by clicking on the white cross in the red box in the top right corner.**

   You return to the Customer window.

You can view customer activity on screen by selecting the relevant customer and then clicking the Activity icon. The top half of the screen that appears shows all transactions and the bottom part shows a breakdown of the item highlighted in the top section of the screen.

Checking Numbers with Supplier Daybook Reports

You can find daybook reports in the customer, supplier, and nominal ledgers. I use the supplier daybook reports regularly to check the invoice number on the last invoice I posted – I double-check to ensure the last filed invoice is in fact the last invoice posted on the system. Starting off a numbering sequence for your new batch of supplier invoices only to find you've duplicated your numbers is very annoying and time-consuming.

A *daybook* is a list of items entered on the system in the same order you input them. The daybook shows transaction numbers, transaction types, account references, details of the transaction, and the net, VAT, and gross amounts. Detailed reports often show the nominal code and the department the transaction has been allocated to. A daybook is important because it lets your accountant prove the original source documents, such as sales and purchase invoices, cheque stubs, paying-in slips, and electronic payments, have been entered on to the computer.

You can choose from a number of different daybooks. Using Sage, you can print daybooks for all invoices, paid invoices, credit notes, and discounts.

To find the last invoice number, choose the Supplier Invoices (Detailed) report from the list of reports that Sage provides. This report clearly shows the invoice reference, so if you scroll down to the bottom of the report you can see the last invoice reference, which is the last invoice posted.

Make sure the invoicing sequence runs in order and you have definitely got the last posted invoice number.

To run a Supplier Daybook report, follow these steps:

1. **From the Navigation bar, click Suppliers and then click the Reports icon.**

   The Supplier reports window opens.

2. **Click on Daybooks on the left side of the screen. Highlight your chosen report from the right side of the screen and click the Preview icon.**

   I use the Day Books: Supplier Invoices (Detailed) report, which shows a list of all purchase invoices entered within your specified date range.

   Specify your criteria in the relevant sections of the Criteria Values box.

3. **Click OK to run the report.**

   If you want the report to list all invoices, don't specify any dates.

To find the last invoice number, scroll to the bottom of the report and check the Invoice Reference column. Check this number agrees with the last invoice filed. If it does, you can start the next batch of invoices with the subsequent number.

Finding the Customers Who Owe You

If your business is running short of cash because customers aren't paying you promptly, you can produce an aged debtors analysis report to tell you who owes you money, how much, and for how long. You can see instantly which customers need a polite kick up the proverbial to help get some cash across to your bank account.

Creating an up-to-date aged debtors analysis report each month helps your business collect debts as efficiently as possible.

An aged debtors analysis report builds up a payment profile of your customers so you can see who pays you within 30 days and who takes more than 90 days to pay. You can use this information to determine who you prefer to continue working with. After all, selling to customers who don't pay you is pointless.

Make sure you reconcile your bank on a regular basis so your aged debtors analysis reports are meaningful. You need to be sure that all the money you receive is allocated to the correct customer accounts so you have the most up-to-date information available.

The most sensible time to run an aged debtors analysis report is at the beginning of the month following the month you're trying to chase. For example, you can run the report for the period ended 30 June in the first week of July, when you know that all the sales invoices for June have been posted on the system and you've reconciled the bank up to the end of June.

You have to wait until you see your paper bank statements, which may take up to a week following the month-end. Or you can run off your bank statements online so you don't have to wait until the end of the month before processing bank entries.

To run off an aged debtors analysis report, follow these steps:

1. **From the Navigation bar, click Customers and then click the Reports icon.**

   The Customer reports window opens.

2. **Click on Aged debtors on the left side of the screen, and then highlight the report of your choice on the right side of the screen.**

   Sage greets you with a raft of options. I suggest you run an Aged Debtors Analysis (Detailed) report (located about a third of the way down the screen), which shows all the individual invoices and credit notes outstanding, or you can run the much shorter Aged Debtors Analysis (Summary) report (located about two-thirds of the way down the screen), which shows only the total debt outstanding from each customer. Both reports show the outstanding balance for each customer and also age the debt. You can see the current-month debt, debts that are 30, 60, and 90 days old, and debts that are older than 90 days.

   Highlight the report you want and then click the Preview icon to open the Criteria Values box. You can also double-click on the report you wish to view to open the Criteria Values box.

3. **Select the customers and dates for which you want to run an aged debtor analysis report.**

   You normally select everyone, so leave the Customer Reference box as it is. Selecting the correct dates is important. You need to pick up all transactions outstanding, from day 1 to the end of the period you've decided to run a report for – the end date of the report is the most important one. Choose the end of a period, such as a month or quarter.

   To run a debtors report to tie in with your accounts at the end of a period, run the report to the period end but then select Exclude Later Payments. For example, if you produce accounts to 30 April but continue to process sales receipts into May and then run the aged debtors analysis to 30 April without checking this box, the current amount outstanding is updated by the May sales receipts and the overall balance of debts outstanding doesn't agree with the balance sheet as at 30 April. By checking Exclude Later Payments, you can run the report to exclude the July receipts and the report then balances as at 30 April.

4. **Click OK to run the report.**

   You can print or email the report, or export it to Excel.

   Figure 20-5 shows a detailed aged debtors report for Jingles.

5. **Click Close to exit the report, or click the white cross in the red box to close the Preview window.**

   You return to the Customer reports window. From here, click the white cross in the red box to return to the Customers screen.

Figure 20-5: Reviewing the aged debtors analysis (detailed) report for Jingles.

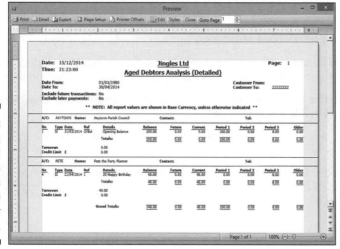

Paying Attention to Your Creditors

If you find going through your credit card bill terrifying, you probably won't like looking at your aged creditors report, which shows a list of all monies owed to your suppliers.

The aged creditors report looks much like the aged debtors analysis report (which I describe in the preceding section 'Finding the Customers Who Owe You'). The report shows how much you owe, to whom, and for how long. You can use the aged creditors report to decide which suppliers you to pay at the end of the month.

Type suggested payments into the Sage Help facility to see how to run a Suggested Payments report.

Make sure you reconcile all your bank accounts from which you make supplier payments, including credit cards, before you prepare your aged creditors report. If you overlook some payments, your aged creditors analysis report won't be accurate and you may end up paying a supplier twice.

To run an aged creditors analysis report, follow these steps:

1. **From the Navigation bar, click Suppliers and then click the Reports icon.**

   The Supplier reports window opens.

2. **Click on Aged creditors on the left side of the screen and highlight the report of your choice from the right side of the screen.**

   I usually select Aged Creditors Analysis (Detailed) from the raft of options. The Criteria Values box opens. Double-clicking on the report you wish to view also opens up the Criteria Values box.

   You can save your regular reports as favourites so you don't have to keep scrolling down the list of reports to find the one you want.

3. **Use the dropdown arrows to select the supplier you want to run an aged creditors report for.**

   If you leave the Supplier Reference fields alone, Sage automatically selects all suppliers.

   Ensure the Date From and To fields are correct. Tick the Exclude Later Payment box to tell Sage to ignore information beyond the To date.

4. Click OK to run the report.

Choose to print, email, or export the report. Figure 20-6 shows a detailed aged creditors report for Jingles.

5. To exit the report, click the white arrow in the red box.

You return to the Supplier reports window. Click the white cross in the red box at the top right corner of the window to return to the Suppliers window.

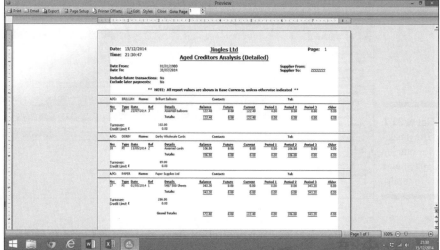

Figure 20-6:
An aged creditors report for Jingles', showing how much Jingles owes.

Handling Unreconciled Bank Transactions

After you reconcile your bank account, you probably have a few transactions that you can't reconcile. They may be unreconciled payments or unreconciled receipts.

You quite often have entries posted in Sage that haven't yet cleared the bank account (see Chapter 15 for more about reconciling). For example, you may post cheques or receipts on Sage before they clear the bank account – these are known as *unpresented cheques* and *outstanding lodgements*.

To print an unpresented cheques report, follow these steps:

1. **From the Navigation bar, click Bank accounts and then click the Reports icon.**

   The Bank reports window opens.

2. **Click Unreconciled transactions.**

   A range of reports appear on the right side of the screen, as in Figure 20-7.

Figure 20-7: The unreconciled payments report.

3. **Highlight the Unreconciled Payments report, and then click the Preview icon.**

   The Criteria Values box opens.

4. **Enter the transaction dates you require.**

   You usually put to the end of the month that you've just reconciled.

5. **Click OK to open the report.**

   You can print, email, or export the report to your required destination.

6. **Click the white cross in the red box to close the Preview window.**

   This returns you to the Bank reports window. Click the white cross in the red box to close the Bank reports window and return to the Bank accounts window.

Figure 20-8 shows an unreconciled payments report for Jingles from 01 January 1980 to 30 June 2014. Putting in such a broad range ensures Sage picks up all transactions, from day 1 to 30 June 2014. Use these dates if you've just performed a bank reconciliation to 30 June 2014. The report shows one entry for cheque number 001234, dated 30 June 2014 – this is an

Figure 20-8:
Viewing
a list of
unpresented
cheques for
Jingles.

unpresented cheque – maybe written on the last day of the month and only posted that day, so it hasn't got as far as the bank yet.

To run an outstanding lodgements report, follow these steps:

1. **From the Navigation bar, click Bank accounts and then click the Reports icon.**

   The Bank reports window opens.

2. **Click Unreconciled transactions.**

   A range of reports appear on the right side of the screen.

3. **Click Unreconciled Receipts and then click the Preview icon.**

   The Criteria Values box opens.

4. **Enter the transaction dates you require.**

   You generally put to the end of the month you've just reconciled.

5. **Click OK to open the report.**

   You can print, email, or export the report to your required destination.

6. **Click the white cross in the red box to exit the Preview window.**

   You return to the Bank reports window. Click the white cross in the red box to close the Bank reports window and return to the Bank accounts window.

Your accountant probably requires a copy of your unreconciled bank transactions at the year-end, so remember to supply them with a copy. Any extra work you do saves on accountancy costs.

Doing a Monthly Breakdown of Profit and Loss

The monthly breakdown report is an incredibly useful report. It shows a month-by-month breakdown of the profit and loss account. You can drill down on any number (except for the totals) to see the breakdown of each number and the nominal code the figures are posted to. Seeing trends developing across the months in income and expenditure is useful.

To run the monthly breakdown report, follow these steps:

1. **From the Navigation bar, click Nominal codes and then click the Reports icon.** The Nominal codes reports window opens.
2. **Click Profit and Loss on the left side of the screen.**

   Double-click Profit and Loss (Monthly Breakdown) on the right side of the screen to open the Criteria Values box.
3. **Select the From and To periods and click OK.**

   The report opens and you can choose to print, export, or email it. Figure 20-9 shows a monthly breakdown report for Jingles.
4. **To close the Preview report, click the white cross in the red box at the top right corner of the window.**

   You return to the Nominal code reports window.
5. **Click the white cross in the red box at the top right corner of the window.**

   You return to the Nominal codes window.

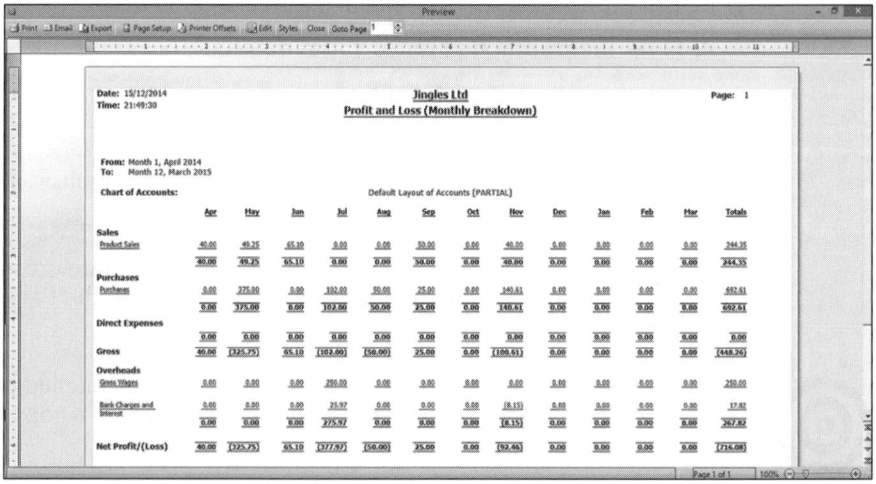

Date: 15/12/2014
Time: 21:49:30

Jingles Ltd
Profit and Loss (Monthly Breakdown)

Page: 1

From: Month 1, April 2014
To: Month 12, March 2015

Chart of Accounts: Default Layout of Accounts (PARTIAL)

	Apr	May	Jun	Jul	Aug	Sep	Oct	Nov	Dec	Jan	Feb	Mar	Totals
Sales													
Product Sales	40.00	49.25	65.10	0.00	0.00	50.00	0.00	40.00	0.00	0.00	0.00	0.00	244.35
	40.00	49.25	65.10	0.00	0.00	50.00	0.00	40.00	0.00	0.00	0.00	0.00	244.35
Purchases													
Purchases	0.00	375.00	0.00	102.00	50.00	25.00	0.00	140.61	0.00	0.00	0.00	0.00	692.61
	0.00	375.00	0.00	102.00	50.00	25.00	0.00	140.61	0.00	0.00	0.00	0.00	692.61
Direct Expenses													
	0.00	0.00	0.00	0.00	0.00	0.00	0.00	0.00	0.00	0.00	0.00	0.00	0.00
Gross	40.00	(325.75)	65.10	(102.00)	(50.00)	25.00	0.00	(100.61)	0.00	0.00	0.00	0.00	(448.26)
Overheads													
Gross Wages	0.00	0.00	0.00	250.00	0.00	0.00	0.00	0.00	0.00	0.00	0.00	0.00	250.00
Bank Charges and Interest	0.00	0.00	0.00	25.97	0.00	0.00	0.00	(8.15)	0.00	0.00	0.00	0.00	17.82
	0.00	0.00	0.00	275.97	0.00	0.00	0.00	(8.15)	0.00	0.00	0.00	0.00	267.82
Net Profit/(Loss)	40.00	(325.75)	65.10	(377.97)	(50.00)	25.00	0.00	(92.46)	0.00	0.00	0.00	0.00	(716.08)

Figure 20-9: An extract from the profit and loss (monthly breakdown) report for Jingles.

Ranking Your Top Customers

The top customers report can be a real eye-opener and is a very useful management tool. You may think you know who your best customers are, but this report can reveal some very surprising results.

The report has a simple layout. It shows you the customer's account and name, contact details, when you last invoiced them, their credit limit, and the year-to-date (YTD) or month-to-date (MTD) turnover.

The report lists your customers in order of turnover, so you see which customers are invoiced with the highest value, showing where the bulk of your sales turnover comes from.

You may find your turnover is generated by your top five customers, or you may find you have 20 customers who spend slightly less individually with you. You may consider the second arrangement to be more beneficial as it spreads the risk across a wider customer base. If one customer disappears, you aren't going to feel the effect quite so dramatically.

To run your top customer report, follow these steps:

1. **From the Navigation bar, click Customers and then click the Reports icon.**

   The Customer reports window opens.

2. **Click on Top customers at the bottom left of the screen.**

   Highlight the Top Customer List – Year and click on the Preview icon. The report opens and you can print, email, or export it.

3. **To close the report, click the white cross in the red box.**

   You return to the Customer reports window.

4. **To close the Customer reports window, click the white cross in the red box at the top right corner of the window.**

   You return to the Customer window.

Try exporting your top customers report and play around with the numbers in a spreadsheet. You can then put the information into graphical format to send to your company managers.

If you run the Top Customer List – Month, make sure you complete regular month-ends and tick the `Clear Turnover Figures` box in the Month-End window, otherwise the information is the same as the YTD report. Check out Chapter 16 for more on running your month-ends.

Figure 20-10 shows a top customer report for Jingles.

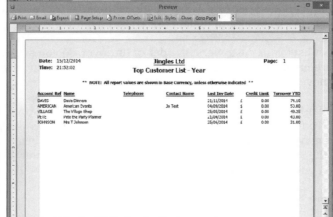

Figure 20-10: The top customer report can provide surprising results.

Chapter 21

Going Mobile

In This Chapter

▶ Using Sage Drive

▶ Installing the Sage Accounts 50 Tracker app

▶ Using the Sage 50 Accounts Mobile Sales app

▶ Connecting users remotely

*I*f you have Sage 50 2015 or newer, you can use Sage Drive to access your data out of the office. If you're playing a round on your favourite golf course, with Sage apps you can still check whether a customer has paid their invoice, add new customer details, or view your price lists. In this chapter I give a brief introduction to the different apps available with Sage 50 Accounts 2015 using Sage Drive.

With the addition of any of these apps, you can improve the mobile capability of your accounting software. Never again are you constrained to your desktop. Now you can really do all your work remotely: You can work from home, you can have remote meetings with your accountant, and you can finalise sales orders and produce invoices out on the road.

Setting up Sage Drive

Sage Drive harnesses cloud technology to let you access your accounts remotely. With Sage Drive you can connect multiple users to your Sage 50 software, access your accounts data using Sage 50 Accounts Tracker via your phone, and use the Sage 50 Accounts Mobile Sales app on your tablet.

Having Sage Drive means you can access your accounts wherever you are, as long as you have an internet connection. You can then work collaboratively with clients or staff in different locations if they also have internet access. Sage Drive also means your accountant can access your data remotely without chasing you for backups.

Any changes you make to your data in the cloud are automatically updated to your local data in real time, so everything is always in sync.

You need to register for Sage Drive before you can use it. To do this, you need to create a Sage ID by doing the following:

1. **Open Sage 50 Accounts 2015 and then click File on the Menu toolbar.**

2. **Click Set up Sage Drive.**

   Click I don't have a Sage ID and follow the instructions to set up a new ID.

3. **Enter your account number and serial number to register for the service.**

4. **To sign in, enter your Sage ID email address and password.**

   Sage may also ask you to enter some Captcha text to verify you're a human and not a device trying to hack into the system.

5. **Confirm you agree to the terms and conditions before you upload your data.**

If you don't have the option to set up Sage Drive, contact Sage and ask for an update to let you access the facility.

For more information about setting up Sage Drive, use the F1 function and type Sage Drive. This brings up lots of useful information on Sage Drive, including sharing additional sets of data, managing shared data, and adding other users such as your accountant.

Tackling Sage 50 Tracker

Sage 50 Tracker is an app that lets you manage your accounts on the move. The app uses Sage Drive, which means your Sage data is held securely in the cloud. With this app, you can log into Sage wherever you are and do the following:

- ✔ Check account balances for customers and suppliers
- ✔ Keep in touch with your key contacts
- ✔ View maps of where your customers are based

    ✔ Review outstanding debtors and creditors

    ✔ Quickly locate sales invoices

To use Sage 50 Tracker you must have Sage 50 version 21 with Sage Drive and a Sage ID.

Installing Sage 50 Tracker

In this section, I demonstrate how to access your accounts data via an iPhone. To have the benefit of using this app, you must have an iPhone 4 or above (and be running IOS 7 or above), alternatively you can use an Android smartphone (version 4 or above). You can download the app free of charge from the App Store on your phone. In Figure 21-1 I show the Sage 50 Tracker Info screen.

Figure 21-1:
Viewing information about Sage 50 Tracker in the iPhone App Store.

On your phone, tap the install button on the Sage 50 Tracker Info screen to download the app. This process takes a minute or so.

After the application loads, tap the Sage 50 Tracker icon on your phone to go to the Login screen, which I show in Figure 21-2.

Figure 21-2:
Looking at
the Login
screen for
Sage 50
Tracker.

Looking at the Sage 50 Tracker dashboard

To log in and access your data on Sage 50 Tracker, you need your Sage
Passport email address and password. In this section, I use the Demo Mode
to demonstrate the features of Sage 50 Tracker.

Click on the Demo Mode button to go to the Sage 50 Tracker Dashboard
screen, which I show in Figure 21-3. The screen shows key data about your
business, such as your bank balance details, who owes you money (debtors),
and who you owe money to (creditors).

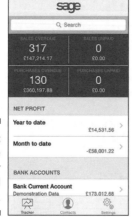

Figure 21-3:
The Sage
50 Tracker
Dashboard
screen.

Chevrons (>) on the Dashboard screen show you can find further information by drilling down into the data. For example, if you tap the Net Profit figure of £14,531.56, the app shows you a breakdown of how that figure has been achieved, as in Figure 21-4.

Figure 21-4: Using the drilldown facility to investigate your net profit.

Clicking on the Sales Overdue line on the dashboard gives you a list of your customers and how much they owe you – I show an example for A1 Design Services in Figure 21-5. You can see the individual invoices outstanding on your phone. You can see the same level of information for your suppliers, so you know who you owe money to.

Figure 21-5: Taking a look at the Sales Overdue Overview screen.

A really useful feature of the Tracker app is the ability to drill down to the contact details for customers and suppliers, which I show in Figure 21-6. You can obtain names, addresses, and phone numbers, and view their locations via a Google map – great if you're on the road and need to find a client quickly.

Figure 21-6:
Finding a customer's contact details

Sussing Out Sage 50 Mobile Sales

The Mobile Sales app has been designed to provide all the tools necessary to enable your sales force to do an effective job. It is only available in tablet format but allows you to process sales on the road.

The user must have Sage 50 Accounts with Sage Drive and must be using an iPad mini or iPad 2 or above. The app can be installed by paying an additional fee to Sage whereupon an activation email will be sent to the user to allow the app to be set up.

Having this app available to the sales force whilst out with the customer enables the sales person to check stock availability online and create a quote instantly for the customer. This can be printed at the customer's premises and even an invoice raised before the sales person has left the client. This is a great tool to gain quick sales and for the sales people to have up to date pricing information and stock information allowing them to make informed decisions when negotiating sales with the customer.

Sage 50 Mobile Sales costs £5 plus VAT.

Keeping Connected with Connected Users

Connected Users is part of the added functionality of having Sage Drive. This app gives you and your staff remote access to accounts data, wherever you all are. You automatically have access to one person connecting when you first buy Sage 50, but any additional users cost £5 plus VAT per user per month.

You can add up to 24 connected users, and you can add and delete users whenever you want. You have total control of who can access your secure company data. Users need an internet connection at all times and a Windows operating system.

Part VI

The Part of Tens

Go to www.dummies.com/extras/sage50accountsuk for some great free bonus content.

In this part . . .

✔ Find out how function keys can help to speed up data processing.

✔ Discover the wonderful ways wizards work their magic to help you with the basic setting up of records and some of the trickier aspects of bookkeeping.

✔ Use the helpful glossary for jargon-busting definitions.

Chapter 22

Ten (Okay, Eleven) Funky Functions

. . . .

In This Chapter

▶ Getting help

▶ Finding out about shortcuts

▶ Opening programs

. . . .

*I*f you want to wow your friends or your boss with a few neat Sage tricks, look no further than this chapter. Here I show you how to use some of the function keys that give you some great shortcuts – for example, the copy key (F6), which speeds up processing no end, and F7, which can get you out of a tight spot if you need to insert an extra line somewhere (particularly useful if you miss a line of information from the middle of a journal).

Browsing for Help with F1

Pressing F1 launches the help system. The Sage help system is intelligent enough to know which part of Sage you're working in and displays the Help screens most suited to your needs. This saves you having to scroll through the Help index list to find the appropriate section. For example, if you're in the Batch Entry screen for suppliers, pressing the F1 key brings up a Help screen related to entering purchase invoices.

Calculating Stuff with F2

Having instant access to a calculator is pretty handy, particularly if you're in the middle of a journal and you need to add something up. Pressing F2 brings up a little calculator on the screen. You can quickly do your sums and then carry on processing information using Sage without having to dive through your office drawers to find a calculator.

Accessing an Edit Item Line for Invoicing with F3

Pressing F3 displays the Edit Item line when you're entering invoices. You can add additional information and comments to your invoice, whether for a product or service. You need to enter some information first before the Edit box opens.

Finding Multiple Functions with F4

Pressing F4 does three different things, depending on which screen or field you're in:

- ✔ In a field with a dropdown arrow, press F4 to display the full list.

- ✔ In a Date field, press F4 to show the calendar.

- ✔ In a numeric field, press F4 to make a mini-calculator appear. (F2 opens a calculator in any screen; F4 opens a calculator only if you're in a screen devoted to numbers.)

Calculating Currency or Checking Spelling with F5

Pressing F5 does two different things, depending on which field you're in:

- ✔ In a numeric box, press F5 to show the currency calculator. (You need to ensure your currencies and exchange rates are set up for this to function properly.)

- ✔ In a text box, press F5 to bring up the spellchecker.

Copying with F6

F6 is one of the best Sage inventions ever. Pressing F6 copies entries from the field above, which is particularly useful when you enter batch invoices. For example, for a batch of invoices with the same date, you can enter the date only once and then press F6 when you get to the Date field as you enter each subsequent invoice. Sage copies the date from the field directly above your line of entry and enters the same date into the invoice on the line of the batch that you're working on.

F6 doesn't work only with dates. You can use the key to copy any field. If you want to enter a mass of invoices from the same customer or supplier, you can use F6 to copy the customer or supplier's details from one invoice into all the other invoices.

F6 has an amazing impact on your data entry speed, and the key is an absolute godsend when you set up a new system.

Inserting a Line with F7

The ability to add a line using F7 may seem pretty mundane, but it's very useful when you enter batches of invoices or journals. If you get halfway through entering a journal and realise you've missed out a line, instead of putting the at the bottom you can press F7 to insert the line exactly where you want it.

Deleting a Line with F8

F8 is one of my favourite function keys in Sage. Many a time I get to the bottom of a long laborious journal and realise I've started to enter a line of journal that shouldn't be there.

After you enter a nominal code, Sage expects you to continue to post that line of the journal and waits for you to enter a value. When you realise yourmistake and try to save the journal with a zero amount on the last line, Sage won't let you post. Instead, it gives you a warning message stating 'No transaction values entered'.

If you click the line you want to delete and press F8, the line miraculously disappears, and Sage lets you save the journal with no further problems.

You can also use the F8 key in other parts of Sage, such as to delete a line from an invoice or order.

Calculating Net Amounts with F9

When you enter an invoice, Sage asks you for the net amount of the invoice, followed by the tax code. After you enter the tax code, Sage calculates the VAT. If you don't know the net amount of the invoice and only have the gross amount, you can type the gross amount in the Net field and press F9. Sage then calculates the net amount for the invoice.

Launching Windows with F11

Pressing F11 launches the Windows control panel. The control panel is useful if you accidentally send a report to the printer and want to cancel the job. Press F11 to open the control panel and select the Printer icon. Double-click the printer where the job is waiting to print and delete the report from the queue. Click the black cross in the right corner to exit the control panel.

You can also configure F11 to launch another program. Use the Help menu for instructions on how to do this.

Opening Report Designer with F12

F12 launches Report Designer, a Sage feature that lets you create your own or modify existing reports. If you can't find a standard report that produces your information in the way that you want, Report Designer lets you design a report with exactly the details you need for your business. (I explain how to use Report Designer properly in Chapter 18.)

You can also configure F12 to launch another program. Use the Help menu for instructions on how to do this.

Chapter 23

Ten (Plus One) Wizards to Conjure Up in Sage

In This Chapter

▶ Looking at how wizards help you perform tricky transactions in Sage

▶ Investigating Sage's most helpful wizards

Sage comes with a number of *wizards*. No, I don't mean little characters with pointy hats and wands – I mean step-by-step instructions on how to carry out specific procedures. Some Sage wizards are a bit laborious to use, but many of them provide much needed expertise. For example, some of the wizards in Sage help you complete complicated journal entries – and even the most dedicated bookkeepers use these sometimes.

In this chapter I talk about the most helpful wizards Sage offers.

Creating a New Customer Account

Using the Navigation bar on the left side of your screen, click Customers and then the Wizard icon. The New Customer wizard starts, taking you step by step through the seven-window process of setting up your customers.

This wizard can take a long time, so I don't use it very often. Instead, I use the quicker method of clicking Customer and then the New icon, which immediately opens up a customer record so you can start entering your data.

To have a look at the questions Sage asks as you work through the wizard, press the F1 function key. The Sage Help facility describes in detail the information you need to enter in each of the seven windows.

The final stage of the New Customer wizard lets you enter your opening balances, so you don't need to do this again when you work through other wizards. I talk about opening balances in detail in Chapter 4.

Setting Up a New Supplier

On the Navigation bar, click Suppliers and then the Wizard icon. The New Supplier wizard walks you through the process of setting up your supplier records. The windows you complete help you set up suppliers' names, addresses, contact details, credit details, bank details, and settlement discounts.

If you want to preview the information Sage needs from you to complete the wizard, press the F1 function key to bring up Sage Help.

You don't have to complete every field in the wizard to set up a supplier, but you do need to click through all seven windows to get to the end and save the information you've entered. You can add information to a supplier's record at a later date if you feel you've missed something – simply open the relevant record, make your changes, and click Save.

The final stage of the New Supplier wizard lets you enter your opening balances, so you don't need to do this again when you work through other wizards. I talk about opening balances in detail in Chapter 4.

Initiating a New Nominal Account

You use the Nominal Record wizard to create new nominal accounts for your chart of accounts. You only need to work through two screens with this wizard. From the Navigation bar, click Nominal codes and then the Wizard icon.

The wizard asks you to enter the name of your new nominal account and confirm what type of account it is – sales, purchase, direct expenses, overheads, assets, liabilities, and so on.

The wizard then asks you to enter your nominal category from within the chart of accounts – for example, product sales – and to type in your nominal code.

Decide on your nominal code before you start the wizard. At this point in the wizard, you don't have the option to search your nominal code list to check whether your code is suitable.

After you click Next, the wizard asks if you want to post an opening balance. Click the appropriate answer, and then click Create. Some new boxes appear asking you whether it's a debit or a credit balance and the date and amount. Click Create and the new account is prepared.

Always check your chart of accounts for any errors after you enter new nominal accounts. You can find details on how to do this in Chapter 2.

Creating a New Bank Account

To access the New Bank Account wizard, click the Bank accounts link from the Navigation bar and then the New/Edit icon. Select Wizard from the drop-down menu that appears. The first four windows ask the usual bank details, such as bank name, sort code, account number, and so on.

The last window lets you enter your opening balances so you don't need to do this again when you work through other wizards. See Chapter 4 for the low-down on opening balances.

Launching a New Product

You use the New Product wizard to create a new product record. To access the wizard, click Products and services on the Navigation bar, and then click the Wizard icon.

The wizard asks you to enter descriptions of the product, selling price, cost price, nominal codes, and supplier details. The wizard also lets you enter your opening balances.

Starting Up a New Project

You use the New Project wizard to create a new project record. In Chapter 13 I talk in more depth about creating projects to keep track of a job's progress. To access the New Project wizard, click Projects on the Navigation bar, and then click the Wizard icon.

The wizard asks you to enter details such as the project name and unique reference, such as a shortened name or number to identify the project. You can also enter information such as the project start and end dates, choose one of five predefined statuses for the project, and link the project to a certain customer. The next couple of windows are optional and contain questions such as the site address and site contact details. The last window asks you to enter the price you quoted for the project.

Helping Out at Month-End: Opening/Closing Stock

The Opening/Closing Stock wizard forms part of the month-end routine and is a welcome method of recording your closing stock. The wizard records the amount of closing stock you have at the end of a period and then transfers it to the start of the next period. To access the wizard, click Modules on the Menu bar, and then click Wizards.

By recording your opening and closing stock figures, the wizard can accurately calculate the cost of sales figures for your profit and loss report. If you don't post opening and closing stock figures, the cost of sales only reflects the purchase cost and doesn't reflect any stock you have left to sell.

The wizard asks you to confirm the closing stock nominal accounts in your balance sheet and your profit and loss report. Sage asks you to enter the value of this month's closing stock and the previous closing stock. Sage then calculates the double-entry bookkeeping when you click the Calculate button and then posts those entries when you click the Post Transactions button.

Fuelling Up: Scale Charges

If your organisation uses company cars, the Scale Charges wizard is really handy. The wizard lets you calculate the fuel-scale charges levied against any fuel used when an employee drives a company car for personal rather than business purposes. You have to enter the fuel-scale charge details, and then Sage creates the journals necessary to post to the nominal ledger.

You can access the wizard from the toolbar by clicking Modules, then Wizards, and then Scale Charges. A new window will open and you need to complete the screen instructions that ask you for a date, details, reference and amount. When you click Next, Sage will confirm the journal post which will take place to post the fuel scale charges to your accounts. Just click Post if you're happy with the details.

Before you proceed with this wizard, you need to calculate the scale charge for each company vehicle using the details held on the HMRC website (www.gov.uk/fuel-scale-charge).

Saving Time: Global Changes

The Global Changes wizard helps you make global changes to information in customer, supplier, or product accounts without changing each account individually. For example, you can raise the selling price of all your products by 10 per cent, as the sample business in Figure 23-1 did. (I don't recommend such an abrupt and significant change, however, lest you lose 10 per cent of your customers!)

You can access the wizard by clicking Modules from the main toolbar and then Wizards, followed by Global Changes. Work through each of the windows of the wizard, selecting the appropriate boxes for your global change. When you're happy with the details and can see the results shown on screen, click Finish. Sage then activates the changes.

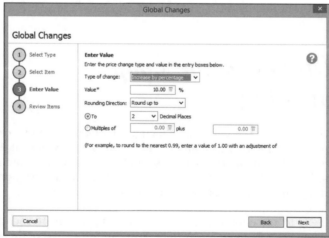

Figure 23-1: The results of applying a 10 per cent increase in selling prices, using the Global Changes wizard.

Handling Currencies: Foreign Bank Revaluation

The Foreign Bank Revaluation wizard takes into account currency rate fluctuations and lets you update currency rates at specific dates so you can report your accounts accurately.

After you activate the Foreign Trader option, you can't switch it off.

You have to complete the Foreign Trader Setup wizard to activate the foreign currency functionality in Sage Accounts Professional. Follow these steps to set it up:

1. **Select your currency followed by the appropriate foreign bank account.**

   Click Next.

2. **Enter the date you want to revalue, for example the month end.**

3. **Enter an exchange rate you want to use for that date.**

   Click Next.

4. **Sage calculates the revaluation figures and shows you what it will post.**

   If you're happy with the calculation, click Post. Otherwise click Back to amend your details.

Keeping Others in the Loop: Accountant Link

The Accountant Link is a very useful facility that lets you send a copy of your data to your accountant via email or post. In the past, if you sent data to your accountant, you had to stop work and wait for any adjustments to your accounts. The Accountant Link lets you send the data and carry on working on the data yourself, minimising disruption within your business.

After you export the data to your accountant, Sage begins to record any material changes you make to the data. You can print a list of these changes to send to your accountant. The accountant can send the data, with adjustments, back to you via a secure file, which you can then import.

The Accountant Link helps you apply your accountant's adjustments to your data to bring it up to date. At this point, Sage stops recording material changes.

You can access the Accountant Link wizard by clicking Modules from the main tool bar, then Wizards, followed by Accountant Link. You then need to choose whether you wish to import data from your accountant or export data to your accountant. Whichever option you choose, you will be taken step by step through the process, following on-screen instructions. I go through this process in more detail in Chapter 19.

You don't need the Accountant Link if you already have Sage Drive, because Sage Drive lets your accountant dip into your live data at any time – with your permission.

Index

About the Author

Jane Kelly trained as a Chartered Management Accountant while working in industry. Her roles ranged from Company Accountant in a small advertising business to Financial Controller for a national house builder. For the last few years Jane has specialised in using Sage accounting software and has taught a wide variety of small businesses and employees the benefits of using Sage. More recently Jane has been involved in writing *For Dummies* books, including *Bookkeeping For Dummies*, 3rd Edition and *Sage One For Dummies*.

Dedication

I would like to dedicate this book to my daughter Megan and my husband Malcolm. Without their support none of my books would ever have been created.

Author's Acknowledgements

I hope that this book will help many of the small business owners that currently struggle keeping up-to-date with their finances. I want people to understand that if a system is set up properly, it's very easy to use and the business gains a huge benefit from it.

I want to thank everyone at Wiley, who have been very kind and supportive, particularly Steve Edwards and the rest of the development team, who have turned my words and pictures into the *For Dummies* book that you see before you.

Finally, I would like to thank my husband Malcolm and my daughter Megan who have put up with me disappearing into the office to work on the book for what must have seemed like a never-ending time.

Publisher's Acknowledgements

We're proud of this book; please send us your comments at `http://dummies.custhelp.com`. For other comments, please contact our Customer Care Department within the U.S. at 877-762-2974, outside the U.S. at (001) 317-572-3993, or fax 317-572-4002.

Some of the people who helped bring this book to market include the following:

Acquisitions, Editorial and Vertical Websites

Project Editor: Steve Edwards

(Previous Edition: Rachael Chilvers)

Production Editor: Suresh Srinivasan

Commissioning Editor: Annie Knight

Assistant Editor: Ben Kemble

Proofreader: Colette Holden

Publisher: Miles Kendall

Front Cover Photos: (c) Getty Images/me4o